Tribal Education for Community Development

About the Author

RUDOLF C. HEREDIA completed his doctorate in sociology from the University of Chicago in 1979. From 1980, he has been the Director of the Social Science Centre at St. Xavier's College, Bombay, and has recently been appointed director of the research department at the Indian Social Institute, New Delhi.

His publications include: "*Structure and Performance of College Education: An Organizational Analysis of Arts and Science Colleges in Bombay*" (Somaiya, Bombay, 1981); "*Religious and Social Change: Behavioural Responses in Bombay University*" (Indian Social Institute, 1984), "*Voluntary Action and Development: Towards a Praxis for Non-Government Agencies*" (Concept, 1988); "*Urban Housing and Voluntary Agencies: Case Studies in Bombay*" (Institute of Social Sciences, New Delhi, 1989). At present he is working on a study of Jesuit seminary training in South Asia.

Tribal Education for Community Development

A Study of Schooling in the Talasari Mission Area

Rudolf C. Heredia
Social Science Centre
St Xavier's College
Bombay

CONCEPT PUBLISHING COMPANY PVT. LTD.
NEW DELHI-110059

ISBN: 978-81-7022-425-9

Edition 2022

Published and Printed by

Concept Since 1974

Concept Publishing Company Pvt. Ltd.
A/15-16, Commercial Block, Mohan Garden,
New Delhi-110059 (India)
T : 91 11 41101460
E : publishing@conceptpub.com, *W*: www.conceptpub.com

Cataloging in Publication Data--Courtesy: D.K. Agencies (P) Ltd. <docinfo@dkagencies.com>

Heredia, Rudolf C., author.
Tribal education for community development : a study of schooling in the Talasari Mission area / Rudolf C. Heredia.
pages cm
Study on the educational work of the Talasari Mission in Talasari Taluka, Maharashtra.
ISBN 9788170224259

1. Talasari (India)--Scheduled tribes--Education. 2. Education--Social aspects--India--Talasari. 3. Educational surveys--India--Talasari. 4. Missions--Educational work--India--Talasari. I. Title.

LCC LC4097.I4H47 2022 | DDC 371.82694095479 23

CONTENTS

PREFACE

In the early 1980s Talasari Mission was consolidating and expanding its network of schools in the area. Talasari taluka at the north west end of Thane district on the Bombay-Ahmedabad highway was rapidly developing numerous industrial estates within convenient reach of Bombay to the south and Surat to the north. Education was considered to be a necessary human investment if the tribals in the area where not to be left behind in the process of development.

As part of this growing investment in education, the mission decided to have a study done not just to review its educational work but to help plan and execute its future orientations as well. This was best done as an action-research following a participative method. Moreover, rather than focus on the mission schools, in isolation, a comparative approach was adopted and government and other private schools were included in the study.

Obviously, the levels of participative involvement would differ with the various persons concerned, but overall it was certainly something that must be mentioned here with generous gratitude. In particular the mission personnel's commitment and diligence, openness and honestly were surely a most rewarding experience while working on the project. But if there's one person without whose sensitivity and insight this study could easily have floundered, it is Ms. Vasudha Ambiye, the research coordinator, who carried the heat and burden of the day in the field and the long hours of preparation and follow-up at home, for this action-research.

The study was begun in July 1983 and carried over a period of two years. It was followed up with another two more years of planning and implementing programmes as an action continuation of this participative research. And though the follow-up was mostly with the mission schools the findings of the study surely have a bearing not just on schooling in this area, but on tribal education elsewhere as well.

This monograph is indeed a documentation of education and development in a well defined taluka of Maharashtra. But it attempts to be more than just this. For the issues and concerns that preoccupy this action research are not unique to this area, nor is the developmental process here un-typical of the mainstream in this country. It is in this larger context that the study must be read, if it is to make a wider contribution to the understanding of tribal education for community development.

St. Xavier's College, Bombay
14 February 1992

Rudolf C. Heredia

1

INTRODUCTION

1. The Present Concern

If as the *Report of the Education Commission (1964-66)* began with a solemn proclamation: "The destiny of India is now being shaped in her classrooms",[1] then it would be tragically true that the first dwellers of this land, the *adivasi* tribals have missed their 'tryst' with destiny. For "while the Indian experiment with tribal development has been hailed as unique in the third world perspective of the treatment of indigenous peoples"[2] it is far from a success story as yet. Tribals have in fact maintained their demographic growth rate and ethnic identity, their political rights and democratic participation.

> "From almost the zero level in the 1930s progress in education and literacy, health care and communication has been remarkable, though critical gaps exist in the utilization of these facilities by tribals as compared to non-tribals. . .on the negative side however they remain the most backward, under-developed and, next only to the Harijans, the most exploited community."[3]

Education is one more arresting instance of their marginalization in society.

Non-government agencies have made a tremendous investment in educational institutions in the country and foremost among these have been church related ones. These have in no small measure contributed to the institutionalization of Western education in the country. The 'convent school' has become the institutional model for most private agencies in the field and admission to such institutions is much sought after.

However one rates the success of these schools, their contribution for better or worse has been largely confined to the urban areas. When transferred to the rural milieu they seem out of context and quite alien to the real educational needs there. The adult illiteracy figures and the school dropout rates testify to the tragic failure of the formal school system to reach the poor and under-privileged in rural India, and nowhere is this more in evidence than for our tribal population.

Surely one of the principal reasons for the failure has been the lack of political will on the part of the government. But many committed private agencies have also failed to make an impact on rural and especially tribal education and all too often this has not been for their want of trying. For the formal school still remains an alien implant from an urban milieu. Even with a capable and committed staff, it cannot overcome its caste-class bias that all too easily excludes the marginalized rural poor.

The crisis of education in India then, demands nothing less than a restructuring of the formal school in a new institutional model. Suggestions and attempts in this direction have indeed been made, the most important in the long list being Gandhi's basic education. However, no venture so far has fulfilled its promise and the problem is too urgent to be left to solve itself.

Talasari mission at the North-West corner of the Thane district in Maharashtra has a long history of primary education among the Warli tribals there. At least one of its eleven schools is over 50 years old and most average about 25. More recently it has launched into secondary education. This commitment to education is a top priority, together with the effort to build the Warli community. This study attempts to link these two priorities under the theme of tribal education for community development.

Educational initiatives and innovations are hardly new in the geographic area under study. Already in 1948 the Wandrekar Committee was appointed by the Government of Bombay to recommend a "Programme of Educational Expansion in the Adivasi Area of the Thana District."[4] The Committee recommended the craft-centred basic education of the Wardha plan. Following up the Committee, primary education was made compulsory in three prominently *adivasi* talukas in the district in 1949: Umbergaon, Dahanu, and Mokhada. Ninety-eight additional schools were opened by 1955 and *adivasi* enrolment rose from 3,762 to 8,280 over the six year period in the three talukas, but was still only 40 per cent of the target for schools and 35 per cent of that for pupils.[5]

Other more innovative educational initiatives were taken by

Acharya Bhise and the Sarvodaya Yojana in 1953, as also by the Adivasi Seva Mandal in 1954. But by far the most innovative was the Vikaswadi project at Bordi initiated by Tarabai Modak in 1953 and later carried on by the Anutai Vagh, beginning with the Gram Bal Shiksha Kendra, the *anganwadis* and *balwadis*, to the Meadow School and experimental teacher training.[6] But the experimental model was not replicated because of "the inability of administrators to encourage experimentation and the lack of special funds for supporting the alternatives to the existing system!"[7]

If the Christian mission and other educational agencies did not quite succeed with a breakthrough in tribal pedagogy and education in this area, in spite of trying over a considerably long time span, it is because the formal school remains an alien implant from another cultural milieu. Even its best efforts cannot overcome the inherent bias of the system against the rural poor, especially the tribal community here.

It would of course be naive to expect a total restructuring with all the vested interests that have now coalesced around the educational system. But small innovations and creative responses on a minor scale now, can make larger changes and structural transformation possible later. For this more micro-level analysis is needed particularly with regard to the school-community linkages. This was the original inspiration of the action-research undertaken here.

The issue, however, is not one of individual advancement and upward mobility through education. Already a very few among the scheduled castes and tribes have taken advantage of reservations in their favour and now constitute a small elite. These are more alienated from the community they leave behind than integrated into the upper strata they have supposedly reached. This is hardly a happy situation and can be cause for concern on its own.

But the real issue here and the explicit concern of this study is not so much individual advancement, but rather tribal education for community development, a development in which the tribals will have their identity and dignity respected, a community that finds its place in the sun in an equitable integration in the national mainstream, making their own distinctive contribution there.

2. The Research Design

This study is not designed to untangle the causal priorities in the relationship between education and society, but as will be shown later, it will follow the emerging consensus regarding the reciprocity between the two. This is most evident at the lower levels of their interaction in a less complex milieu, i.e., the village school and the tribal community. In such a situation it is the school that is the more easily manipulated variable of the two, precisely because as a formal institution it lends itself more easily to experimentation and restructuring. For an action-research project, then it is a convenient starting point to investigate and orient the school-community relationship.

The objective of this research would be to study not so much how tribal education can be oriented more efficiently to individual advancement, but rather how it can become more effective for developing communities. The questions under investigation would, then, concern:

1. the institutional impact of the school on the student,
2. the institutional influence of the school on the village.

The first would focus on ways in which the school could be adapted to the culture of the student, the second on how the school can be adjusted to the needs of the community. In both these instances the opposite has often been attempted with unfortunate consequences for student, school and community.

For an action-research project, the participatory method was seen to be the most appropriate. This study was designed to involve as many as conveniently possible: administrators and teachers, students and parents, alumni and community leaders. Obviously there were different degrees of involvement and different kinds of contributions that each group could make; all this would have to be properly balanced in an integrated effort.

The analysis involved a three-way comparison between mission, government and other private schools, made at three levels: the individual, (students and ex-students, teachers and parents, school administrators and community leaders), the institutional or school, and community or the village.

Besides the mission schools, the sample included matching ones from the other two categories. The various individuals required were then chosen from the school selected, and the village community in which the school is located. Thus besides the 11 primary, and the one mission high school, 3 others run by private agencies, 2 government *ashramshalas,* and one private one were included. Three zilla parishad schools in the study were chosen by the local education officer (EO) as the best from the many in the area.

Two kinds of data collection were planned:

1. more quantitative: from school records and close-ended questionnaires for the individuals concerned, i.e., students, teachers, parents.
2. more qualitative: from open-ended in-depth interviews with some significant individuals and with school staff and community leaders.

The data collection instruments are presented in the appendix, unabridged. Here they are briefly described. A separate closed-ended questionnaire for each of the three groups, students, parents and teachers (Appendix II) was put together in consultation with a cross-section of participants in the study.

The first questionnaire for students (App. V. 1. pp. 214-219) covered basic socio-economic information about their family and its support for their children's schooling; information on their performance in school in curricular and extra-curricular activities; questions about their preferences for various kinds of occupations, reference persons and groups; and their relationships with other students and with their teachers.

The questionnaire for parents (App. V. 2. pp. 219-225) covered much of the same information on socio-economic background and educational support, and extended it somewhat. This overlap provided a simple test for validity and made for a more refined matched-pair analysis. Other additions included a section on parents' participation in the village and their contact with the school.

The teacher questionnaire (App. V. 3. pp. 225-232) was more elaborate. Besides the usual data on their socio-economic and educational background, their pedagogic practices, their perceptions of their students, supervisors, and the parents, as also their involvement in the village community, were queried. Lastly, the teachers were given a questionnaire on institutional goals, (App. V. 4. pp. 232-237) to be responded to at the 'is' and the 'ought' level of importance. This provided a useful extension and validation of the other data.

The open-ended discussion schedule (App. V. 5. pp. 237-239) was designed to go into some depth with significant individuals in the school and the community with regard to the changing culture and historical context of both the tribal society and the community school. These were meant to elicit concrete particulars as well as to gain insight into their perspectives as in keeping with the participatory method. Some 25 such interviews were done of approximately 1 to 2 hours each, over some months. They covered a wide spectrum of educational perspectives, institutional allegiances, political commitments and social positions.

The execution of this study was a difficult and delicate matter. For although Talasari is only 150 km from Bombay, it is still a very impoverished and deprived area. It is extremely polarised along party and ideological, communal and religious divisions. Any effort at constructive social intervention is all too often dissipated in a political struggle that sidetracks the real issues, leaving the people even more entangled in their difficulties than before.

Education would seem to provide a point of entry for a voluntary agency willing to make a long term investment to develop the social infrastructure so lacking in this area and yet so necessary for equitable and just community-building today. More than simply a means of individual mobility, the school can be a centre for critical awareness and community change. The school has often been seen as the most effective contribution of any social action agency trying to steer clear of the imbroglio of party politics and the violence it so easily precipitates. However, in the context of the failure of the formal school to reach the marginalized rural poor, the kind of schooling offered needs to be examined and reoriented more effectively for this group.

After a careful consideration of its present social situation, and a realistic appraisal of its resources, the Talasari mission has explicitly chosen education as one of its top priorities. This study will not merely evaluate the past, but rather attempt to orient the present work to the future, in terms of the new possibilities already beginning to appear and the new perspectives already being accepted.

The study began in July 1983, and was planned for two years in two stages: the first, more concerned with the design and execution of the study, the second more with the follow-up, planning and implementation. But these stages were more a matter of preferential emphasis, than a distinct division.

Thus already in the first stage, as the various categories of participants in the project were involved in designing the research instruments and collecting the data in the field, there was also a feedback process to initiate the action stage of the study. For instance, meetings with teachers and administrators of the schools to propose new school programmes, or village meetings with tribal leaders to examine possibilities of community support for the school, etc.

So too the second stage of planning and implementation included a reflective process to interpret the findings and examine their implications in a dialogic process with the various participants involved: the researchers, the local educationists, the community activists, etc. This second stage also included programmes for teacher training, student assistance, village awareness, etc.. Hopefully the approach chosen has combined action research and planned implementation in a creative praxis.

The study itself was substantially complete in a little over two years by early 1985. A follow-up to it extended another two years and was concerned mostly with planned inputs on the basis of the findings, like workshops on teaching aids, seminars on teaching skills, mobilization of community awareness and support through village level meetings and discussions.

This monograph does not document the further follow-up. A separate volume would be required for that. Here a detailed presentation of the findings will made and discussed within the contexts set out in the next chapters, before some pertinent conclusions are drawn.

3. A Preview

After presenting the research design in this chapter, an attempt will be made to situate the study in the two chapters following. Chapter 2 will discuss the complex relationship between education and society, with special reference to the situation in the Indian arena and the policy and practice in elementary education there, before concluding with how alien and alienating this is for tribals.

Chapter 3 sketches the history of the Talasari mission in this area, beginning with the land and its people, the early experience of the mission and its transformation over the years, to the pertinent issues and concerns that arise from this.

Chapter 4 tabulates the data from the closed-ended questionnaires on the students, parents and teachers in a straightforward descriptive presentation. This constitutes a first level analysis.

A second more refined statistical analysis follows in Chapter 5 and the results are discussed and summed up in the light of the qualitative data from the open-ended interviews and discussions, though these are not directly presented here.

The last chapter brings together the more significant conclusions with regard to the students and their families, the community and its school, the mission and its education. These are finally interpreted in the broader social context and against the historical background of the earlier chapters. Lastly, the crucial problem of overcoming the alienating effects of formal education on the tribals as contextualized within the earlier discourse is addressed, and some recommendations, which derive from this study but might have a more universal application as well, are made.

The appendices present a summary index of the variables used, the detail tabulation for the analysis of variance, regression and matched-pairs. The various questionnaires used are also reproduced here.

NOTES

1. *Report of the Education Commission (1964-66)*, Ministry of Education, Delhi, 1966, p.1, no.1.01.
2. K. S. Singh, "Transformation of Tribal Society: Integration Vs assimilation," *Economic and Political Weekly*, Vol.XVI. No.33, 14 Aug.'82, p.1322.
3. *Ibid.*
4. *Cf.* N.R. Paranis, *The History and Survey of Education in Thana District (Formerly Bombay State, now Maharashtra State)*, University of Bombay, 1967, pp.311 & ff.
5. *Cf. Ibid.* p.314.
6. *Cf.* Chitra Naik, *Growing up at Kosbad Hill: A Study of the Vikaswadi Experiment*, Gram Bal Shiksha Kendra, Kosbad, Thane District., 1978.
7. *Ibid.* p.91.

2

THE SOCIAL CONTEXT

1. Introduction

This study must needs be situated within three overlapping and concentric contexts, from the broader and more generalized to the narrower and more concrete. Not only will such a contextualization help to grasp the specific significance of the findings here more comprehensively, but it will also make it possible for the conclusions to be more insightfully extended and generalized. This is precisely what must make an in-depth case study relevant to a wider theory.

First, the broadest context is that of society at large and more specifically the relationship of the education system to the other sub-systems in Indian society; the focus here will be on education and social change, particularly as illustrated by elementary education.

Second, the tribal community in India and the integration of educational institutions in it; here the emphasis will be on the socio-cultural alienation these have caused. And finally, the Talasari mission to the Warlis and its contribution to the tribal community there; here the concrete local circumstances will form the geographic context and historical background of the discussion. The purpose, however, will not be an exhaustive description of each, but more limitedly to situate one in relation to the other.

Thus, the first context is a more general socio-economic one; the second a more specific socio-cultural one; while the last becomes a specific historical-geographic backdrop for the study. The first two contexts are treated in this chapter, while the last one is taken up in the next.

2. Society and Education: Single or Multiple Causality

The relationship of education to society is a problematic one. As a sub-system of society it must interface with the other ones, but there is still no complete consensus on the causal relationships that obtain. Earlier an optimistic philosophy prevailed:

> "It was uncritically assumed that education could cure all kinds of social problems and, particularly, that it could bring about more equality among men. As the sociology of education developed, this was progressively reversed and a new philosophy, a pessimistic one, emerged more and more convincingly. It may be summarized in the statement that schooling is unable to reduce to any considerable extent the inequalities among individuals which result from social background."[1]

The Education Commission Report (1964-66) subtitled "Education and National Development" reflected this earlier optimism when it emphatically affirmed, that for "change on a grand scale. . . there is one instrument and one instrument only, that can be used: Education."[2]

Generally those who would use a more consensus model of social order, give causal priority to "fiduciary institutions", in the Parsonian sense,[3] and to value change. These are the ones more optimistic about the causal efficacy of education. Not unexpectedly, they favour evolutionary over revolutionary change, initiated and sustained by educational institutions.

At the other extreme is the view that the education system merely reflects the political economy of a society; the social relations in education are but a reproduction of the social relations of production. Education merely reproduces the class system and extends the capitalist mode of production. Education is thus relegated to an effect not a cause, a dependent not an independent variable.

Generally, this has been the position of those who adopt a more conflict model of social order, give causal priority to the political economy, and use interest analysis. Given their pessimistic view of education changing society, it is not surprising that they favour revolutionary change precipitated in the political and economic systems.

In the optimistic liberal view, as expressed best by John Dewey, the "democratic school"[4] was to integrate the young into adult roles in society by promoting social equality and human development. Empirical studies, however, have not confirmed this but rather pointed to the opposite, by underlining the minimal role of the school.

In the pessimistic neo-Marxist view, best expressed by Althusser[5] and Gramsci[6] education becomes the ideological instrument of class domination and control. It merely produces "officers of the ruling class for the exercise of subordinate functions of social hegemony and political government".[7] Thus the modern school replaces the medieval Church as the dominant ideological state apparatus.[8]

In the complex, multi-causal situation of a changing society, neither of the two extreme positions sketched above are very helpful. The reciprocity between these various subsystems in modern society cannot be ignored by policy-makers and social-planning today, even while conceding that one or the other is the dominant system. Moreover, it is hardly possible to deny all causal efficacy to education, especially in the Third World. For "when we have clear evidence of the role of education creating conditions of change, it is usually from the Third world rather than the West."[9]

Conceptualizing society in terms of sub- and super-structures today must allow for a multiplicity of dialectic contradictions if it is not to fall into a simplistic reductionism. This has meant conceding the 'relative autonomy' of various structures, even the less determinant super structural ones. In this 'cultural Marxists' would go further than 'structural' ones.

The emerging consensus now would seem to be that no one system or structure of a complex society can be changed without its impacting on the others, and their interface can help or hinder the change in varying degrees. Here no attempt is being made to settle the controversy or sort out all the ambiguities. Rather the stance taken is in line with this emerging consensus, while trying to be sensitive to the kinds of issues that have agitated the controversy. Obviously, the issues that concern the relationship of the education system to the others must be contextualized within that particular society, a task which must now be addressed in the next section.

3. The Indian Arena: Contest or Sponsorship

In the developing world as the optimism of the 60s gave way to the crises of the 70s, education too was subject to this change. The dominant strategy was:

> "to achieve rapid quantitative expansion of the existing education system substantially in its old image, in the belief that this would equalize opportunity and generate the human skills and leadership needed for general development."[10]

The expansion was spectacular, but so too was the crisis that followed. And it was not just financial, but one of "serious maladjustment, taking many forms, between inherited educational institutions and the realities of their rapidly changing societies".[11]

In India, the Education Commission (1964-66) was a unique attempt at a comprehensive approach to re-structure the old colonial institutions into a national system of education. But the Commission presumed a change towards a more democratic and egalitarian society that was belied. No wonder some of its insightful and incisive recommendations were non-starters: "priority to elementary and adult education, selective admissions at higher levels, a common neighborhood school system. . . . With the exception of a few individuals, no political party was committed to a radical restructuring of education, which remains a populist slogan still, a carry-over from the national freedom movement."[12]

By 1977-78 formal education expanded into "a gigantic structure with about 700,000 educational institutions, 100 million students more than 3.5 million teachers, and an expenditure of about Rs. 25,000 million which is next only to that on defence."[13] But the inequity of the system as yet remains to be redressed. Illiteracy is still near 60 per cent; of the 80 per cent of children who enroll in school half drop out by standard V, three quarters by standard VIII, 15 per cent reach standard XII, and one per cent the first degree; in short the system's "entire ethos is oriented to the needs and aspirations of the upper and middle classes."[14] The National Policy on Education in 1986, and the Ramamurthy Commission's report, "Towards an Enlightened and Humane Society", have yet to make any perceptible change in this ethos. They only further accentuate the chasm between policy and practice.

Raymond Boudon, postulates "a two-stage filtering process" for the social status of individuals: "In the first they go from a given social background to a given educational level. In the second stage they go from educational level to achieved status."[15] With regard to the first stage, J.P.Naik's remark on Indian education is pertinent: "In fact, the primary object of the system is not to spread education among the people but to function as an efficient and merciless mechanism to select individuals who should continue to remain in the privileged sector or enter it afresh."[16] And with regard to the second stage, the ascribed status of caste, still leaves very little scope to achieve any upwardly mobile occupational status, especially for the scheduled castes and tribes, as the stark statistics of numerous government reports establish. The iniquitous bias of the system falls hardest on the ones lowest in the social hierarchy and it is most crucial at the earliest stages of education.

There is within the system a "key dialectic" that operates through two crucial mechanisms: "early selection and mass examinations."[17] Already at their point of entry into the education system the children are streamed at two levels: on the one hand the rather expensive, and generally privately run, urban based English medium schools which prepare them for an elite status in later life; on the other hand, the freely offered, generally rural based, vernacular medium schools run by local government bodies, that prepare young people to accept lower status occupations. In a formally democratic system, what legitimates the blatant inequality of this early selection, is "the ritual of mass examinations" which "carry a symbolic message – that all individuals have an equal chance. Thus, while emphasis on early selection ensures special treatment to the children of those who can afford to make extra inputs, mass examination promises total parity among all the candidates."[18]

This makes for "sponsored" not "contest" mobility.[19] Such supposed 'equality' between 'unequals' perpetuates and legitimates the *status quo* even while keeping "the confidence and aspirations of the masses alive."[20] Elementary education in India provides a stark illustration of this "key dialectic", as the next section will elaborate.

4. Elementary Education: Policy and Practice

Article 45 of the Constitution of India stipulated that

> "the State shall endeavour to provide, within a period of ten years from the commencement of this Constitution, for free and compulsory education for all children until they complete the age of fourteen years."

From time to time though the period has been extended, the

commitment has been reaffirmed. But the national statistics tell the sad story of an as yet unfulfilled promise.

Certainly this is no mean task. For in the West, "the general economic development of the society and the improvement in the economic conditions of the people preceded rather than followed the universalization of elementary education",[21] which then led to further growth and improvement in a continuing reciprocal relationship between the economy and education. In India the situation was somewhat different, and in trying to use education to initiate and support development, the nationalist leaders looked to indigenous models since the colonial ones had failed. The best known was Mahatma Gandhi's 'basic education', or 'nai talim'.

In a recent examination of the official statistics, after making all the necessary corrections, John Kurien pessimistically concludes that "it will be impossible to achieve universal elementary education for many decades to come".[22]

Kurien assumes that the present constraints are not likely to change, and he rejects Gandhi's basic education as utopian. He finds the reasons for the educational failure not so much in the lack of implementation but in the very approach used for this purpose.[23] His own proposal goes back to an earlier model of R. V. Parulekar.[24] It amounts to a scaled down alternative for universalizing primary not elementary education, i.e., up to standard V not VIII; a shortening of the school day to three hours not six; and focusing on the three 'R's not on a craft.[25]

But this would only further accentuate the dualism in the system between elite and mass education. Rather what is needed is to revive the Gandhian debate so as to initiate a mass movement not just for educational reform but also to reorient our developmental model and plans towards a more participative and just society. Already the tensions of an unjust social order are boiling over into violence; even the ecological crisis is forcing a reconsideration of developmental priorities. The example of Kerala, a relatively poor state but far ahead of richer ones in education, demonstrates that lack of resources is not the main obstacle; yet class based power still resists any challenge to the privileges entrenched in the status quo, and education is no exception.

The allocations in the education budget dramatically under-score this bias. In the past thirty years from the first to the seventh plan, the overall expenditure on education decreased from 7.86 to 3.55 per cent, the relative allocation for primary education has been halved from 56 to 28 per cent while that for higher education has more than doubled from 8 to 18 per cent. Further while primary education, which is clearly the need of the masses, has expanded threefold, university education, which ofcourse helps the elites, has increased sixfold! Obviously then, achieving educational goals set by the Constitution will involve more than restructuring the educational system. It must include other deep seated social changes as well. So too must any sustained social development involve the educational system in very basic ways. When it comes to the weaker sections of society this is all the more apparent even as it becomes increasingly difficult to initiate change in one or the other system. With the scheduled tribes in India this reciprocity actually becomes a vicious circle or rather a downward spiral that is still difficult to reverse, as will be demonstrated in the following section.

5. Tribal Education: Alien and Alienating

The educational backwardness of the scheduled castes and tribes is too well documented in numerous government reports and official statistics to need further repetition here. However, a brief presentation of some significant statistics will help to set a backdrop for the later discussion.

According to the Indian Census in 1981 the national literary rate was 46.74 per cent, while for scheduled castes and tribes it was 21.38 and 16.35 per cent, though in Maharashtra these were higher at 33.63 and 22.23 per cent respectively. Moreover, although the enrolment for primary education for scheduled tribes in 1978-79 started at 70 per cent of the corresponding age group,[26] the wastage at this level was 79.8 per cent for SCs and 79.2 per cent for STs in Maharashtra.[27] Female education among these weaker sections is even more depressingly backward.

The statistics can be elaborated further, but the conclusion is beyond dispute: the *adivasis*, the first dwellers in this land, are very much the last in education, reservations and other positive measures notwithstanding. Obviously, this is closely correlated with their economic backwardness as well. For by far, a vastly disproportionate majority of them live below the poverty line or close to subsistence levels.

For *adivasis*, particularly, the opportunity cost of education is high. It "entails dislocation in the traditional pattern of the division of labour."[28] No wonder then

> "where school and work conflict at this level of income, work always wins. Poverty coupled with familial agricultural production has the effect of drawing children out of school as they are needed in the fields."[29]

A direct attack on their poverty is the obvious first step for any development of the tribals but they must also be concientized to the extra-advantage of education if this development is to make self-sustained progress.

The reasons then for the failure of tribal education in India are not just economic. For too long have the internal constraints of the system and socio-cultural context of the community been neglected. The resulting mismatch between educational institutions and tribal life has been responsible for a colossal economic and human wastage. It is this that will be the focus of the discussion here.

To begin with, "prevailing assumptions concerning the relationship between mass poverty and poor attendance at primary schools" needs to be challenged.[30] When more than half the drop outs over the first five standards of primary school drop out between the first and the second, and these are mostly from the weaker sections, a pertinent question must be raised: does the economic value of the children's labour suddenly jump between these two standards, roughly between the ages of six and seven years? Obviously the answer is negative and "the question takes away the bottom out of the theory that early elimination has a satisfactorily economic explanation in our conditions in the late twentieth century."[31] The alienating effect on the adivasi children of their first contact with the school surely cannot be ignored.

Even so it is tempting to fall back on a "culture of poverty" theory that 'blames the victim' and "perpetuates the belief that the poor are responsible for their backwardness."[32] But again this is but an easy explanation that refuses to question the prevailing assumptions. Rather what is required is to examine the educational institutions and their relationship to the marginal communities. It will then become apparent that the apathy of parents and the children are a response to an alien and alienating system.[33]

To begin with language; Verrier Elwin writes:

> "An important reason why the schools do not fulfil the real function in tribal society is the astonishing indifference on the part of educationists to the local languages."[34]

The Dhebar Commission had proposed that the first two classes be taught in the local tribal dialect and from the third standard on that the classes be in the regional language.[35] But this has yet to be implemented, in spite of the Constitutional obligation of providing primary education in one's mother-tongue. According to the Census in 1961, of the 1652 mother-tongues in the country, hardly 50 have been used for this purpose, and the minority tribal languages are hardly the ones counted among these.[36]

The content of the syllabus too is alien, and since the "text-books do not contain anything pertaining to their society and culture they fail to create and sustain interest among the tribals."[37] Participation in extra- and co-curricular activities is again low because neither are these oriented to tribal children.[38] Rote learning too, so commonly used and so necessary to prepare for the mass examination, are alien to the informal manner of traditional tribal education.[39] No wonder, then, that those students who stay on in the system, cannot but be eventually alienated from their people by the socialization processes and the hidden agenda prevalent in the system.

All this does not by any chance mean relegating tribals to a 'primitive' education. For as with any traditional society there is as much scope for creative and constructive educational programmes that will not leave them marginalized in society, ones that will be respectful of tribals and sensitive to their culture, where they no longer are an "invisible people",[40] subject to the "symbolic violence" of the system; where "tribal identity is not a matter of shame",[41] but of pride. For this, a fourfold isolation must be overcome: that of "the community as whole, the school within the community, the pupil within the classroom and the teacher within the education system".[42] This no doubt is a task as gigantic as it is urgent, but not an uncommon situation with tribal communities here and elsewhere.

An ideally integrated educational programme is yet to be attained, but it has been approached by missionary agencies and voluntary organizations.[43] However, these are only a small presence in a much larger are only context, where unfortunately, "a section of people in he Government treat the tribal problem as one of law and order . . . aspects intimately connected with tribal life style are treated as transgression of laws promulgated by and for non-tribals. The tribal is then punished for his cultural values, his life style and his ethos about which judgement has already been passed by a ruling society which has determined the 'mainstream' in its own image and to its best advantage. This, the tribal naturally regards as inimical to his interest. There is no wonder that the tribal people are not keen to take advantage of an education which appears to them to be a calculated move to destroy their social fabric."[44]

Such systemic ethnocentricity, perpetuated by governmental officials themselves, eventually de-tribalized the *adivasis* and destroy their dignity with their identity. "Just as the native is made to feel ashamed of his world and is prescribed a new way of seeing the world by the western anthropologist so children are prescribed refilled forms of knowledge which produce a view of social reality that is mechanistic and deterministic."[45] The 'primitive' is made to adjust to 'modern' society and the child must be fitted into school system.

Reformist measures have been proposed, but as yet there has been no breakthrough in tribal education as the statistics unambiguously testify. And the vicious circle of educational change waiting on social change and vice versa persists, as also the downward spiral of the adivasis towards tribal marginalization in society.

NOTES

1. Raymond Boudon, *Education, Opportunity, and Social Inequality: Changing Prospects in Western Society,* John Wiley and Sons, New York, 1974, p.xii.
2. *Report of the Education Commission (1964-66), op. cit.*, p.79.
3. Talcott Parsons and Gerald M. Platt, *The American University,* Harvard Univ.Press, Cambridge, Mass., 1973, p. 8 & ff... *Cf.* Samuel Bowles and Herbert Gintis, *Schooling in Capitalist America,* Routledge and Kegan Paul, London, 1976.
4. John Dewey, *Education for Democracy,* Macmillan, New York, 1961.
5. Louis Althusser, *Lenin and Philosophy and Other Essays,* New Left Books, New York, 1971.
6. Antonio Gramsci, *The Modern Prince and Other writings,* International Publishers, New York, 1957.
7. *Ibid.*, p.124.
8. Louis Althusser, "Ideology and Ideological State Apparatus," in *Education: Structure and Society,* ed. B.R.Cosin, Penguin Books, England, 1972.

9. Joseph Di Bona, and R. P. Singh, "Modernity of Tradition in Indian Education," in *Education and the Process of Change,* eds. Ratna Ghosh and Mathew Zachariah, Sage Publishers, N. Delhi, 1987, p.226.
10. Philip H. Coombs with Manzoor Ahmed, *Attacking Rural Poverty: How Non-formal Education Can Help,* John Hopkins Univ. Press, Baltimore 1974, p.3.
11. *Ibid.*
12. *Cf.* J. P. Naik, *The Education Commission and After,* Allied Pub., N. Delhi, 1982, p.44.
13. *Ibid.* p.169-170.
14. *Ibid.* p.170.
15. Boudon, *op.cit.* p.21.
16. J. P. Naik, *op.cit.*, p.170.
17. Krishna Kumar, "Reproduction or Change? Education and Elites in India," in R. Ghosh and Z. Mathew eds., *op.cit.*, p. 27-41.
18. *Ibid.* p.32.
19. *Cf.* R.H. Turner, "Modes of Social Ascent Through Education: Sponsored and Contest Mobility," in A. H. Halsey, J. Floud, and C. A. Anderson eds., *Education, Economy and Society,* Free Press, Glencoe, Ill., 1961.
20. K. Kumar, *Ibid.*
21. J.P. Naik, *Elementary Education in India: A Promise to Keep,* Allied Pub., Bombay, 1975, p.12.
22. John Kurien, *Elementary Education in India: Myth, Reality, Alternative,* Vikas Pub. House, N.Delhi, 1983, p.32.
23. *Ibid.* p.42.
24. R.V. Parulekar, *Mass Education in India,* Local Government Institute, Bombay, 1934 and *Literacy in India,* Macmillan, Bombay, 1939.
25. Kurien, *op.cit.*, pp 180 & ff.
26. Source, the Ministry of Education, *A Handbook of Education and Allied Statistics,* Delhi, 1983.
27. Source, NIEPA, *Selected Indicators of Educational Development in India,* Delhi, 1984.
28. *Report of the Scheduled Areas and Scheduled Tribes Commission,* Government of India, N. Delhi, 1961, p.223.
29. Manning Nash, "The Role of the Village School in the Process of Cultural and Economic Modernization," in *Education in Comparative and International Perspectives,* Kalil I. Gezi, ed., Holt, Rinehart and Winston, New York, 1971. p.150.
30. Krishna Kumar, "Children and the Research Mill", *Economic and Political Weekly,* Vol.23, No.41, 8 Oct.88, p.2107.
31. *Ibid.* p.2108.
32. *Ibid.*
33. *Cf.* E. V. Rathnaiah, *Structural Constraints in Tribal Education: A Regional Study,* Sterling Pub., N. Delhi, 1977, p.10.
34. Government of India, *Report of the Committee on Special Multipurpose Tribal Blocks,* N.Delhi, 1960, p.90.
35. Government of India, *Report of the Scheduled Areas and Scheduled Tribes Commission, op.cit.* 1962, p.226.

36. *Cf.* D. P. Pattanayak, *Multi-lingualism and Mother-tongue Education,* Oxford Univ.Press, Delhi, 1981, p.xiii.
37. E. V. Rathnaiah, *op.cit.*, p.151.
38. *Ibid.*
39. *Ibid.*, p.162.
40. Krishna Kumar, "Educational Experience of Scheduled Castes and Tribes," *Economic and Political Weekly,* Vol.18, No.36 and 37, 3 Sept "83 p.1568.
41. B. P. Pattanayak, *op.cit.*, p.187.
42. E. V. Rathnaiah, *op.cit.*, p.9.
43. *Cf. Report of the Committee on Special Multipurpose Tribal Blocks, op.cit.*, p.86, and N. K. Ambast, *A Critical Study of Tribal Education,* S. Chand and Co., N. Delhi, 1970,pp.43-60.
44. D. P. Pattanayak, *op.cit.*, pp.87-88.
45. Madan Sarup, *Marxism and Education,* Routledge and Kegan Paul, London, 1978, pp.25-26.

3

THE HISTORICAL BACKGROUND

1. Introduction

Religious communalism and fundamentalism have more recently escalated the issue of tribal conversions into a national one, just as the greater awareness among the tribals of their own identity and the injustices they are subjected to has precipitated many local movements for change at the grass-roots. Though religious conversion is no longer as urgent an objective as it used to be at the Talasari mission, other more secular movements for change among the tribals have certainly gathered momentum and have often resulted in 'violent' conflicts.

How did the inspiration of the first missionaries who set out to convert the tribals in the area change over the years? What kind of opposition did it provoke and why? How did this change as the mission developed? In attempting to answer such questions we expect to arrive at a better understanding of the role of the mission in "the service of the faith and the promotion of justice," as articulated by the Jesuit missionaries there.[1]

2. The Tribal Situation

A brief sketch of the historical context of the tribals in the mission area will attempt to set the background for further discussion. This will be put together by drawing on the ethnographic research that has already been published, especially on the Warlis,[2] and on the oral history still very much alive among the people. What emerges is a picture of tribal exploitation and resistance, a struggle for survival that has not quite ended.

(a) *The Land and the People*

The mission to the Warlis was first started in 1922 at Zaroli, now in

Gujarat, and spread southwards to make its headquarters eventually at Talasari. Today a string of chapels and schools, boarding hostels and Christian families, are scattered through the talukas of Talasari and Dahanu and even as far south as Palghar taluka.

The mission area is divided into two areas: a narrow coastal belt called the *banderpatti* to the west, which consists of a coastline of shallow creeks and salty marshes while more inland there are older rice fields and newer fruit orchards; and to the east the *junglepatti*, a once unbroken tract of forest, which has since been cleared in patches for shifting cultivation. Now cultivation is more stabilized even though there are continuing encroachments on the forests and a rapid deforestation that is leaving behind bare and denuded hills.

The non-tribal population is fairly diverse and resides mostly in the coastal area, though it has large vested interests in the forest as well. Muslims had migrated to the area during the Bahamani rule. The Portuguese too left behind some Christians when they were displaced in 1740 by the Marathas, who introduced Brahmins and Prabhus, locally called "Panderpeshas", to colonize the area. With the advent of British rule in 1818 other groups began to establish their dominance in the area, notably the Parsis, who had first landed on the cost at Sanjan some centuries before. Most recently the Uttar Pradesh 'Bhaiyas', who have been part of the labour force in Bombay for some generations, have been brought into the area as strongmen for the landlords. Petty trade is mostly in the hands of the Vani Marwaris and Brahmins, while the Parsis and Muslims are mainly concerned with orchard farming and trading in timber and grain.

The tribal population inhabits mostly the hilly tracts, but forms a substantial overall majority in the area. According to the 1981 census, Maharashtra has a scheduled tribal population of 9.2 per cent and Thane district more than double the state percentage at 21.8 per cent. In the area under study the proportion of tribals is even higher: 90.8, 65.7 and 36.2 per cent for the Talukas of Talasari, Dahanu and Palghar respectively. This works out to a majority of 54.7 per cent for all three but a very substantial 71.5 per cent for the first two.[3] However, the percentage of tribals must have been even higher, for in the 1872 census the overall percentage of tribals in Thane District was 40, and the talukas being considered here, at the northern end of the state, are the mostly intensely tribal in the district.

With regard to the sub-divisions of the tribal population, the largest single group are the Warlis who, according to the 1941 census, numbered 932,733 or 13.5 per cent of the Thane district population. They were concentrated mostly in the northern-most talukas of Umbergaon and Dahanu, which then included Talasari, with 41.3 and 29.5 per cent respectively. Palghar Taluka had just 9.5 per cent Warlis, though more to the east in Vada and Mokada where their numbers were 18.2 and 29.6 per cent respectively.

Other scheduled tribes in the district at the time were: Thakurs (45,949), Katkaris (37,051), Dublas (15,659), Dhodias (11,660), Mahadev Kolis (9,376) and Koknas (9,245). Clearly the Warlis are the dominant tribal group in the area.

(b) *A History of Exploitation*

Yet the tribals have not been able to protect themselves or assert their rights. The *Report on the Aboriginal Hill Tribes of the Partially Excluded Areas in the Province of Bombay* by Symington in 1938 records that their lives were "wretched in the extreme and constitute a blot on the administration".[4] Symington reports that rack-renting, forced labour or vetu, and widespread indebtedness were rampant, resulting in a progressive alienation of tribal lands: a process begun under the Portuguese, intensified under the Marathas, and culminating with the British.

> "Over a short span of three decades the British introduced in this region the raiyatwari land settlement and settled the tribals into a semblance of regular cultivation."[5]

This change represented a transposition from a tribal economy of slash and burn cultivation oriented to consumption needs, to a monetized , colonial system with regularized property rights. So great was this transition that it is hardly surprising that these tribals did not emerge as independent peasant proprietors.

> "The absence of any institutional infrastructural facilities like credit, markets, protection against alienation and lack of education rendered the tribal an easy prey to the exploitation of the money lenders and landlord".[6]

(c) *Resistance and Rebellion*

There were of course protests and rebellion against such exploitation.

Occasionally there was violent retaliation, as when a particularly brutal landlord would be murdered. A more organized opposition is in evidence with the Shetkari Sabha formed at the end of the last century.[7] But the most common response of the tribals to their exploitation was to flee deeper into the forest. However, as this became more difficult, they were forced to face their situation with more than passive acceptance of this downward spiral of exploitation, and to assert themselves in a more organized and effective way.

In 1940 the Adivasi Seva Mandal was founded by B.G. Kher, a prominent Gandhian and later the first chief minister of Bombay State. The Mandal adopted a gradualist and reconciliatory approach to tribal uplift. However, this reformist response was inadequate to effect the radical changes needed to end tribal exploitation.

From 1945 to 1947 the communist inspired Kisan Sabha led the Warli movement against bonded labour, rack-renting and subsistence wages. The struggle escalated to a Telengana type revolt which was finally quelled by armed police, but not without first achieving a measure of reprieve for the tribals.[8] However, as the communist party consolidated its hold in the area and settled down to electoral politics, it soon lost its radical stance with the inevitable compromises it made to broaden its appeal and enter into coalitions with other parties, as it did in the Samyuktha Maharashtra movement in the late 1950s and with the opposition front in the late 1970s.

Most recently in the 1980s a new tribal movement of the toiling masses called the Kashtakari Sanghatana has arisen and is rapidly spreading. It claims to be of Marxist-Leninist, or Naxalite inspiration, but its roots were not entirely unconnected with the mission.

3. The Mission Experience

The mission encounter with the tribals in the area was mainly, if not almost exclusively, with Warlis, the largest tribal group in the area. The mission experience was truly a heroic saga of pioneering beginnings, patient consolidation and persevering growth. It cannot be set out here in all its engaging detail. However, though this outline cannot really capture that experience in all its dimensions, we hope it will help to provide a context for the issues we will debate later.

(a) *The Pioneering Beginnings (1922-1937)*

The Missionary Society of St. Francis of Assisi was officially established in 1901 in Nagpur. In 1907 the archbishop of Daman, Dom Sebastino Jose Pereira, invited the congregation to start an orphanage at Mount Poinsur, Borivili, which is now the mother house of the congregation.

Most of the brothers were of German origin and during the first World War, they were interned. So it was only in 1921 that the society was officially registered with the government "as an authorized Mission Society to conduct mission-work in India".[9]

At the time no religious orders or congregations were allowed to work in the Portuguese possessions so the first mission outpost was set up on British Indian territory in November 1927 at Zaroli, a village about 180 km north of Bombay, near the railway station of Bhilad. The beginnings were already made difficult by opposition from the landed class, but the brothers soon established themselves and began their "tent-touring". They would set out in a bullock-cart and pitch their tent near a village. Here they would attract the tribals with some form of entertainment, a magic lantern or a gramophone. The people called these "*tamashas*"! Having thus gathered the people they would talk to them about the Christian faith and at an appropriate time urge the need for baptism as an assurance against evil spirits, the "*bhuts*", that so filled the tribals with fears and anxieties.

In the very first year 400 persons were baptized, including 25 adults. As their activity moved south, residential mission centres were established at Nagzeri, Gangangaon, Dhamangaon and Sambarpada, and in 1926 at Talasari.

In November of 1926 the sisters of St. Francis Xavier, with their mother house in Bellari, South India, and a convent at Agashi in Vasai, joined the mission at Zaroli and soon began touring the villages on their own, working mostly with women and children. In 1930 a convent was opened at Damangaon, but eventually closed in 1938. Finally in 1943 this congregation was replaced by the Canossian sisters.

All through this period the brothers were themselves spiritually assisted by priests in the capacity of chaplains. But the mission was very overstretched in more ways than one. Archbishop Lima of Bombay, who visited the mission in 1930 and acquainted himself first hand with the situation, attempted to put the mission on a firm footing financially, administratively and spiritually. However, in spite of his wise directions, the criticism of the brothers' methods of conversion began to mount.

It was the priests, working as chaplains to the brothers, who made a sustained and sober critique, and when Monsignor Andrew D'Souza toured the area and made an official report dated 12th May 1936, his recommendations were accepted by Archbishop Lima, though it was his successor, Archbishop Roberts, who finally implemented the decision to invite the Jesuits to assist the mission in 1937.

(b) *Consolidation and Expansion (1937-1958)*

The arrival of the Jesuits in the mission was not without friction with the brothers, who felt them to be a dampener on their enthusiasm. The more serious theological and pastoral difficulties with their missionary method seem to have been lost on them. Basically at issue were two approaches to the missionary endeavour. The brothers' "race to baptize" as many as possible had resulted in a large number of baptisms but very few Christians. Of the 8,000 baptized at this time, the Jesuit fathers estimated that about 700 would call themselves Christians.

To cope with this situation the Jesuits' approach was one of consolidation, of catechizing the Christians in their faith, educating them in the schools founded by the mission, and organizing them into cooperative societies.

The Franciscan brothers never quite accepted this new situation with the Jesuits in charge. They found it too constricting, and as the opposition to the church from the outside began to escalate, their activities were more and more restricted until they effectively withdrew from the mission. The Gangangaon centre was closed in 1946, though the one at Dabchari lingered on till 1955, with little or no activity.

Given the mission practices of the brothers, it is not at all surprising that in the face of insistent opposition to the church large numbers gave up the faith, if indeed it could be said they had it in the first place. The Jesuits immediately put a stop to the indiscriminate baptizing, especially of children and others, when there was no reasonable chance of their being brought up and educated as Christians. Their first priority now was to shore up the faith of the Christians still in the fold. This was done with a vigorous catechizing and pastoral effort, which had to be carried out with the help of lay catechists as the brothers began to withdraw from the area.

Educating the tribals to keep up with a changing world was also offering them the best chance of breaking their dependence on the landlord and moneylenders. At the time the Jesuits took over the mission, it boasted of sixteen primary schools. These schools were a natural extension of the pastoral work of the mission, where parish and school have traditionally gone together. However there were only 226 students on the rolls and none of the masters had passed the "vernacular final examination" of the middle school.

This system was now consolidated and expanded so that eventually there were eleven primary schools, all recognized and qualifying for the government's grant-in-aid. Some of the more important ones of this period are thriving today: Varkhandha (1926), Gangangaon (1930), Savroli (1933), Talasari (1934), Uplat (1936), Shisne (1950), Kurje (1953), Karazgaon and Udwa (1954), Bahre (1958). Some of these schools have boarding hostels attached to them for children living too far to be able to commute daily.

Considering the odds against them, education notwithstanding, for these tribals survival can only be a collective endeavour. To this end two multipurpose cooperative societies were established, at Varkhandha in 1951, and at Uplat in 1958. Rice banks in six different villages were also established to tide over the lean months before the harvest. To counteract the Kisan Sabha of the communists a Christi Sabha was also started, very much on the lines of the Young Christian workers movement in Europe. It included all the prominent members of the community, village leaders, teachers, catechists, etc.. However, as the multiplication of government schemes for the tribals has rendered such efforts superfluous, they were terminated.

A mention must be made of the health care and medical work of the mission. This was begun by the Xaverian sisters and later became mainly the responsibility of the Canossian who established several centres, especially to tackle the prevalence of leprosy in the area. A moving testimony to the sisters' dedication can be seen in the fact that in the early days, the mother general of the Xaverian died of the leprosy contracted through her constant care of her patients.

(c) *Development and Change (1958-1980)*

The surge for national development after Independence was, not surprisingly, reflected in the mission. During this period various other kinds of socio-economic benefit schemes were started with regard to agricultural improvements, e.g., the Japanese method of intensive rice cultivation, the use of chemical fertilizer and of high yield varieties of rice, etc. Under the Catholic Relief Service (CRS) of the United States, a large scale programme of food for work was introduced, to develop community assets like roads, wells, tanks, etc., and to generate employment in the dry season. Many of the boarding hostels attached to the mission schools were subsidized by CRS.

Much of this effort was mainly secular though its inspiration was religious. The preoccupation with conversions now had clearly shifted. Evangelization *versus* social-work was a much debated controversy during this transition period. But finally with the second Vatican Council the autonomy of the secular and the legitimacy of the Christian involvement in it was emphatically asserted.

But scarcely had an integration between such developmental work and the missionary endeavour been accepted when a new and more controversial inspiration came into prominence with 'liberation theology,' and the Jesuits' understanding of their mission today in terms of "the service of the faith and the promotion of justice" as one integrated mission, at the General Congregation of the Society in 1974.

Following on this, the emphasis shifted from developmental work to 'conscientization' and organizing people's movements. However, the conflicts and controversies this gave rise to eventually led the mission to adopt a more reconciliatory stand with adult literacy and educational work. Non-formal educational efforts have been given much encouragement, but the main investment of the mission today is clearly in its school system, which consists of eleven primary and three secondary schools. If in the early stages of the mission education was an adjunct to pastoral work, today it has certainly come into its own.

4. Issues and Concerns

The issue of conversion is a sensitive one and difficult to handle to the satisfaction of all. Here it is presented from the perspective of an 'insider', which cannot but give it an orientation that not all may be comfortable with. Hence to correct this bias to the extent possible an attempt will be made to present in like manner the concerns of the local opposition to the mission, if not empathetically then at least as fairly as we can. We hope this procedure will be more acceptable than a mere disclaimer of any prejudice.

(a) *The Issue of Conversion*

The discussion of the issue of conversion here will not entail a theological analysis of this issue. Without negating the importance of such an approach, especially in this time of dialogue and religious pluralism, our attempt is rather to reflect on the social significance and meaning of such religious phenomena. This is indeed a necessary step for theological discussion, which becomes meaningful only in the social context in which much religious phenomena become intelligible and significant.

The "tent touring" of the Fransican brothers is an example of what has come to be called "the direct proclamation of the gospel". This has been a time honoured strategy of missionaries from the time of St. Paul ("Woe to me if I do not preach the gospel," 1 Cor 9:16) to the days of St. Francis Xavier and after. Indeed this "tent touring" surely has some parallel with the missionary activity of Xavier, who would recite the "Credo" or preach a sermon that he had learned by heart in a language he did not comprehend, and then baptize thousands of 'pagans' before moving on to newer pastures. Now if our judgement of Xavier must be in the historical context of his time, then our discussion of "tent-touring" must be contextualized in ours.

It is rather presumptuous to conclude that such conversions are the result of a mass realization of the 'truth' of the new religion as opposed to the inadequacies of the old one, or that material inducements and clever persuasion have led such people to change their religious allegiance *en masse*. Such presumptions seem to derive less from historical fact than from the ethnocentric perspective and paternalist prejudice of the outsider, who has too much regard for his own religion and/or too little for the integrity of these other people. A realistic appreciation of tribal society and culture would demand a less facile explanation.

The religious conversion of a group represents a change in social allegiance that is more than just religious. It is the function which the new allegiance fulfils, and the new social context which it creates, wherein the significance and meaning of this change must be sought in any sociological reflection.[10]

From the historical context of the Warlis sketched above it is apparent that the tribal situation at this time was one of oppression, both religious and social. Their animistic faith was not a bedrock of assurance against the fears and anxieties that seemed to crowd in on them with the political, economic and social changes that left them increasingly more oppressed and defenceless. Yet a change of religious allegiance meant cultural and tribal isolation. This made individual conversion socially rather costly and difficult. Group conversion provided more security. While it is true that the earliest converts were somewhat scattered, marginalized persons, eventually those who persevered were more likely to have been helped by the support of a family and even of a larger group of families in the village or at least in its hamlets (*padas*).

The earliest efforts of the brothers at evangelization addressed themselves to the condition of spiritual distress the tribals seemed to experience in their changing world. But their endeavour was never confined to religion alone. From the very beginning the mission did make efforts to buffer the social isolation of conversion and lessen tribal dependence on landlords, moneylenders and other exploiters. They supported the neophytes as best they could by building small communities of them, providing some measure of charitable relief for the needy, and especially education for the tribals who wanted it.

From its early endeavours the mission's social involvement progressively increased, as it consolidated the school system, expanded into development work, and eventually into non-formal education and conscientization. The tribal response to these efforts can hardly be explained by force or fraud. Some genuine need, some deep aspiration of these people, must have been touched for them to choose an allegiance to the mission in spite of the opposition they had to brave.

When social change adversely affects a people and they find no adequate ways of coping with their insecurities from within their prevailing religion and culture, then religious renewal or conversion can easily be precipitated. In the oppressive situation of the Warlis at the time, the brothers' preaching must have represented such a spiritual liberation from their fear of evil-spirits and a new assurance against their anxieties in their fast deteriorating situation. Obviously the social involvement of the mission in their lives had something to do with this change in their religious allegiance. But to dismiss the importance of the religious factor and its significance for these tribals is to discount their religious sensibilities because of our own secular prejudices.

Certainly the religious promise and hope the missionaries brought these tribals was rendered more credible by their endeavour to uplift them socially. For the religious does not exist in isolation from the human, either in the individual nor in society.

Over the years we have seen how the understanding of the missionary endeavour did change in the direction of a broader commitment to social development and human liberation, though the religious inspiration is not lost. If then the early conversions among these people were fróm an experience of spiritual and religious liberation, their perseverance in the face of persecution and violence becomes intelligible only when it is seen in the light of a larger experience, a wider and more integrated liberation in their struggle for justice, and not just in that of the faith.

(b) *The Opposition from Vested Interests*

If we have rejected the facile explanations of tribal conversions which seem to derive from ethnocentric or paternalistic assumptions, then here too we must not be naive with the mission's opponents. To discuss the opposition to the mission in terms of demonic forces and evil inspirations or the inevitable burden of the cross may go better with some theological perspectives than with others. But we are engaged in a sociological reflection, not a theological controversy. Hence our attempt will be to contextualize the concerns of the mission's opponents in terms of the social situation from which they derive. For even apparently accidental events and individual motivations ought to be seen in this context. Only then is it possible to discern the structure into which they fall, and make an analysis at the level of social significance and meaning, as we did earlier for the issue of conversion.

How one comes across to one's opponents must surely be included somehow in one's self-understanding. For their perception can often come from an entirely different perspective, and precisely as such can provide some interesting and revealing insights, once a proper context has been set. It would be unfortunate to discount them as merely subjective and prejudiced, and to miss the opportunity of seeing oneself through the eyes of one's opponents, for whatever it is worth, which sometimes does amount to rather much. Hopefully we will not make this mistake with the mission here.

Although the brothers first pitched their tent near Bhilad railway station in November 1921, it was only in 1926 that they were able to secure land at Zaroli nearby. For, roused by a visiting brahmin priest, the landlords began a campaign of protest to the government to keep the brothers out of the area. This opposition seems to have increased even though it never quite succeeded in stopping the progress of the mission.

Frequently the opposition was expressed in a landlord expelling his Christian Warli tenants, who were not much more than bonded labourers. So it fell to the mission to rehabilitate them on land it acquired on their behalf. Thus in 1939 the Christians of Thakurpada, a village near Dapchari, were expelled by their landlord for refusing to give up their faith and were resettled by the mission at Varkhandha. Eventually the land legislation enacted after Independence did provide some means of legal redress, however inadequate.

At times the opposition was more organized and planned. In 1936 Brother Sales, a Franciscan, converted to Hinduism, assumed the name of Narayan Sharma, and with the active support of the landlords and moneylenders (*saukars*), mounted a vigorous campaign against the mission, trying to wean people away from it. On occasion the confrontation took a violent turn, as when on the 13th November, 1939, Narayan Sharma called a large public meeting at Numberpada near Nagzari, and the mission mobilized Christians to oppose it.

In the end the faithful persistence of the missionaries in following their flock led to the diminishing of Sharma's impact. By 1943 his influence seems to have waned, to go by the people's response to the meetings he called. By 1947 he moved out of the mission area to the coast. He was finally reconciled to the church in 1954, and his brahmin wife received into the faith in 1955.

Obviously there were religious, political and economic concerns involved in this opposition. For the Hindu priests and tribal *shamans* (*bhagats*), the new faith represented a religious and cultural challenge they could not take lightly. Hence their attempts to isolate and ostracize the neophytes. However, the converts' response, encouraged by their priests, was to preserve as much of their tribal culture and religion as was compatible with their new faith. Becoming Christian was not to alienate themselves from being Warlis. They would authentically be both. This approach served to buffer the change of conversion for both sides. Later it was developed into a full-fledged policy of 'inculturation'.

Interestingly it is only more recently, and rather as a response to tribal conversions to Christianity, that Hindus have claimed them as their own. Earlier their animistic religion was not regarded as part of the 'sanatana dharma', and certainly tribal gods were not part of the Hindu pantheon, though tribals had adopted some of these deities. Today this claim that primitive tribal religion is part of Hinduism seems to be more politically inspired than historically or sociologically founded.

Moreover, much of the opposition to the mission came from Muslim and especially Parsi landlords, who could have little religious concern over conversions that did not directly affect their religious community. It seems then that underlying the expressed religious concerns of the mission's opponents were political and economic ones. These could only come from perceiving the mission as a threat to their interests in this area, which must lead us to conclude that the mission brought more than spiritual or religious liberation (*moksha*) to these tribals. Its involvement in social welfare and development, in education and conscientization, was rightly perceived as a threat to the social structure that had served the vested interests in the area so well. Surely this was a threat even less acceptable than the religious challenge the mission posed.

(c) *The Conflict with the Communists*

If the mission was seen as an instrument of change on behalf of the oppressed by the established interests, then it becomes problematic indeed to explain the confrontation with a political party struggling for the same goal. The adivasi revolt led by the Communist party in the area provoked a harsh response from the state,[11] and the mission by and large seems to have sided with the state and against the Communists. They in turn seem to have perceived the mission as supporting the status quo and opposing genuine structural change.

At first sight a conflict between an atheistic political party and a property-conscious church might well seem inevitable. However, we cannot but be skeptical as to how atheistic these tribal communists were — though their party leaders may well have been — or how property-conscious Christian tribals were — though their missionary institutions may well have been. The hostility of these two protagonists is not easily explained in terms of the local situation alone, but must be seen in a larger context.

This was the time of the cold war on the international scene, when the Catholic Church and the Communist Party were implacable enemies. The Catholic Church in India clearly took its cue from the Roman Church just as the Communist Party in India did from the international communist movement. Thus in 1937, Pius XI in his encyclical "On Atheistic Communism" condemned communism as "intrinsically perverse" and forbade Christians to "collaborate with it in any undertaking whatsoever". A decree of the Holy Office in 1949, which was reiterated again in 1959, excommunicated Catholics who collaborated with the Communist Party. And this could hardly have remained as a one-sided antagonism.

On the national scene, the Congress party in power was firmly opposed to the Communist Party and its ideology. The Indian Church, with its sensitivity to its minority status, took the safer option of siding with the state. The Communist Party, with its revolutionary pretensions, took the one against the government.

Moreover, the preoccupation of the Indian Church with the communist threat is well reflected in the *Reports of the Catholic Bishops' Conference of India* (CBCI). In 1946 the entire report dealt with communism, claiming that

> "the gravest danger to faith and right social order is present day communism. . . . Extensive rioting and lawlessness in big cities can be traced to communist activities."[12]

And as late as 1960, the bishops wanted to "protect the people in general and Catholics in particular, against the virus of communist ideology."[13] And once again, on the international as on the national level, the communist party was not about to respond to such a stance by turning the other cheek.

It seems then that it was really the religious-political conflict on the international scene, and the political-economic one in the nation, that oriented and triggered the confrontation between the local church and local party in the mission area. Today the context has changed. Internationally the religious cold war between Catholics and Marxists has thawed. The two sides have become more appreciative of each other since liberation theology made its appearance. Nationally too, there has been change. The communist parties have entered parliamentary politics, and a more indigenous church is more willing to oppose the government on issues of justice. Such changes have slowly begun to filter down to the local level at Talasari, where the hostility is less overt, though the suspicions remain.

Eventually both the protagonists settled down to a working arrangement. The mission withdrew its overt opposition to the communist vote, and the party refrained from actively harassing the Christians in the villages. The tribals still vote communist in the area, and the Christians still practice and preach their faith. Such co-existence makes for a precarious peace, which easily breaks down whenever the mission has attempted anything that may threaten the party's political base, which it jealously guards.

In 1978 the Kashtakari Sanghatana was launched as a movement to fight for the rights of the toiling masses, under the guidance of two Jesuit priests who were inspired by liberation theology. Many educated tribal youth, mostly Christian, participated. This was seen by the party to be a direct threat to its political dominance in the area and there followed a series of violent attacks on mission property and personnel, on Christian villages and sympathizers. The two priests were expelled from the Order by 1982 and only when the mission completely dissociated itself from the movement was there some reprieve from such violence.

The Kashtakari Sanghatana has evolved into a Marxist-Leninist inspired movement, and is actively involved in the political struggle of the area. However the hostility between the two Marxist-inspired protagonists is unabated and often spills over into violence. This situation is hardly to the best advantage of the tribals but it is not uncommon with grass-roots movements of the left and a dominant communist party in the area.

5. Summing Up

The questions pertinent to conversion and confrontation are not peculiar to Talasari. The dynamics of the issues involved are more general, and this makes them relevant to a wider discussion.

The shift in the mission's focus from a narrow religious approach to a broader social involvement and eventually to a political concern is not an exceptional problem. Two complementary processes are at work here. From the outside, the experiences in the field of the interrelatedness of the religious and the social, and the response this calls for; and on the inside, a reflection on this experience, questioning the old and inspiring a new vision for mission work.

The confrontation that the mission met with is very much a part of the mission's experience, just as the perceptions of its opponents are also very revealing. The extra-religious involvement of the mission in the lives of the people to liberate them is indeed authenticated by this opposition of the landlords and moneylenders,. especially when religious conversion was not an issue for the non-Hindus among these, why else were they so opposed to the mission!

It was the same vested interests that had earlier opposed the Devi cult that had swept through this area in 1922.[14] It was a religious movement which advocated vegetarianism and ritual cleanliness, banned liquor and boycotted the Parsis. Thus it was both an "act of assertion against the most rapacious of the local exploiters, the Parsis" and an attempt "to appropriate (and thus democratize and implicitly change) the values associated with the regionally dominant high caste Hindus (and Jains).[15] Eventually the movement was suppressed by the British when it took on a nationalist turn. But the centrality of religious symbolism to the movement and the challenge it posed to the tribal exploiters are crucial to our understanding of the tribals' conversion to Christianity and its implication for the local vested interests, as part of the saga of the mission.

The conflict with the communist party seems to have ideological overtones, a religious 'ideology' for the mission and a political one for the party. These seem to derive from the international affiliations of both, the Roman Church for the mission and the international communist movement for the party. At the national level too, the opposition between the government and the communist party disinclined a church conscious of its minority status from supporting any radical opposition to the government or the status quo.

The conflict then between the Christians and the communists seems to have been precipitated less by the local situation itself than by factors extraneous to it. Only when the church posed a threat to the political vote of the party did they retaliate. Otherwise a co-existence seems to have been worked out. More recently, with the mission's connection with the initial stages of the Kashtakari movement, there were violent reprisals by the party. However, now that the mission has distanced itself from the movement the status quo ante prevails. This of course is not an appraisal of the role of any of the parties to this conflict, it is only a comment on the relationship between two of the protagonists.

The mission to Warlis in Talasari represents a small missionary endeavor in the church's history. But its evolution does have parallels elsewhere in the country. Though we cannot develop them here we will do well to at least indicate one of them, so the broader implication of our conclusions for Talasari are not lost.

The Ranchi mission to the tribals in Chota Nagpur, begun in the 18th century, has been a model for Talasari. Here too the initial efforts at evangelization soon included a social involvement, as epitomized by the struggle of Constance Lievans on behalf of the tribals against their oppressors. There have been tribal movements, from Birsa Munda in 1895 onwards, that revolted against this oppression,[16] but the local church was not in confrontation with them. These movements were by tribal leaders, not communist outsiders. The local situation did not warrant any conflict and extraneous factors did not intervene. The Jharkhand movement today with its demand for a separate tribal state represents a coalescence of earlier movements against the 'dikhu', the outsider. But Christians were not considered so. In fact they are largely supportive of the movement.

The parallel between Talasari and Chota Nagpur should not be overplayed, but it can be instructive in understanding the saga of the Talasari mission. To see this saga as the secularization of the mission is to miss the really critical issue : the quest of the mission to liberate the people, a quest as old as the Exodus and enlivened today with the inspiration of liberation theology. It is beyond the scope of this study to trace the development of the theology implied in this quest, and how the 'liberationist' elements have been articulated at various times. This has been documented and made explicit in numerous theological studies now available. Here we have tried to underline the social processes which have moved the mission in this direction, processes which do in fact embrace the religious and the social, including the political and economic dimensions as well.

At one level, the service of the faith and the promotion of justice must be explicitly integrated in an apostolic endeavour. There is a tension between them that must be transcended. And yet at another level, the very interrelatedness of the realities encountered in the field demands a correspondingly integrated approach, which any genuine involvement must meet or become marginal to the real needs of the situation. At Talasari both these levels were operative, at times perhaps one more than the other, though the general trend of the shift has been from the implicit to the explicit articulation of the liberation perspective operative here.

And so, it is only in such a total context of the interrelatedness of these aspects, and their connectedness to the situation beyond the local one, that the true saga of the Talasari mission can be told. It is a tale not without its share of lost opportunities and unintended consequences, but certainly also one of dedication and perseverance, of quiet heroism and selfless sacrifice. But this is not the end of the story. We feel sure the saga of the Talasari mission will continue and be retold many times.

6. Conclusions

The contextualization in the earlier chapter has helped to establish some crucial points. The critical importance of education for the tribal community if they are not to be left behind by the development process is not contested anymore. That the place to begin this is by universalizing primary education, and making it effectively available among them is also recognized. That the acceptable way to do this is not by 'assimilating' them so that they are merged in the mainstream where they lose their identity, but rather to 'integrate' them is that they keep their dignity even if they must change; just as other groups will have to as well.

Hence the need for an education programme that will reach them where they are now, to take them where they will be better off tomorrow. The historical sketch of the Talasari mission in this chapter has shown that this has been the inspiration behind the more recent and intensified effort of mission through its network of schools. It is surely not the only service it offers these tribals, but it is certainly in continuity with their endeavour to uplift and liberate these people they have dedicated themselves to serve, in religious as well as social ways.

NOTES

1. *Documents of the 32nd General Congregation of the Society of Jesus*, Dec. 4. "Our Mission Today" Nos. 47-130, Anand Press, Anand, 1976, pp. 107-138.

2. *Cf.* K. J. Save, *The Warlis*, Padma Pub., Bombay, 1945..
3. *Cf. Census of India 1981: Figures of Total Population, Scheduled Caste Population and Scheduled Tribe Population, Series 12*, Maharashtra Directory of Census Operations, Maharashtra, 1982, pp.1-2.
4. Bombay Government Central Press, 1939, Cited in *Repression in Dahanu: Where It Comes From*, Lok Hakk Sanghatana, Maharashtra, Bombay, 1983.
5. Ashok K. Upadhaya, "Peasantization of Adivasis in Thane District", *Economic and Political Weekly*, V15, N 52, 27 Dec. 1980, Review of Agricultural p. A.134.
6. *Ibid*., p. A-137.
7. *Cf. Quarterly Journal of the Poona Sarvajanik Sabha*, V.19, N.1-2, 1896, p.33.
8. *Cf.* Godavari Parulekar, *Adivasis Revolt: The Story of the Warli Peasants in Struggle*, National Book Agency, Calcutta, 1975.
9. *Cf.* Henry Comes, S.J, *A Historical Sketch of the Zaroli Mission*, Diocesan Seminary, Bombay 1959, unpublished typescript p.8.
10. *Cf.* Augustine Kanjamala, *Religion and Modernization of India*, Ishvani, Pune,1981, esp. Ch.2, Mass Conversion to Christianity and Social Changes before 1949, p.55 and ff.
11. *Cf.* Godavari Parulekar, *Adivasis Revolt, op. cit.* Ch.10, p.116 and ff.
12. Cited by John Desrochers, *The Social Teaching of the Church*, published by the author, Bangalore,1982, p.408,from the CBCI Report, 1946, pp. 57 and 59.
13. *Ibid*., from the CBCI Report, 1960, p. 40.
14. David Hardiman, *The Coming of the Devi: Adivasi Assertion in Western India*, Oxford Univ. Press, Bombay,1987.
15. *Ibid*., p. 164.
16. Stephen Fuchs, *Rebellious Prophets: A Study of Messianic Movements in Indian Religions*, Asia Pub. House, Bombay, 1965.

4

THE DATA PRESENTATION

Introduction

The tabulated data presented in this chapter constitute a first level description, that begins to make a coherent picture of a mass of detail, lest the wood be missed for the trees. An index of the variables used is reproduced in the appendix. The tabulation itself is fairly straight forward and uncomplicated. But sketching the more subtle contours within a broad outline will require a fairly comprehensive grasp of the tables so that underlying patterns can be later perceived. The descriptive analysis here begins this discussion on the data but does not complete it. A more refined statistical analysis will ransack the data more thoroughly in the next chapter (i.e., Chapter 5) and make for a more in-depth and comprehensive discussion. However, the final interpretation will be made only in the concluding chapter which will bring together the qualitative analysis in the light of the qualitative data.

The presentation here is in four rather lengthy parts: (1) the students, (2) the parents, (3) the teachers and (4) institutional goals. The various sections in each of these represent the different sub-groups in the sample, separated out for more controlled comparisons.

1. THE STUDENTS

(1) The Sample

The students in the sample were selected to represent both the primary and the secondary levels in the schools surveyed. For the primary level, all the 7th standard students in the school were included, and for the secondary one, all the 10th standard students. The zilla parishad schools (Talasari, Zari, Udhwa) (ZP) and the

Dhundalwadi ashramshala (DW) were primary schools up to the 7th only, so they are not represented at the secondary level. The mission schools (MS) at the primary level included two schools: Varkhanda with 18 students, and Talasari with 59 students, making a total of 77 students.

At the secondary level the mission school at Uplat Patilpada had only the 8th standard. Rather than leave this level unrepresented, these students were included with all the 10th standard students of the other schools : Thakkarbapa High School (TB), Dapchari High School (DC), and the two ashramshalas (AS) i.e., Saune and Uplat.

TABLE 4.1: Student Distribution of Sample

	School						
	MS	TB	DW	DC	AS	ZP	Total
Primary	77	14	20	33	23	25	192
Secondary	48	55	0	22	26	0	151
	125	69	20	55	49	25	343

(2) **Students' Background Variables**

(a) *Age*

The average age of the student sample is 14.6 years. There are minimal differences across the schools at the primary level, and at the secondary one too, if one considers that the mission school 8th standard students are two years behind the students in the 10th. Here the ashramshala students appear to be a year above the average age.

TABLE 4.2: Average Age in Years

% ave. age (N)	School						
	MS	TB	DW	DC	AS	ZP	ALL
Primary	13.14 (77)	13.43 (14)	12.60 (20)	13.29 (31)	13.61 (23)	13.96 (25)	13.29 (190)
Secondary	14.92 (48)	16.70 (54)	–	16.27 (22)	17.25 (26)	–	16.15 (150)
Total	13.82 (125)	16.03 (68)	12.60 (20)	14.53 (53)	15.54 (49)	13.96 (25)	14.55 (340)

(b) *Religion*

Christian children almost exclusively attend mission schools at the primary level. At the secondary one, they mostly attend Thakkarbapa from the mission boarding in Talasari in the 9th and 10th, since the mission high school does not as yet have these standards.

TABLE 4.3: Percentage Christian Children (N)

	School						
	MS	TB	DW	DC	AS	ZP	ALL
Primary							
Percentage	68.8	0.0	0.0	0.0	4.3	0.0	28.1
(N)	(55)	(0)	(0)	(0)	(1)	(0)	(56)
Secondary							
Percentage	79.2	41.8	—	0.0	0.0	—	40.4
(N)	(38)	(23)		(0)	(0)		(61)
Total	74.4	33.3	0.0	0.0	2.0	0.0	30.6
	(93)	(23)	(0)	(0)	(1)	(0)	(117)

(c) *Caste*

The Dapchari High School has the lowest proportion of adivasis because it draws its students from the government dairy scheme which employs many non-adivasis. The zilla parishad schools in the sample were situated in towns with a sizeable non-adivasi presence as is reflected in their enrollment. The non-adivasis in the mission schools are represented only in the primary school at Talasari. Ashramshalas can of course admit adivasis only.

TABLE 4.4: Percentage of Adivasis (N)

	School						
	MS	TB	DW	DC	AS	ZP	ALL
Primary							
Percentage	76.6	92.9	95.0	45.5	100.0	80.0	77.6
(N)	(59)	(13)	(19)	(15)	(23)	(20)	(149)
Secondary							
Percentage	100.0	81.8	—	36.4	100.0	—	84.1
(N)	(48)	(45)		(8)	(26)		(127)
Both	85.6	84.1	95.0	41.8	100.0	80.0	80.5
	(107)	(58)	(19)	(23)	(49)	(20)	(276)

(d) *Sex*

The proportion of female students is highest in Dapchari H.S., very probably because of the highest proportion of non-adivasis there, but there is a decline from the primary (39.4%) to the secondary level (18.2%). Mission schools show an increase across these levels (16.9% to 22.9%) and ashramshalas a drop (8.7% to 0.0%).

TABLE 4.5: Percentage of Female Students

	School						
	MS	TB	DW	DC	AS	ZP	ALL
Primary							
Percentage	16.9	14.3	10.0	39.4	8.7	8.0	17.7
(N)	(13)	(2)	(2)	(13)	(2)	(2)	(34)
Secondary							
Percentage	22.9	16.4	—	18.2	0.0	—	15.9
(N)	(11)	(9)		(4)	(0)		(24)
Both	19.2	15.9	10.0	30.9	4.1	8.0	16.9
	(24)	(11)	(2)	(17)	(2)	(2)	(58)

(e) *Parental Occupation*

Parental occupations were categorized as follows:

1. Landless, daily wage labourers who were seasonal workers ("*mazuri*", LL)
2. Landed farmers including those who worked on others' land as well as their own land ("*shethi kam*", FA)
3. Regularly employed manual workers, skilled and unskilled ("*naukari*", MW)
4. Regularly employed non-manual workers, clerical, white-collar ("office *kam*", WC)
5. Business ("*dhanda*", BU)

The most common parental occupation is farming (72.9% of farmers) followed by white-collar workers (11.4%). Business is least common (4.7%) and the landless labourers and manual workers next (5.5% each).

TABLE 4.6: Father's Occupation N = 343

Occupation % (N)	School						
	MS	TB	DW	DC	AS	ZP	ALL
1. LL	6	7	1	1	3	1	19
	(4.8)	(10.1)	(5.0)	(1.8)	(6.1)	(4.0)	(5.5)
2. FA	89	50	16	31	44	20	250
	(71.2)	(72.5)	(80.0)	(56.4)	(89.8)	(80.0)	(72.9)
3. MW	6	1	3	7	0	2	19
	(4.8)	(1.4)	(15.0)	(12.7)	(0.0)	(8.0)	(5.5)
4. WC	13	9	0	14	1	2	39
	(10.4)	(13.)	(0.0)	(25.5)	(2.0)	(8.0)	(11.4)
5. BU	11	2	0	2	1	0	16
	(8.8)	(2.9)	(0.0)	(3.6)	(2.0)	(0.0)	(4.7)
Total	125	69	20	55	49	25	343
	(100.0)	(100.0)	(100.0)	(100.0)	(100.0)	(100.0)	(100.0)

With agriculture as the main occupation, some breakdown of the sample in terms of agricultural assets would be in order. Moreover, even those in non-agricultural occupations would generally have some such assets as well. The assets were graded in ascending order thus : land, bullocks, well, pump. Each was given a single point to form an additive scale of range 0 = landless, no assets, to 4 = a farmer with all assets and so capable of a second crop. The assumption underlying the scale is that those with the higher order assets would have the lower ones too, i.e., someone who owned a well would have land and bullocks, etc.

TABLE 4.7: Agricultural Assets (N = 343, Range = 0-4)

	School						
	MS	TB	DW	DC	AS	ZP	ALL
Primary	1.38	1.29	1.65	0.94	1.13	1.20	1.27
Secondary	1.17	1.09	—	1.23	1.23	—	1.16
Both	1.30	1.13	1.65	1.06	1.18	1.20	1.22

(f) *Parental Education*

To compare the educational level of the students' families, two variables were used: father's level of education (FAEDUC) and parental level of education i.e., father's and mother's level of education (FAMED)

The levels of education were categorized as follows:

1 = no education
2 = 1st std to 4th std
3 = 5th std to 7th std
4 = 8th std to SSC
5 = SSC and above

Thus the scale range for father's education would be 1 to 5, for family education 2 to 10.

The average educational level of the father is 2.17, i.e. between the 1st and 4th standard of the lower primary level. The level of the primary school parents is slightly higher (2.30) than that of the secondary school ones (2.01). The mother's education is lower (1.46) than the father's.

TABLE 4.8: Father's Education (N = 343, Range = 1-5)

	School						
	MS	TB	DW	DC	AS	ZP	ALL
Primary	2.44	2.64	1.25	3.18	1.70	1.92	2.30
Secondary	2.17	1.95	—	2.55	1.38	—	2.01
Both	2.34	2.09	1.25	2.93	1.53	1.92	2.17

TABLE 4.9: Parental Education (N = 343, Range = 1-5)

	School						
	MS	TB	DW	DC	AS	ZP	ALL
Primary	4.04	4.00	2.35	5.58	2.74	3.16	3.85
Secondary	3.46	3.29	—	4.41	2.38	—	3.35
Both	3.82	3.43	2.35	5.11	2.55	3.16	3.63

(g) *Educational Support*

The support and encouragement a child gets outside school from family and friends is an important factor in the child's performance in school. This was looked at in two ways:

(a) *from where the support came:* whether parents or others (relatives, friends, teachers, social workers, etc.) encouraged the child to go to school and brought them back if they ran away from school.

(b) *the strength of this parental support*: how insistent the parents were on regular attendance at school and whether the text and copy books, etc, were obtained for the child at the beginning of school year or later. The scale for this measure was 0 to 4.

TABLE 4.10: Who encourages you to go school? (Breakdown by school level)

%age (N) Encouraged by	School level		
	Primary	Secondary	Both
Nobody	3.6 (7)	2.0 (3)	2.9 (10)
Parents only	78.6 (151)	56.3 (85)	68.8 (236)
Parents and others	17.7 (34)	41.7 (63)	27.3 (97)
Total	100.0 (192)	100.0 (151)	100.0 (343)

TABLE 4.11: Who encourages you to go to school? (Breakdown by school type)

%age (N) Encouraged By	School						
	MS	TB	DW	DC	AS	ZP	ALL
Nobody	3.2 (4)	2.9 (2)	0.0 (0)	1.8 (1)	2.0 (1)	8.0 (2)	2.9 (10)
Parents only	77.6 (97)	49.3 (34)	100.0 (20)	70.9 (39)	69.4 (34)	48.0 (12)	68.8 (236)
Parents & Others	19.2 (24)	47.8 (33)	0.0 (0)	27.3 (15)	28.6 (14)	44.0 (11)	28.3 (97)
Total	100.0 (125)	100.0 (69)	100.0 (20)	100.0 (55)	100.0 (49)	100.0 (25)	100.0 (343)

TABLE 4.12: Who encourages you back to school if you run away? (Breakdown by school level)

%age (N) Brought back by	School level		
	Primary	Secondary	All
No one 5.2	4.0 (10)	4.7 (6)	(16)
Parents only	74.0 (142)	53.0 (80)	64.7 (222)
Parents and others	20.8 (40)	43.0 (65)	30.6 (105)
Total	100.0 (192)	100.0 (151)	100.0 (343)

TABLE 4.13: Who brings you back to school if you run away? (Breakdown by School Type)

%age (N) Brought back by	School type						
	MS	TB	DW	DC	AS	ZP	ALL
No one	4.8 (6)	4.3 (3)	0.0 (0)	1.8 (1)	6.1 (3)	12.0 (3)	4.7 (16)
Parents only	71.2 (89)	42.0 (29)	100 (20)	74.5 (41)	63.3 (31)	48.0 (12)	64.7 (222)
Parents and others	24.0 (30)	53.6 (37)	0.0 (0)	23.6 (13)	30.6 (15)	40.0 (10)	30.6 (105)
Total	100.0 (125)	100.0 (69)	100.0 (20)	100.0 (55)	100.0 (49)	100.0 (25)	100.0 (343)

TABLE 4.14: Strength of Parental Support (Range = 0-4)

Score (N) School level	School Type						
	MS	TB	DW	DC	AS	ZP	ALL
Primary	3.35 (77)	2.93 (14)	3.05 (20)	3.52 (33)	3.22 (23)	2.92 (25)	3.24 (192)
Secondary	3.00 (48)	2.93 (55)	–	3.32 (22)	3.15 (26)	–	3.05 (151)
Both	3.22 (125)	2.93 (69)	3.05 (20)	3.44 (55)	3.18 (49)	2.92 (25)	3.16 (343)

From Tables 4.10 to 4.14 on parental support, it is apparent that the strongest source of support and encouragement for school-going comes from the parents, both at primary and secondary levels. But there is a decrease in this from the primary to the secondary, while there is a corresponding increase in support from others, mainly teachers. Among the schools the zilla parishad ones and Thakkarbapa have the lowest parental support while the mission schools and the Dapchari one have the highest.

(3) Student Performance Variables

The data describing the students in school must be seen against their family and social background. We have already presented some information on this, obtained from the students themselves. A more detailed analysis of the relationship between home and school will be made after the data from the parents' questionnaire is presented.

(a) *The Boarding*

The educational advantage of a boarding in the situation we are studying is not contested. The ashram school was mooted precisely because of this. But boardings are an expensive proposition and indicate an intensive rather than an extensive investment in education.

The overall percentage of boarders is high (72.3%), lower in the primary (65.6%) than the secondary (81.5%).

TABLE 4.15: Percentage of Boarders

%age (N)	School						
	MS	TB	DW	DC	AS	ZP	ALL
Primary	61.0 (47)	92.9 (13)	90.0 (18)	30.3 (10)	100 (23)	60.0 (15)	65.6 (126)
Secondary	95.8 (46)	85.5 (47)	—	22.7 (5)	96.2 (25)	—	81.5 (123)
Both	74.4 (93)	87.0 (60)	90.0 (18)	27.3 (15)	98.0 (48)	60.0 (15)	72.3 (249)

(b) *The Subjects*

Students were asked which subjects they liked best and which they found most difficult. Their answers were classified as follows:

1. English Language (Eng)
2. Indian Languages i.e., Hindi, Marathi, Sanskrit (IL)
3. Social Sciences i.e., History, Civics, Geography (SS)
4. Mathematics i.e., Arithmetic, Geometry, Algebra (Mat)
5. Science i.e., Physics, Chemistry, Biology (Sc)
6. Art i.e., Drawing (Art)

TABLE 4.16: Best Liked Subject

%age (N)	Subject						
	Eng	IL	SS	Mat	Sc	Art	All
	1	2	3	4	5	6	7
Primary	13.0 (25)	36.5 (70)	16.7 (32)	10.9 (21)	15.1 (29)	7.8 (15)	100.0 (192)
Secondary	8.6 (13)	36.4 (55)	25.8 (39)	12.6 (19)	10.6 (16)	6.0 (9)	100.0 (151)
Both	11.1 (38)	36.4 (125)	20.7 (71)	11.7 (40)	13.1 (45)	7.0 (24)	100.0 (343)

TABLE 4.17: Most Difficult Subjects

%age (N)	Subject						
	Eng	IL	SS	Mat	Sc	Art	All
	1	2	3	4	5	6	7
Primary	44.3 (85)	3.6 (7)	12.0 (23)	32.8 (63)	0.0 (0)	7.3 (14)	100 (192)
Secondary	49.0 (74)	1.3 (2)	3.3 (5)	40.4 (61)	2.0 (3)	4.0 (6)	100.0 (151)
Both	46.4 (159)	2.6 (9)	8.2 (28)	36.2 (124)	0.9 (3)	5.8 (20)	100.0 (343)

From Tables 4.16 to 4.17 we see that Indian languages and the social sciences are the best liked subjects and among the least difficult ones. English and mathematics are among the least liked and they are the most difficult ones. So far this seems consistent. However, science and art are among the least liked but among the least difficult ones too.

(c) *Class Difficulties*

Asked if they could follow the teacher in class, the students by and large responded positively: 28 per cent say they can follow easily, 70 per cent can if they make the effort and only two per cent say they cannot. Between levels of schooling, the primary students found it easier to follow their teachers than the secondary ones, and among the schools the ones with a higher percentage of adivasis found it more difficult than those with a lower percentage, i.e., Dapchari students with the least difficulty and Dhundalwadi ones with the most. The Table 4.18 presents the responses to this question on a scale of 1 = can't follow to 3 = follow easily.

TABLE 4.18: Difficulty in Following the Teacher (Range = 1-3)

	MS	TB	DW	DC	AS	ZP	ALL
Primary	2.30	2.50	2.10	2.61	2.43	2.36	2.37
Secondary	2.02	2.09	—	2.50	2.04	—	2.12
Both	2.19	2.17	2.10	2.57	2.22	2.36	2.26

Furthermore, the difficulties of the students arise more from the subject than the method of teaching. Thus, 42 per cent had difficulty with the subject matter, nine per cent with the language, 19 per cent with the lack of clear explanation, 14 per cent with the classroom facilities, and 15 per cent had other difficulties.

(d) *Study Time*

Regarding study time to do their homework, 78 per cent report having enough time: the secondary level report a slightly higher percentage, 81 to the primary 74. In the Dhundalwadi school, zilla parishad and the ashram ones, a substantially lower percentage of students report having enough time to study, while Dapchari, the mission schools and Thakkarbapa are substantially higher.

TABLE 4.19: Study Time for Homework

	MS	TB	DW	DC	AS	ZP	ALL
Primary (%)	78	93	45	91	70	60	75
Secondary (%)	94	76	–	86	65	–	81
Both	84	80	45	89	67	60	78

At the primary level it is the students at Thakkarbapa and Dapchari that are most satisfied with their study time, at the secondary one it is those at the mission schools and Dapchari again.

(e) *Reading Habits*

The reading habits of the students are tabulated in Table 4.20:

TABLE 4.20: Student Reading Habits

	Read			
	Seldom	Now and then	Frequently	(N=100%)
Text books (%)	11	19	70	(332)
Guide books (%)	24	46	30	(331)
Story books (%)	43	52	5	(327)

It would seem that the students do not go much beyond, and some hardly as far as, reading text books. Of course encouraging reading habits depends not only on the teacher but on the availability of text books as well. On this, *more government-run* zilla parishad and ashram schools *do better than* private ones, except the Dapchari, school where the support of non-adivasi parents seems to make the difference. Table 4.21 below, reading habits on the three *aspects* above are scored on a scale of 0-9.

TABLE 4.21: Student Reading Habits by School (Range = 0-9)

	School						
	MS	TB	DW	DC	AS	ZP	ALL
Primary	5.47	5.86	5.70	6.67	6.13	6.64	5.96
Secondary	5.77	6.07	—	6.41	6.81	—	6.15
Both	5.58	6.03	5.70	6.57	6.49	6.64	6.04

(f) *Examination Performance*

While examination performance cannot be the most important criterion of evaluating students, it cannot be ignored entirely either. For failure, here, often results in drop-outs, stagnation, i.e., repeating the year. Moreover, examinations do allow crude though not completely useless, comparisons.

TABLE 4.22: Students Passing in All Subjects

%age (N)	School						
	MS	TB	DW	DC	AS	ZP	ALL
Students 4th std.	89.5 (68)	92.6 (13)	95.0 (19)	93.5 (29)	95.7 (22)	84.0 (21)	91.0 (172)
Students 7th std.	54.4 (26)	76.4 (42)	—	95.2 (20)	88.5 (23)	—	74.0 (111)

The differences at the primary level are minimal, and the general performance rather good. This is perhaps because in the last year before middle school, the marking is lenient to encourage students to study further. At the secondary level, the mission school is far less selective than the others, drawing as it does from a wider network of primary schools.

(g) *Teacher Availability*

From the students' perspective, the availability of the teacher to answer their difficulties is an important input in the learning process.

The responses show that teachers are not very available outside school or at home.

TABLE 4.23: Teachers Responding to Student Difficulties

	In class	In school (outside school)	Outside school	At home
%age who don't respond (N)	7% (22)	11% (36)	38% (124)	41% (133)

The four categories above were collapsed on a scale of 0 to 8 and tabulated as below (Table 4.24). Not unexpectedly, the school with a higher percentage of resident teachers scored higher.

TABLE 4.24: Teachers' Availability for Student Difficulties (N = 343, Range = 0-8)

	MS	TB	DW	DC	AS	ZP	ALL
Primary	4.46	4.29	5.25	3.70	4.52	4.16	4.37
Secondary	4.85	4.56	—	4.09	5.42	—	4.73
Both	4.61	4.51	5.25	3.86	5.00	4.16	4.53

(h) *Extra-Curricular Activities*

Among the extra-curricular activities, sport is much liked by most students (73%) followed by dramatics (36%), singing (34%), and craft (30%). Moreover 52 per cent say they have enough time for such activities as against 27 per cent who find the time too little. The primary schools have more time for this than the secondary ones. The ashram schools have substantially less time than the others at both levels, Thakkarbapa and Dapchari especially.

TABLE 4.25: Time for Extra-curricular Activities (N = 343)

	School						
	MS	TB	DW	DC	AS	ZP	ALL
Primary	65%	64%	60%	52%	35%	64%	58%
Secondary	60%	45%	—	18%	27%	—	43%
Both	63%	49%	60%	38%	31%	64%	52%

(i) *Work Experience*

Part of the explanation for the insufficient time given for extra-curricular activities may be found in the time given to work-experience. Of the 78 per cent who had such programmes in the school, 77 per cent said it was useful to themselves, 79 per cent to the school. The usefulness of such programmes on both these aspects was collapsed in a scale from 0 to 2 (see Table 4.26).

TABLE 4.26: Usefulness of Work-Experience (N= 343 Range 0-2)

	School						
	MS	TB	DW	DC	AS	ZP	ALL
Primary	.44	1.36	1.25	.97	1.30	.76	.83
Secondary	1.69	1.49	—	1.64	1.38	—	1.56
Both	.92	1.46	1.25	1.24	1.35	.76	1.15

Interestingly enough, the students in schools which gave less time to extra-curricular activities are the ones who have found work-experience more useful. But this should not pre-judge the relevance of one over the other.

(j) *Village Programmes*

The students' participation in village programmes is an important aspect of the school-community relationship. Only 14 per cent of the students said they did not participate in such programmes, while 47 per cent did, with 40 per cent even taking the initiative in a leadership role for such occasions. Table 4.27 shows their responses on a 0 to 2 scale of participation.

TABLE 4.27: Participation in Village Programmes (N= 343 Range = 0-2)

	School						
	MS	TB	DW	DC	AS	ZP	ALL
Primary	1.38	1.29	1.65	.94	1.13	1.20	1.27
Secondary	1.17	1.09	—	1.23	1.23	—	1.16
Both	1.30	1.13	1.65	1.06	1.18	1.20	1.22

The very low level of participation of Dapchari students is in contrast to the high level of participation among its own secondary school students. The ashram schools follow this pattern but the mission schools and Thakkarbapa reverse it. This pattern of participation must be further studied in the broader context of teacher participation in such village programmes and of the village contact with the school (See 3. The Teachers (6) School-Community Relationship, pp. 134-139).

(4) The Students' Attitudes

(a) *Educational Commitment*

The questionnaire attempted to study how committed the students were to their further education. If they were offered a job, would they prefer to pursue their education rather than accept the offer? On a scale of 1 to 3 their educational commitment is shown in Table 4.28.

TABLE 4.28: Educational Ambition (N= 343 Range= 1-3)

	School						
	MS	TB	DW	DC	AS	ZP	ALL
Primary	2.43	2.71	2.70	2.52	2.39	2.40	2.49
Secondary	2.29	2.69	—	2.86	2.46	—	2.55
Both	2.38	2.70	2.70	2.66	2.43	2.40	2.52

These scores do seem very high: overall 2.52, for the primary 2.48, and for the secondary 2.55. How realistic they are would depends on how committed the parents are to the further education of their child. (See Part 2: The Parents (4) (b) Parental Support for Education, pp. 89-93).

(b) *Occupational Preferences*

With reference to their future occupations, the students seem to be modestly ambitious. Only 47 per cent of the boys would like to follow their father's occupation and only 36 per cent of the girls the[illegible] preferences are. But once again how realistic these are would depend on their parental preference and support as well.

TABLE 4.29: Occupation Preferences

Occupation:	Level:	School						
		MS	TB	DW	DC	AS	ZP	ALL
Farmer:	Primary	53.2 (41)	7.1 (1)	65.0 (13)	6.1 (2)	52.2 (12)	32.0 (8)	40.1 (77)
	Secondary	50.0 (24)	25.5 (14)	–	4.5 (1)	80.8 (21)	–	39.7 (60)
Manual Worker:	Primary	29.9 (23)	57.1 (8)	10.0 (2)	6.1 (2)	30.4 (7)	16.0 (4)	24.0 (46)
	Secondary	33.3 (16)	21.8 (12)	–	40.9 (9)	34.6 (9)	–	30.5 (46)
Clerical Work:	Primary	11.7 (9)	0.0 (0)	25.0 (5)	0.0 (0)	26.1 (6)	20.0 (5)	13.0 (25)
	Secondary	6.3 (3)	7.3 (4)	–	0.0 (0)	26.9 (7)	–	9.3 (14)
Business:	Primary	16.9 (13)	21.4 (3)	20.0 (4)	0.0 (0)	30.4 (7)	4.0 (1)	14.6 (28)
	Secondary	6.3 (3)	7.3 (4)	–	9.1 (2)	19.2 (5)	–	9.3 (14)
Teacher:	Primary	55.8 (43)	71.4 (10)	65.0 (13)	18.2 (6)	87.0 (20)	72.0 (18)	57.3 (110)
	Secondary	60.4 (29)	52.7 (29)	–	27.3 (6)	88.5 (23)	–	57.6 (87)
Nurse:	Primary	19.5 (15)	7.1 (1)	20.0 (4)	15.2 (5)	26.1 (6)	16.0 (4)	18.2 (35)
	Secondary	20.8 (10)	12.7 (7)	–	0.0 (0)	11.5 (3)	–	13.2 (20)
Policeman:	Primary	10.4 (8)	21.4 (3)	55.0 (11)	0.0 (0)	34.8 (8)	32.0 (8)	19.8 (38)
	Secondary	14.6 (7)	9.1 (5)	–	4.5 (1)	38.5 (10)	–	15.2 (23)
Military Service:	Primary	14.3 (11)	35.7 (5)	80.0 (16)	9.1 (3)	30.4 (7)	20.0 (5)	24.5 (47)
	Secondary	22.9 (11)	40.0 (22)	–	27.3 (6)	38.5 (10)	–	32.5 (49)
Doctor:	Primary	40.3 (31)	42.9 (6)	50.0 (10)	24.2 (8)	47.8 (11)	44.0 (11)	40.1 (77)
	Secondary	25.0 (12)	32.7 (18)	–	22.7 (5)	34.6 (9)	–	29.1 (44)
Lawyer:	Primary	23.4 (18)	7.1 (1)	40.0 (8)	3.0 (1)	39.1 (9)	36.0 (9)	24.0 (46)
	Secondary	18.8 (9)	18.2 (10)	–	18.2 (4)	34.6 (9)	–	21.2 (32)

Farming and teaching are the preferred occupations, probably because they are the most familiar ones for these students. Business and clerical work were the least preferred. Given the high percentage of adivasis in this sample this is not surprising. Nursing too scores low because only the girls seem to choose it. Police service is less preferred to military service which scores about the same as manual work. Medicine is also a highly preferred occupation but not law, surely because it is seen to be the more prestigious of the two. However, it scores lower with the secondary students who seem more realistic about ambitions to such professions.

Looking now at the school-wise breakdown of the most preferred occupations: farming is least preferred in Dapchari and Thakkarbapa schools, specially at the primary level. In the ashram schools at the secondary level it is highest. Teaching is least preferred at Dapchari where regular manual employment scores high with the high school students.

The impression, then, from this analysis of occupational preferences is that students would rather choose the familiar occupations and they do get more realistic in their preferences as they reach high school. Once again these preferences must be seen together with those of their parents for a more complete view. (See Part: 2 The Parents (4) (c) Parental Occupational Aspirations, pp. 94-97).

(c) *Occupational Support*

The students preferences just indicated must be seen together with the encouragement they feel to pursue them. This seems to be rather high. They were asked whether they felt encouraged by parents, teachers, relatives, or friends and their answers are shown in Table 4.30 on a scale of 0 to 4.

TABLE 4.30: Occupational Support (N = 343, Range = 0-4)

	School						
	MS	TB	DW	DC	AS	ZP	ALL
Primary	2.42	3.21	2.45	1.42	2.39	2.12	2.27
Secondary	2.40	2.56	—	2.27	2.69	—	2.49
Both	2.41	2.69	2.45	1.76	2.55	2.12	2.36

Secondary school students feel more supported than primary school ones. Thakkarbapa and mission school students seem most supported and Dapchari ones the least, especially at the primary stage.

(d) *Awareness of Schedule Tribe Reservations*

Besides parental support, the government policy of positive discrimination in favour of certain socially under-privileged groups does reserve for the adivasis special educational and employment opportunities.

Among these students 71 per cent knew of the special educational facilities but only 49 per cent knew of the job reservations. As expected, secondary school students were more aware of these opportunities than the primary school ones. This awareness is least pronounced at Dapchari, especially with the primary school students where there are fewer adivasis, as also in the mission schools which, however, have proportionately more adivasis. Awareness of educational and employment opportunities are shown in Table 4.31 on a 0 to 2 scale.

TABLE 4.31: Awareness of Opportunities for Schedule Tribe (N= 343 Range = 0-2)

	School						
	MS	TB	DW	DC	AS	ZP	ALL
Primary	.95	1.43	1.45	.42	1.52	1.04	1.03
Secondary	.79	1.55	—	1.36	1.69	—	1.30
Both	.89	1.53	1.45	.80	1.61	1.04	1.15

(e) *Reference Persons*

Asking young students whom they admire and want to imitate is a useful way of ascertaining how they see themselves in relation to others. The persons most admired were listed by the students and grouped together in the three broad categories (Table 4.32).

TABLE 4.32: Reference Persons

%age (N)	MS	TB	DW	DC	AS	ZP	ALL
Historical Persons	79.3 (96)	62.3 (43)	50.0 (10)	59.6 (31)	77.6 (38)	81.8 (18)	70.9 (236)
Contemporary Leaders	9.1 (11)	24.6 (17)	45.0 (9)	11.5 (6)	20.4 (10)	13.6 (3)	16.8 (56)
School/Institution Personnel	11.6 (14)	13.0 (9)	5.0 (1)	28.8 (15)	2.0 (1)	4.5 (1)	12.3 (41)
Total	100.0 (121)	100.0 (69)	100.0 (20)	100.0 (52)	100.0 (49)	100.0 (22)	100.0 (333)

Among these categories of reference persons, historical ones are the most frequently chosen and contemporary leaders rate about the same as school personnel. A comparison between the schools shows that historical persons rate highest in zilla parishad, mission and ashram schools, and lowest at Dhundalwadi where contemporary leaders rate highest, followed by Thakkarbapa. mission schools rate these the lowest. Finally school and institutional personnel are rated lowest by ashram schools, zilla parishad ones and Dhundalwadi, and highest at Dapchari.

In terms of the comparative ratings then, in mission schools, historical persons are rated high while contemporary leaders are low. At Thakkarbapa the opposite is obtained. In Dhundalwadi, contemporary leaders are rated high and the others low. In Dapchari school personnel are rated high and the other two low, while in ashram schools, the school personnel is rated very low and the other categories are high. In zilla parishad schools once again school personnel are rated low but historical persons are high.

Not surprisingly, what the student wanted to be followed closely on whom they admired: 70 per cent liked historical persons, 16.8 per cent liked contemporary leaders, and 12.3 per cent liked school and/or institutional personnel.

Asked which groups were the most progressive/advanced, the students responded as shown in Table 4.33.

TABLE 4.33: Reference Groups

Category % age (N)	School						
	MS	TB	DW	DC	AS	ZP	ALL
Farmers	8.1 (10)	5.8 (4)	10.0 (2)	11.0 (6)	4.1 (2)	36.0 (9)	9.7 (33)
Businessmen	17.7 (22)	23.2 (16)	5.0 (1)	27.8 (15)	18.4 (9)	4.0 (1)	18.8 (64)
Workers	1.6 (2)	0.0 (0)	5.0 (1)	7.4 (4)	20.4 (10)	12.0 (3)	5.8 (20)
Landlords	4.0 (5)	5.8 (4)	0.0 (0)	9.3 (5)	8.2 (4)	8.0 (2)	5.8 (20)
Politicians	30.7 (38)	26.1 (18)	55.0 (11)	14.8 (8)	22.4 (11)	28.0 (7)	27.3 (93)
Mission Personnel, Social Workers	37.9 (47)	39.1 (27)	25.0 (5)	29.6 (16)	26.5 (13)	12.0 (3)	32.6 (111)
Total	100.0 (124)	100.0 (69)	100.0 (20)	100.0 (54)	100.0 (49)	100.0 (25)	100.0 (343)

Mission personnel and social workers are regarded to be the most progressive groups, followed by politicians. Landlords and workers are the least progressive, followed by farmers and businessmen. Comparing the schools, mission schools rate their personnel and politicians high, while workers and landlords are low. In Thakkarbapa the ratings are similar except that politicians are rated about the group average. In Dhundalwadi politicians rate the highest and landlords the lowest. In Dapchari businessmen rate high, in ashram schools workers rate noticeably higher than in others while in zilla parishad schools it is the farmers that rate thus.

In general it is the service occupations that seem to be regarded as the most progressive, except among the zilla parishad students where farming is regarded as the most progressive, whereas in Thakkarbapa and Dapchari, businessmen are seen as rather progressive and in ashram schools it is the worker who is so regarded. It could well be that these differences are due to the way these students understand what progressive or advanced means. But this itself is an interesting comment not on the occupations but on the students themselves.

(f) *School and Boarding Satisfaction*

Generally, the students seem somewhat more satisfied with their school's personnel than its facilities. Only 6 per cent say they are dissatisfied with their teachers, 7 per cent with their fellow students, but 14 per cent with the school facilities. However, on a 0 to 2 scale of satisfaction the scores show very little differences, because the very satisfied students seem to balance those dissatisfied with school facilities.

TABLE 4.34: Students' Satisfaction (N= 343 Range= 0-2)

Teachers	1.28
Fellow Students	1.21
School Facilities	1.20
Total Score	3.69

These three categories were collapsed to give a scale of satisfaction ranging from 0 to 6. The primary school students seem to be more appreciative of their school, especially at Thakkarbapa and Dhundalwadi.

TABLE 4.35: School Satisfaction (N= 343 Range=06)

Level	School						
	MS	TB	DW	DC	AS	ZP	ALL
Primary	3.91	4.43	4.30	3.42	3.61	3.44	3.81
Secondary	3.56	3.53	—	3.45	3.54	—	3.53
Both	3.78	3.71	4.30	3.44	3.57	3.44	3.69

The boarders seem somewhat less satisfied with their boardings. 19 per cent are dissatisfied with their boarding superintendents, 12 per cent with the facilities, and only five per cent with fellow boarders. Using a 0 to 2 scale of satisfaction the scores show below that there are enough students very satisfied with their superintendents to balance the score, but not enough for the facilities:

TABLE 4.36: Boarders' Satisfaction (N = 249 Range = 0-2)

Boarding superintendents	1.03
Boarders	1.33
Boarding facilities	1.32
Total Score	3.68

TABLE 4.37: Boarding Satisfaction (Range = 0-6)

Level	School						
	MS	TB	DW	DC	AS	ZP	ALL
Primary	4.24	4.15	3.39	4.67	3.64	3.71	4.08
Secondary	3.09	3.87	—	3.20	3.20	—	3.43
Both	3.80	3.93	3.39	4.08	3.41	3.71	3.79

The boarders, however, seem to be more satisfied with their lot. Only 23 per cent of them would rather be day scholars as against 48 per cent of day scholars who would rather be boarders.

(5) *Conclusion*

This presentation of the data collected on students must be seen with the data on parents and teachers, presented in the subsequent parts of this study.

2. THE PARENTS

(1) **The Sample**

The parents of the students interviewed formed the next source of data for this project. Not all these parents could be surveyed. Many had left the area, or were in inaccessible villages or untraceable in the cities and towns. But a very substantial number were interviewed, spread through 65 villages, covering 2 talukas, making a total of 265 parents, or 77 per cent of the 343 students, with 243 matched pairs, or 68 per cent of the students and 89 per cent of the parents. In most cases the parent is missing from the unmatched pair, in a few cases it is the student. The presentation in this section will concern only the data from the parents.

TABLE 4.38: Parents and Matched Pairs by School (N)

	MS	TB	DW	DC	AS	ZP	ALL
Students	125	69	20	55	49	25	343
Parents	112	52	17	30	29	24	264
No. of matched pairs	113	45	15	27	24	19	243

In each case the head of the household was interviewed. Only seven per cent or 19 of these were women, either because the husband was dead, or away and so she was effectively the household head. In fact six per cent or 16 were widows.

(2) The Parents' Background

(a) *Caste*

The non-adivasi component of this sample is small, 14 per cent, the largest adivasi group being the Warlis, 79 per cent, followed by the Koknas with four per cent and smaller groups of other tribes, making a total of 86 per cent adivasi. The sub-castes were collapsed to give the schoolwise breakdown in Table 4.39.

TABLE 4.39: Percentage of Adivasi Parents by School

	School						
%age (N)	MS	TB	DW	DC	AS	ZP	ALL
	88.4 (99)	82.0 (41)	100.0 (17)	56.7 (17)	100.0 (29)	91.7 (22)	85.9 (225)

If we compare this to the percentage of adivasi students in the sample, which is 80.5 per cent, we see there is a slight over-sampling of adivasis among the parents, probably because they were more accessible to the interviewers who were adivasis mostly, and perhaps because they were more available and willing to be interviewed. This five per cent over-sampling does not invalidate the results, though it should be kept in mind while interpreting them.

(b) *Religion*

The Christians are over-represented in the sample because it was designed to include a higher number of students and consequently parents from the mission schools so as to study them in greater depth.

TABLE 4.40: Percentage of Christian Parents by School

Religion %age (N)	School						
	MS	TB	DW	DC	AS	ZP	ALL
	75.9 (85)	38.0 (19)	11.8 (2)	3.3 (1)	20.7 (6)	4.2 (1)	43.5 (114)

Once again there is a slight over-sampling of Christian parents, 43.5 per cent Christian parents to 30.6 per cent Christian students. In Dhundalwadi, Dapchari, the ashram and zilla parishad schools, more Christian parents than Christian students were interviewed, an unfortunate mismatch of pairs.

(c) *Age*

The parents seem to be quite middle-aged, average 44.7 years, ranging from 22 to 68 years. The difference between schools is not much, with Dapchari having the youngest parents, average age 41.5 years, and Dhundalwadi the oldest, average age 47.6 years. Caste and religious differences too are slight: adivasi parents 44.9 years to non-adivasis 43.2, Christians 45.2 and non-Christians 44.2 years.

TABLE 4.41: Parents' Age in Years

MS	TB	DW	DC	AS	ZP	ALL
45.0	45.9	47.6	41.5	42.8	44.5	44.7

(d) *Family Size*

The average number of children in the family is 5.3, ranging from 1 to 11, with the lowest average of 4 in Dapchari and the highest of 5.8 in mission schools. Adivasis tend to have larger families than non-adivasis: 5.5 to 4.3 average number of children and Christians larger than non-Christians: 6.3 to 4.6 children.

TABLE 4.42: Family Size (N = 262)

MS	TB	DW	DC	AS	ZP	ALL
5.8	5.6	5.4	4.5	4.3	5.1	5.3

(e) *Occupation*

The occupational categories used for the fathers were the same as for the students, except that manual work was sub-divided into skilled and unskilled. There is a slight discrepancy between the categorization of occupations given by students and by the parents because the two groups are not completely matched in pairs and the categories themselves could be interpreted with some latitude. However, the basic pattern of the data as reflected in Table 4.43 is very much the same.

TABLE 4.43: Occupation of Household Head

Occupation %age (N)	School						
	MS	TB	DW	DC	AS	ZP	ALL
Daily Wage Labourer (DL)	8 (7.1)	1 (2.0)	1 (5.9)	3 (10.0)	2 (6.9)	1 (4.2)	16 (6.1)
Farmer (FA)	74 (66.1)	32 (64.0)	15 (88.2)	20 (66.7)	25 (86.2)	21 (87.5)	187 (71.4)
Unskilled Worker (UW)	8 (7.1)	5 (10.0)	0 (0.0)	2 (6.7)	1 (3.4)	0 (0.0)	16 (6.1)
Skilled Worker (SW)	7 (6.3)	3 (6.0)	1 (5.9)	2 (6.7)	0 (0.0)	0 (0.0)	13 (5.0)
Office Worker White Collar (WC)	10 (8.9)	4 (8.0)	0 (0.0)	2 (6.7)	1 (3.4)	2 (8.3)	19 (7.3)
Business (BU)	5 (4.5)	5 (10.0)	0 (0.0)	1 (3.3)	0 (0.0)	0 (0.0)	11 (4.2)
Total	112 (42.7)	50 (19.1)	17 (6.5)	30 (11.5)	29 (11.1)	24 (9.2)	262 (100)

The wives are much less inclined to outside employment than their husbands: a larger percentage work on their land, 77.9 per cent, and at home, 13.0 per cent; a smaller one at unskilled or office work, 2.3 and 0.4 per cent respectively.

TABLE 4.44: Occupation of Wives

Occupation %age (N)	School						
	MS	TB	DW	DC	AS	ZP	ALL
Daily Wage Labourer (DL)	6 (5.4)	4 (8.0)	2 (11.8)	3 (10.0)	1 (3.4)	1 (4.2)	17 (6.5)
Farmer (FA)	89 (79.5)	34 (68.0)	15 (88.2)	19 (63.3)	25 (86.2)	22 (91.7)	204 (77.9)
Unskilled Worker (US)	1 (0.9)	3 (6.0)	0 (0.0)	1 (3.3)	0 (0.0)	1 (4.2)	6 (2.3)
Office Worker White Collar (WC)	0 (0.0)	0 (0.0)	0 (0.0)	1 (3.3)	0 (0.0)	0 (0.0)	1 (0.4)
Domestic Work (DW)	16 (14.3)	9 (18.0)	0 (0.0)	6 (20.0)	3 (10.3)	0 (0.0)	34 (13.0)
Total	112 (42.7)	50 (19.1)	17 (6.5)	30 (11.5)	29 (11.1)	24 (9.2)	262 (100.0)

TABLE 4.45: Occupation of Wives by Caste and Religion

Occupation (N) row %age Col %age	Adivasi	Non-Adivasi	Christian	Non-Christian	
Daily Wage Labourer	16 94.1 7.0	1 5.9 2.7	5 29.5 4.3	12 70.6 8.1	17 6.4
Farmer	195 94.7 85.9	11 5.3 29.7	103 50.0 69.6	103 50.0 88.8	206 78.0
Unskilled Worker	3 50.0 1.3	3 50.0 8.1	4 66.7 2.7	2 33.3 1.7	6 2.3
Office Work	0.0 0.0 0.0	1 100.0 2.7	1 100.0 0.7	0 0.0 0.0	1 0.4
Domestic Work	13 38.2 5.7	21 61.8 56.8	28 82.4 18.9	6 17.6 5.2	34 12.9
Total	227 86.0	37 14.0	141 56.1	123 43.97	264 100.0

A caste-wise breakdown of the wives' occupation reveal some interesting differences. Many more adivasi women work on the land than non-adivasi ones, and the women landless labourers too are all adivasis. A majority of non-adivasi women do only domestic work. There is a greater proportion of unskilled employees among non-adivasis than adivasis, but there are no skilled workers among them either.

A breakdown by religion shows that Christian wives work more on the land and less at home than non-Christian ones. But this is due to the large number of Christians among the adivasis in the sample.

To indicate the occupational mobility of the group, the occupation of the household head's father was asked. Interesting comparisons emerged.

TABLE 4.46: Occupation of Fathers of Household Heads

Occupation % age (N)	School						
	MS	TB	DW	DC	AS	ZP	ALL
DL	2 (1.8)	3 (6.0)	2 (11.8)	1 (3.3)	1 (3.4)	0 (0.0)	9 (3.4)
FA	103 (92.0)	40 (80.0)	15 (88.2)	24 (80.0)	28 (96.6)	23 (95.8)	233 (88.9)
UW	1 (0.9)	2 (4.0)	0 (0.0)	1 (3.3)	0 (0.0)	0 (0.0)	4 (1.5)
SW	0 (0.0)	2 (4.0)	0 (0.0)	1 (3.3)	0 (0.0)	0 (0.0)	3 (1.1)
WC	0 (0.0)	2 (4.0)	0 (0.0)	3 (10.0)	0 (0.0)	0 (0.0)	5 (1.9)
BU	6 (5.4)	1 (2.0)	0 (0.0)	0 (0.0)	0 (0.0)	1 (4.2)	8 (3.1)
Total	112 (42.7)	50 (19.1)	17 (6.5)	30 (11.5)	29 (11.1)	24 (9.2)	262 (100.0)

(f) *Occupational Mobility*

Comparing the fathers' occupations to those of the present household heads or parents, there is clearly a movement away from the land, 88.9 per cent of fathers to 71.4 per cent of their sons being farmers. One direction of this movement is towards other occcupations, especially regular employment, rather than self-employment in business. But another direction of this is towards landless daily wage labour, 3.4 per cent of fathers to 6.1 per cent of their sons. These are parents who can afford to send their children to school so they would be only a small percentage of the total landless labourers and not really typical of them. These differences represent generational changes of occupations between matched pairs and hence are so much more significant. Table 4.47 highlights this.

TABLE 4.47: Generational Differences of Occupations

%age (N)	Occupation						
	DL	FA	UW	SW	WC	BU	ALL
Father's	9 (3.4)	233 (88.9)	4 (1.5)	3 (1.1)	5 (1.9)	8 (3.1)	262 (100.0)
Son's	16 (6.1)	187 (71.4)	16 (6.1)	13 (5.0)	19 (7.3)	11 (4.2)	262 (100.0)

TABLE 4.48: Occupational Difference by Religion of Household Heads

Religions %age (N)	Occupation						
	DL	FA	UW	SW	WC	BU	ALL
Christians	6 (5.2)	89 (76.7)	6 (5.2)	9 (7.8)	6 (5.2)	0 (0.0)	116 (43.9)
Non-Christians	10 (6.8)	100 (67.6)	10 (6.8)	4 (2.7)	13 (8.8)	11 (7.4)	148 (56.1)

There seems to be a higher percentage of farmers among Christians than non-Christians, but a lower percentage of white collar workers and businessmen too.

TABLE 4.49: Occupational Differences by Religion of Fathers of Household Heads

Religious %age (N)	Occupation						
	DWL	FA	UW	SW	WC	BU	ALL
Christian	2 (1.7)	113 (97.4)	0 (0.0)	1 (0.9)	0 (0.0)	0 (0.0)	116 (43.9)
Non-Christian	7 (4.7)	122 (82.4)	4 (2.7)	2 (1.4)	5 (3.4)	8 (5.4)	148 (56.1)

The pattern of differences by religion among the fathers of these heads of households is very similar to that among the household heads themselves.

Further, this mobility is strongly influenced by caste. The movement away from farming is about equal for non-adivasis (45.9 to 27.0 per cent or 18.9 percentage points) and adivasis (96.0 to 78.9 or 17.1 points). But for adivasis, downward mobility to landless labour almost doubles from 3.5 to 6.6 per cent or 3.1 percentage points while for non-adivasis it stays constant at 2.7 per cent. Mobility to skilled and unskilled manual work increases from 0.4 to 10.1 or 9.7 percentage points for adivasis and stays almost constant for non-adivasis at 16.2 per cent. However, mobility for white collar office work and business increases only 4.4 percentage points for adivasis but 18.9 points (from 35.1 to 54.0) for non-adivasis. Thus mobility to the low status occupations of manual work is higher among adivasis, while to the high status occupation of non-manual work it is higher among non-adivasis. Indeed this latter is almost double that of the former. Table 4.50 summarizes these findings.

TABLE 4.50: Generational Differences of Occupation by Caste (N=262)

Occupation (N) %age	DWL	FA	UW	SW	WC	BU	ALL
Adivasi	8	218	0	1	0	0	227
	(3.5)	(96.0)	(0.0)	(0.4)	(0.0)	(0.0)	(86.0)
Fathers'	15	179	11	12	10	0	227
Adivasi	(6.6)	(78.9)	(4.8)	(5.3)	(4.4)	(0.0)	(86.0)
son							
Non-Adivasi	1	17	4	2	5	8	37
Fathers	(2.7)	(45.9)	(10.8)	(5.4)	(13.5)	(21.6)	(14.0)
Non-Adivasi	1	10	5	1	9	11	37
Sons	(2.7)	(27.0)	(13.5)	(2.7)	(24.3)	(29.7)	(14.0)

These occupations can be graded in terms of status from the more manual and less remunerative ones to the non-manual and more rewarding ones. Thus we can have a six point scale: 1 = daily wage labourer, 2 = farmer, 3 = unskilled worker with regular employment, 4 = skilled worker with the same, 5 = office or white collar worker, and 6 = businessman. Using the differences between the parents' score and their fathers' occupational status we find that parents at Dapchari are the least mobile and the overall direction is towards upward mobility. This is highest at Thakkarbapa and lowest at Dapchari school and higher for non-adivasis than adivasis, 0.62 to 0.26.

TABLE 4.51: Occupational Mobility by School (N=262)

Occupational Mobility	School						
	MS	TB	DW	DC	AS	ZP	ALL
Father' score	2.20	2.26	1.88	2.36	1.96	2.16	2.18
Son's score	2.57	2.84	2.05	2.43	2.06	2.20	2.48
Differences	0.37	0.58	0.17	0.07	0.10	0.04	0.30

(g) *Agricultural Assets*

Agricultural assets were scaled in the same way as explained earlier for the students. The general impression is that students tended to make slightly lower estimates of their parents' assets than the parents themselves. Of the parents, 82 per cent owned some land, 73 per cent bullocks, but only 13 per cent had wells and 8 per cent pumps. The scale used was from 0 to 4.

TABLE 4.52: Agricultural Assets by School, Caste and Religion (N = 262, Range = 0-4)

	School							
	MS	TB	DW	DC	AS	ZP	ALL	(N)
Agr. Assets	1.86	1.80	1.94	1.17	1.79	1.83	1.76	262

TABLE 4.53: Agricultural Assets by Caste and Religion (Range = 0-4)

	Adivasi	Non-Adivasi	(N)	Christian	Non-Christian	(N)
Agr. Assets	1.90	0.89	262	1.99	1.56	264

Dapchari school parents have less agricultural assets since most are not working on the land but employed in the dairy. So too do non-adivasis and non-Christians generally. But this does not as yet mean a lower economic status. For this we must look at economic consumption as well.

(h) *Economic Consumption*

This was measured in terms of the number of sets of clothing bought in a year, kind of food taken, and consumption of alcohol, this last being scored negatively. Here it is not Dapchari, but the adivasi parents at Dhundalwadi and the ashram school parents, who rate the lowest, as do adivasis generally. Religious differences were marginal. The scale used ranged from -3 to +6.

TABLE 4.54: Economic Consumption by School, Caste and Religion (Range= -3 to +6)

	School							
	MS	TB	DW	DC	AS	ZP	ALL	(N)
Eco.Consp	1.64	1.78	0.41	1.60	0.90	1.33	1.47	262

TABLE 4.55: Economic Consumption by Caste and Religion

	Adivasi	Non-Adivasi	(N)	Christian	Non-Christian	(N)
Eco.Consp	1.16	3.35	262	1.38	1.45	264

(3) The Parents' Education

(a) *Educational Level*

Levels of education were categorized as earlier for the students on a 5-point scale from no formal education, through primary, middle, secondary and after.

A caste-wise breakdown shows adivasis markedly less educated than non-adivasis. Thus 96.5 per cent of those with no formal education are adivasis, while only 27.3 per cent of those with a post-secondary one are.

The parents with no formal education constitute 43 per cent. A school-wise breakdown shows that the older schools like Thakkarbapa and the mission one have about a third of such parents, while the newer ones like Dhundalwadi and the ashram schools have about three quarters of them. Dapchari, however, has a larger percentage of parents with secondary and post-secondary education.

TABLE 4.56: Education Level of Parents by Caste (Range = 1-5)

Caste	Education Level					
N (%)	No Education	Std. 1-4	Std. 5-7	Std. 8-SSC	Std. SSC	Total
Adivasi	110 (96.5)	61 (95.3)	42 (77.8)	11 (52.4)	3 (27.3)	227 (86.0)
Non-Adivasi	4 (3.5)	3 (4.7)	12 (22.2)	10 (47.6)	8 (72.7)	37 (14.0)
Total	114 (43.2)	64 (24.2)	54 (20.5)	21 (8.0)	11 (4.2)	264 (100.0)

TABLE 4.57: Educational Level of Parents

Education Level % (N)	School						
	MS	TB	DW	DC	AS	ZP	ALL
No education	34.8 (39)	32.0 (16)	82.4 (14)	40.0 (12)	72.4 (21)	50.0 (12)	43.5 (114)
1st-4th Std.	25.0 (28)	36.0 (18)	17.6 (3)	6.7 (2)	17.2 (5)	25.0 (6)	23.7 (62)
5th-7th Std.	29.5 (33)	20.0 (10)	0.0 (0)	20.0 (6)	6.9 (2)	12.5 (3)	20.6 (54)
8th-SSC	6.3 (7)	10.0 (5)	0.0 (0)	23.3 (7)	3.4 (1)	4.2 (1)	8.0 (21)
Post SSC	4.5 (5)	2.0 (1)	0.0 (0)	10.0 (3)	0.0 (0)	8.3 (2)	4.2 (11)
Total	42.7 (112)	19.1 (50)	6.5 (17)	11.5 (30)	11.1 (29)	9.2 (24)	100.0 (262)

The pattern is similar to the education of the fathers of these parents (Table 4.58).

A breakdown of levels of education by religion showed the Christians to be better educated than the non-Christians, but at the lower levels only. Thus, only 37.7 per cent of those with no formal education are Christians, but only 27.3 per cent of those with post-secondary education are.

TABLE 4.58: Educational Level of Parents' Fathers

Education Level %age (N)	School MS	TB	DW	DC	AS	ZP	ALL
No education	78.6 (88)	80.0 (40)	100.0 (17)	66.7 (20)	96.6 (28)	100.0 (24)	82.8 (217)
1st-4th Std.	16.1 (18)	4.0 (2)	0.0 (0)	13.3 (4)	3.4 (1)	0.0 (0)	9.5 (25)
5th-7th Std.	5.4 (6)	12.0 (6)	0.0 (0)	3.3 (1)	0.0 (0)	0.0 (0)	5.0 (13)
8th-SSC.	0.0 (0)	4.0 (2)	0.0 (0)	10.0 (3)	0.0 (0)	0.0 (0)	1.9 (5)
Post SSC	0.0 (0)	0.0 (0)	0.0 (0)	6.7 (2)	0.0 (0)	0.0 (0)	0.8 (2)
Total	42.7 (112)	*19.1 (50)	6.5 (17)	11.5 (30)	11.1 (29)	9.2 (24)	100.0 (262)

TABLE 4.59: Education Level of Parents by Religion

Religion N (%)	Education Level No edu.	Std. 1-4	Std. 5-7	Std. 8-SSC	Post SSC	Total
Christian	43 (37.7)	35 (54.7)	30 (55.6)	5 (23.8)	3 (27.3)	116 (43.9)
Non-Christian	71 (62.3)	29 (45.3)	24 (44.4)	16 (76.2)	8 (72.7)	148 (56.1)
Total	114 (43.2)	64 (24.2)	54 (20.5)	21 (8.0)	11 (4.2)	264 (100.0)

A cross-tabulation between the educational level of parents and of their fathers shows a very strong positive relationship: of the 83 per cent of fathers who had no education, 50.7 per cent did not educate their sons whereas of the 17 per cent of fathers with some education, only 2.6 per cent did not educate their sons. Looking a: it the other way around, 97.4 per cent of educated sons had educated fathers.

Collapsing columns 2 to 5 and rows 2 to 5 we have a clear picture of the differences between the educated and the uneducated.

(b) *Education and Literacy*

It has been found that a certain minimum number of years of schooling and some access to reading materials are necessary for permanent literacy. Hence to find out what level of education would lead to permanent functional literacy, the parents were asked if they read when they had the chance.

TABLE 4.60: Education of Fathers and Sons

Fathers' ed.level Row % Col % Total %	Sons' Education Level: 1. No.Ed.	2. 1-4 Std	3. 5-7 Std.	4. 8-SSC SSC	5. Post	Total
1. No Ed.	111 50.7 97.4 42.0	58 26.3 90.6 22.0	37 16.9 68.5 14.0	10 4.6 47.6 3.8	3 1.4 27.3 1.1	219 83.0
2. Std.1-4	2 8.0 1.8 0.8	3 12.0 4.7 1.1	9 36.0 16.7 3.4	6 24.0 28.6 2.3	5 20.0 45.5 1.9	25 9.5
3. Std. 5-7	1 7.7 0.9 0.4	2 15.4 3.1 0.8	6 46.2 11.1 2.3	3 23.1 14.3 1.1	1 7.7 9.1 0.4	13 4.9
4. Std.8-SSC	0 0.0 0.0 0.0	1 20.0 1.6 0.4	1 20.0 1.9 0.4	2 40.0 4.5 0.8	1 20.0 9.1 0.4	1.9
5. Post SSC	0 0.0 0.0 0.0	0 0.0 0.0 0.0	1 50.0 1.9 0.4	0 0.0 0.0 0.0	1 50.0 9.1 0.4	2 0.8
Total	114 43.2	64 24.2	54 20.5	21 8.0	11 4.2	264 100.0

TABLE 4.61: Education of Father and Sons

(N) Row % Col % Total %	Sons: Uneducated	Educated	
Fathers: Uneduca- ted	111 50.7 97.4 42.0	108 49.3 72.0 41.0	219 83.0
Educated	3 6.7 2.6 *1.1*	42 93.3 28.0 *15.9*	45 17.0
	114 43.2	150 56.8	264 100.0

TABLE 4.62: Education and Reading

N Col. (%age)	Level of ed. 1 no edu.	2 Std.1-4	3 Std.5-7	4 Std.8-SSC	5 SSC+	Total
1. Don't read Col.	7 (6.1)	0 (0.0)	0 (0.0)	0 (0.0)	0 (0.0)	7 (2.7)
2. Would like to but don't get the chance	105 (92.1)	34 (53.1)	17 (31.5)	1 (4.8)	0 (0.0)	157 (59.5)
3. Reading when they get the chance	2 (1.8)	30 (46.9)	37 (68.5)	20 (95.2)	11 (100.0)	100 (37.9)
Total	114 (43.2)	64 (24.2)	54 (20.5)	21 (8.0)	11 (4.2)	264 (100.0)

Of the 114 parents who had no formal education only two do any reading, 92.1 per cent would like to but can't read, and 6.1 per cent don't read or seem to miss it. Of the 64 with a 4th standard education 46.9 per cent still read, of the 54 with a 7th standard education 68.5 per cent do. Thus with a 4th standard education there is less than a 50 per cent chance of permanent literacy and with a 7th standard one, a 2/3 chance.

Moreover, proportionately fewer adivasis and more Christians are permanently literate.

TABLE 4.63: Reading and Caste and Religion

N (row%)	1 Don't Read	2 Would like to but can't	3 Read when they can	Total
Adivasis	6 (2.6)	151 (66.5)	70 (30.8)	227 (100.0)
Non-Adivasis	1 (2.7)	6 (16.2)	30 (81.1)	37 (100.0)
Christian	1 (.9)	67 (57.8)	48 (41.4)	116 (100.0)
Non-Christian	6 (4.1)	90 (60.8)	52 (35.1)	148 (100.0)

A school breakdown of reading habits showed Dapchari with the highest percentage of parents who still read (50.0%) followed by Thakkarbapa (46.0%) and mission schools (45.5%), Zilla parishad schools (20.8%), Dhundalwadi (11.8%) and ashram schools (10.3%) rate much lower.

TABLE 4.64: Reading Habits of Parents (school-wise)

N (%)	School						
	MS	TB	DW	DC	AS	ZP	Total
Don't read	2 (1.8)	1 (2.0)	0 (0.0)	2 (6.7)	2 (6.9)	0 (0.0)	7 (2.7)
Would like to but can't	59 (52.7)	26 (52.0)	15 (88.2)	13 (43.3)	24 (82.8)	19 (79.2)	156 (59.5)
Read when they can	51 (45.5)	23 (46.0)	2 (11.8)	15 (50.0)	3 (10.3)	5 (20.8)	99 (37.8)
Total	112 (42.7)	50 (19.1)	17 (6.5)	30 (11.5)	29 (11.1)	24 (9.2)	262 (100.0)

(c) *Educational Mobility: Comparisons*

These five levels can be scaled in ascending order from 1 to 5 so as to provide easier comparisons between groups, as also a measure of generation mobility in education as was done earlier with occupation.

TABLE 4.65: Educational Mobility and School Type

Education of	School						
	MS	TB	DW	DC	AS	ZP	ALL
Parents	2.21	2.14	1.18	2.57	1.42	1.96	2.06
"Fathers	1.27	1.04	1.00	1.76	1.03	1.00	1.28
Generational mobility	.94	1.10	.18	.81	.39	.96	.78
(N)	(112)	(50)	(17)	(30)	(29)	(24)	(262)

The pattern between schools mentioned earlier is confirmed. Schools with better educated parents are the ones where they are more upwardly mobile as well, i.e., Dapchari, Thakkarbapa and the mission Schools, the exception being the zilla parishad ones.

TABLE 4.66: Educational Mobility and Religion

	Religion		
Education of	Christian	Non-Christian	Both
Parents'	2.06	2.06	2.06
Fathers	1.17	1.36	1.28
Generational mobility	0.89	0.70	0.78
(N)	(114)	(148)	(262)

There was no difference between the two religious groups in the present generation of parents and an extremely slight one in the earlier one. The greater generational mobility of Christians here is evidence of the educational impact of the Church.

TABLE 4.67: Educational Mobility and Caste

Education of	Caste		
	Adivasis	Non-Adivasis	Both
Parents'	1.83	3.40	2.06
Fathers	1.12	2.24	1.28
Generational mobility	0.71	1.16	0.78
(N)	(227)	(37)	(264)

TABLE 4.68: Education and Occupation of Parents

Occupation N row% col%	Level of Education						
	1 no ed.	2 std 1-4	3 std 4-7	4 std 8-SSC	5 SSC+	Ed. level score	Total
1. Daily wage labourer (DL)	12 75.0 10.5	3 18.8 4.7	1 6.3 1.9	0 0.0 0.0	0 0.0 0.0	1.31	16 6.1
2. Farmer (FA)	96 50.8 84.2	51 27.0 79.7	30 15.9 55.6	8 4.2 38.1	4 2.1 36.4	1.80	189 71.6
3. Unskilled worker(UW)	3 18.8 2.6	6 37.5 9.4	6 37.5 11.1	1 6.3 4.8	0 0.0 0.0	2.31	16 6.1
4. Skilled worker(SW)	2 15.4 1.8	3 23.1 4.7	7 53.8 13.0	1 7.7 4.8	0 0.0 0.0	2.54	13 4.9
5. Office work white collar (WC)	0 0.0 0.0	0 0.0 0.0	3 15.8 5.6	10 52.6 47.6	6 31.6 54.5	4.16	19 7.2
6. Business (BU)	1 9.1 .9	1 9.1 1.6	7 63.6 13.0	1 9.1 4.8	1 9.1 9.1	3.00	11 4.2
Occupational status score	1.92	2.20	3.04	3.76	4.45		2.47
Total	114 43.2	64 24.2	54 20.5	21 8.0	11 4.2	2.06	264 100.0

(d) *Education and Occupation*

The stronger positive relationship of educational level to occupational status for the present generation of parents is underlined by cross-tabulating the two.

Of the 114 with no education 10.5 per cent are landless labourers and 84.2 per cent are farmers. Only 5.3 per cent are not on the land. Again 75.0 per cent of the landless labourers and 50.8 per cent of the farmers have had no education. Of the 118 who had primary education only 3.4 per cent are landless labourers, while 68.6 are still farmers. The rest, 9.3 per cent, are employed off the land. Among the 32 with secondary education there are no landless labourers, 37.5 per cent are farmers and 56.3 per cent are off the land.

The occupational status score and the educational level one, computed as earlier, show the higher status associated with higher levels of education and *vice versa*. The level of education then seems crucial in saving people from becoming landless labourers and getting them employment off the land. This is illustrated when Table 4.69 on education and employment is simplified.

TABLE 4.69: Education and Occupation of Parents

Occupation N (%)	Level of education			
	No education	Primary	Secondary +	Total
On the land (DL + FA)	108 (94.7)	85 (72.0)	12 (37.5)	205 (77.7)
Blue collar Worker (UN+SW)	5 (4.4)	22 (18.6)	2 (6.3)	29 (11.0)
White collar Worker (WC+BU)	1 (.9)	11 (9.3)	18 (56.3)	30 (11.4)
Total	114 (43.2)	118 (44.7)	32 (12.2)	264 (100.0)

(e) *Socio-economic Status*

A scale of socio-economic status was computed, with range -1 to 21, by adding the scores on educational level, occupational status, agricultural assets and level of economic consumption, the last two being approximate measures of income. As expected, adivasis have a much lower socio-economic status than non-adivasis, though Christians and non-Christians do not differ much. Again the schools with the highest percentage adivasis have parents with a lower socio-economic status, i.e. Dhundalwadi and the ashram schools. Thakkarbapa and the mission schools have parents with the highest status.

TABLE 4.70: Socio-economic status (SES) of Parents by Caste and Religion (Range = -1 to 21)

(N)	Adivasis	Non-Adi.	Total	Christian	Non-Christ.	Total
SES	7.12 (227)	11.73 (37)	7.77 (264)	7.77 (114)	7.79 (148)	7.78 (262)

TABLE 4.71: Socio-economic Status (SES) of Parents by School

	MS	TB	DW	DC	AS	ZP	ALL	(N)
SES	8.28	8.56	5.59	7.77	6.17	7.33	7.78	264

(4) The Parents' Attitudes

(a) *Urban Contact*

Town contact was measured by the frequency (1 to 3) and the size (1 to 3) of towns visited (1 to 3) on a scale of 1 to 18. There was greater urban contact for non-adivasis, for Christians and for the mission schools, Dapchari and Thakkarbapa.

TABLE 4.72: Urban Contact Score of Parents by Caste and Religion (Range 1-18)

	Caste			Religion		
(N)	Adivasi	Non-Adi.	Total	Christ.	Non-Chris.	Total
Score	9.84 (227)	13.32 (37)	10.33 (264)	10.55 (114)	10.16 (148)	10.33 (262)

TABLE 4.73: Urban Contact of Parents by School

	School							
	MS	TB	DW	DC	AS	ZP	ALL	(N)
Score	11.32	10.06	8.94	10.43	8.35	9.5	10.33	264

(b) *Parental Support for Education*

The support parents give to their child's education was operationalized in terms of the benefits they perceived from education, and their commitment to educate all their children, especially the girls, postponing the more immediate advantage of early employment for boys or marriage for girls.

While education is clearly seen as beneficial, for the family the benefit of educating the child is seen to be more social than economic (94.7 to 87.5%), while for the individual child it is opposite, more economic than social, (95.8 to 86.7%). But taken together for both family and child, economic and social benefit seem to even out, 83.3 to 81.3 per cent respectively.

TABLE 4.74: Educational Benefits

N (%age)	No benefits	Benefits	Total
For the family:			
Economic	33 (12.5)	231 (87.5)	264 (100.0)
Social	14 (5.3)	250 (94.7)	264 (100.0)
For the child:			
Economic	11 (4.2)	253 (95.8)	264 (100.0)
Social	35 (13.3)	229 (86.7)	264 (100.0)
Total:			
Economic	44 (16.7)	220 (83.3)	264 (100.0)
Social	49 (18.6)	215 (81.4)	264 (100.0)

Asked whether, in terms of the money spent on the child and the lost labour of the child, they experienced a loss in educating the child, 41 per cent said they did not.

A single consolidated measure of the awareness of education benefits was constructed by adding up the scores ranging from 0 to 2 on the 4 measures on the perception of the benefits (i.e. economic and social for the family and the individual) and subtracting 4 times the score (ranging from 0 to 1) on the one measure for the perception of loss. The range of this scale was -4 to +4.

This awareness of the benefits of education among the parents is higher at Thakkarbapa and the mission schools than the other schools, higher for non-adivasis, higher for Christians than non-Christians. Thus educational awareness prevails among the groups which have had longer contact with education (e.g., the older more established schools, the non-adivasis) or where a more persistent educational effort has been made, (e.g., Christians).

TABLE 4.75: Awareness of Educational Benefits (Range = -4 to +4)

	School						
	MS	TB	DW	DC	AS	ZP	ALL
Score	2.45	2.84	1.24	1.57	1.14	1.63	2.13
(N)	(112)	(50)	(17)	(30)	(29)	(24)	(262)
	Caste:						
	Adivasi			Non-Adivasi			
Score	1.84			3.81			2.11
(N)	(227)			(37)			(264)
	Religion:						
Score	Christian			Non-Christian			
(N)	2.70			1.69			2.13
	(114)			(148)			(262)

Parental commitment to education was measured on three dimensions. First, with regard to educating all their children: 30.3 per cent said they would not, 16.3 per cent said they would if they could, and 53.4 per cent said they would. Here again it is the non-adivasis, the Christians, and the better educated who are the more committed.

TABLE 4.76: Educating All One's Children

N=264 (%ge)	Will not educate all	Will if I can all	Will educate	Total
Caste:				
Adivasi	76 (33.5)	42 (18.5)	109 (48.0)	227 (86.0)
Non-Adivasi	4 (10.8)	1 (2.7)	32 (86.5)	37 (14.0)
Religion:				
Christian	25 (21.6)	21 (18.1)	70 (60.3)	116 (43.9)
Non-Christian	55 (37.2)	22 (14.9)	71 (47.9)	148 (56.1)
Education:				
No formal ed.	47 (41.2)	21 (18.4)	46 (40.4)	114 (43.2)
Primary Ed.	29 (24.6)	21 (17.8)	68 (57.6)	118 (44.7)
Secondary ed.	4 (12.5)	1 (3.1)	27 (84.4)	32 (12.1)

TABLE 4.77: Educating All One's Children

N (%)	School						
	MS	TB	DW	DC	AS	AP	Total
Will not educate all	26 (23.2)	14 (28.0)	6 (35.3)	11 (36.7)	8 (27.6)	15 (62.5)	80 (30.5)
Will if can	19 (17.0)	5 (10.0)	8 (47.1)	1 (3.3)	7 (24.1)	2 (8.3)	42 (16.0)
Will educate all	67 (59.8)	31 (62.0)	3 (17.6)	18 (60.0)	14 (48.3)	7 (29.2)	140 (53.4)
Total	112 (42.7)	50 (19.1)	17 (6.5)	30 (11.5)	29 (11.1)	24 (9.2)	262 (100.0)

A schoolwise breakdown of the parents' willingness to educate all their children shows that the highest number of such parents came from Thakkarbapa (62.0%), Dapchari (60.0%), and mission schools (59.8%). The lowest number came from Dhundalwadi (17.6%) and the zilla parishad schools (29.2%) with ashram schools in between (48.3%).

The second measure of educational commitment was in terms of female education: 13.3 per cent are not prepared to sacrifice to educate their girls, 44.7 per cent are but not as much as for their boys, and 42.0 per cent would sacrifice equally for their girls and boys. Once again the same categories as mentioned earlier are those more committed to female education: non-adivasis, Christian and the educated.

TABLE 4.78: Willingness to Sacrifice for their Girls' Education

(N) (%)	Will not sacrifice for boys	Will sacrifice but less than for boys	Will sacrifice the same as	Total
Caste:				
Adivasi	31 (13.7)	114 (50.2)	82 (36.1)	227 (86.0)
Non-Adivasi	4 (10.8)	4 (10.8)	29 (78.4)	37 (14.0)
Religion:				
Christian	3 (2.6)	53 (45.7)	60 (51.7)	116 (43.9)
Non-Christian	32 (21.6)	65 (43.9)	51 (34.5)	148 (56.1)
Education:				
No formal ed.	17 (14.9)	72 (63.2)	25 (21.9)	114 (43.2)
Primary ed.	16 (13.6)	43 (36.4)	59 (50.0)	118 (44.7)
Secondary ed.	2 (6.3)	3 (9.4)	27 (84.3)	32 (12.1)

A third measure of educational commitment was in terms of continuing the education of the child, and postponing more immediate employment for boys or marriage for girls. Regarding how far they would want to continue their children's education, only seven per cent said they would not want to continue it, 23 per cent would up to the SSC, and 69 per cent would want to go beyond that too. If offered an opportunity for more immediate employment for boys or marriage for girls, 27 per cent would not want to continue the child's education, 31 per cent would up to the SSC and 25 per cent would want to go beyond that even, while 17 per cent could not decide.

Adding up these 3 measures to form a consolidated measure of educational commitment (range 0 to 8) once again confirmed the stronger commitment of the parents from the older schools, i.e., Thakkarbapa and the mission schools, from among the non-adivasis and the Christians. It is not surprising that these are the same groups that were found to be more aware of the benefits of education as well. A schoolwise breakdown of the parent's willingness to sacrifice for their daughter's education showed once again that the highest number of such parents came from Thakkarbapa (58.0%) mission schools (50.9%) and Dapchari (50.0%). The lowest number again came from Dhundalwadi (0.0%) with the zilla parishad schools (12.5%) and the ashram ones (20.7%) very low too.

TABLE 4.79: Willingness to Sacrifice for their Girls' Education

N (%)	School						
	MS	TB	DW	DC	AS	ZP	Total
Will not sacrifice	10 (8.9)	4 (8.0)	5 (29.4)	9 (30.0)	3 (10.3)	4 (16.7)	35 (13.4)
Will sacrifice but less than for boys	45 (40.2)	17 (34.0)	12 (70.6)	6 (20.0)	20 (69.0)	17 (70.8)	117 (44.7)
Will sacrifice the same as for boys	57 (50.9)	29 (58.0)	0 (0.0)	15 (50.0)	6 (20.7)	3 (12.5)	110 (42.0)
Total	112 (42.7)	50 (19.1)	17 (6.5)	30 (11.5)	29 (11.1)	24 (9.2)	262 (100.0)

TABLE 4.80: Educational Commitment (Range = 0-8)

	School						
	MS	TB	DW	DC	AS	ZP	ALL
Score	5.56	5.9	3.71	5.2	4.69	4.08	5.23
(N)	(112)	(50)	(17)	(30)	(29)	(24)	(262)
	Caste:						
Score		Adivasi		Non-Adivasi			5.23
(N)		5.02		6.57			(262)
	Religion:						
Score		Christian		Non-Christian			
(N)		5.50		4.79			5.23
		(114)		(148)			(262)

(c) *Parental Occupational Aspirations*

An important aspect of the family background of these students is the occupational aspiration their parents have for them. This would affect not only the parents' commitment to their education but their own performance as well. Assuming that parents who do not want their children to take up the same occupation they themselves have would want something better for them, these parents do indeed have high aspirations for their children. However, they are higher for boys than for girls. Thus only six per cent of household heads want their sons to follow their fathers' occupations while 39 per cent want their daughters to follow their mothers'.

No parents wanted their sons to be daily wage labourers, but very few wanted them to be farmers either, only 2.5 per cent of the 241 who answered. It is office work or white collar employment that is preferred by most parents for their sons, and more so by adivasis than non-adivasis, 67.3 per cent to 50.0 per cent preferring this for their sons. This is probably because white collar work is a high status occupation more within their reach than business, which no adivasi chooses for his son as against 10 per cent of non-adivasis who do. The Christians' preference for unskilled work is higher than that of non-Christians, 32.7 per cent to 13.4, but less than for skilled work, .9 per cent to 15.7. This would seem to indicate a lesser prejudice against manual labour among the Christians but a lesser awareness of the possibilities of manual skills as well.

TABLE 4.81: Parents' Occupational Aspirations for Sons by Caste

N (%)	Occupation					
	Farming	Unskilled work	Skilled work	Office work	Business	Total
Caste:						
Adivasi	4 (1.9)	46 (21.8)	19 (9.0)	142 (67.3)	0 (0.0)	211 (87.6)
Non-Adivasi	2 (6.7)	7 (23.3)	3 (10.0)	15 (50.0)	3 (10.0)	30 (12.4)
Total	6 (2.5)	53 (22.0)	22 (9.1)	157 (65.1)	3 (1.2)	241 (100.0)

TABLE 4.82: Parents' Occupational Aspirations for Sons by Religion

N (%) Religion	Occupation					
	FA	UW	SW	WC	BU	Total
Christian	2 (1.9)	35 (32.7)	1 (.9)	69 (64.5)	0 (0.0)	107 (44.4)
Non-Christian	4 (3.0)	18 (13.4)	21 (15.7)	88 (65.7)	3 (2.2)	134 (55.6)
Total	6 (2.5)	53 (22.0)	22 (9.1)	157 (65.1)	3 (1.2)	241 (100.0)

TABLE 4.83: Parents' Occupational Aspirations by Education

N (%) Education	Occupation					
	FA	UW	SW	WC	BU	Total
No formal education	2 (1.9)	14 (13.6)	10 (9.7)	77 (74.8)	0 (0.0)	103 (42.8)
Primary education	3 (2.8)	29 (26.6)	9 (8.3)	66 (60.5)	2 (1.8)	109 (45.2)
Secondary education	1 (3.4)	10 (34.5)	3 (10.4)	14 (48.3)	1 (3.4)	29 (12.0)
Total	6 (2.5)	53 (22.0)	22 (9.1)	157 (65.1)	3 (1.2)	241 (100.0)

In the relationship between level of education and occupational aspirations, it would seem that education does not so much raise aspirations as make them more realistic. Thus the parents with no formal education are less inclined to choose for their sons the low status occupations (like farming and unskilled labour) than high status ones (like white collar employment). However, for the educated parents this is reversed, except for business which seems to be a choice only for these educated parents.

Parental aspirations for their daughters' occupations is decidedly lower than that for their sons and this is more so among adivasis than non-adivasis. The preferred occupation among the adivasis is farming (42.0%) and next white collar employment (34.2%). A very few even choose daily wage labour for their daughters (1.6%)! Among non-adivasis their preference is clearly for white collar employment (76.9%) and next domestic work (11.5%).

TABLE 4.84: Parents' Occupational Aspirations for Daughters by Caste

N (%) Caste	Occupation						
	DWL	FA	UW	SW	WC	Domestic work (DW)	Total
Adivasi	3 (1.6)	81 (42.0)	35 (18.1)	7 (3.6)	66 (34.2)	1 (.5)	193 (88.1)
Non-Adivasi	0 (0.0)	1 (3.8)	1 (3.8)	1 (3.8)	20 (76.9)	3 (11.5)	26 (11.9)
Total	3 (1.4)	82 (37.4)	36 (16.4)	8 (3.7)	86 (39.3)	4 (1.8)	219 (100.0)

TABLE 4.85: Parents' Occupational Aspirations for Daughters by Religion

Religion (N) (%)	Occupation						
	DWL	FA	UW	SW	WC	DW	Total
Christian	0 (0.0)	29 (27.4)	28 (26.4)	4 (3.8)	45 (42.5)	0 (0.0)	106 (48.4)
Non-Christian	3 (2.7)	53 (46.9)	8 (7.1)	4 (3.5)	41 (36.3)	4 (3.5)	113 (51.6)
Total	3 (1.4)	82 (37.4)	36 (16.4)	8 (3.7)	86 (39.3)	4 (1.8)	219 (100.0)

The Christians' aspirations for their daughters are higher than the non-Christians'. Thus out of 219 parents, 42.3 per cent of them choose white collar employment as against 36.3 per cent among the non-Christians, 26.4 per cent unskilled manual work as against 7.1 per cent among the others, none of them choose daily wage labour or domestic work for their daughters though some non-Christians do.

TABLE 4.86: Parents' Occupational Aspirations for Daughters by Education

N % Education	Occupation						
	DWL	FA	UW	SW	WC	DW	Total
No-formal education:	1 (1.1)	53 (56.4)	10 (10.6)	4 (4.3)	5 (26.6)	1 (1.1)	94 (42.9)
Primary education:	2 (2.0)	26 (26.5)	20 (20.4)	3 (3.1)	47 (48.0)	0 (0.0)	98 (44.8)
Secondary education:	0 (0.0)	3 (11.1)	6 (22.2)	1 (3.7)	14 (51.9)	3 (11.1)	27 (12.3)
Total	3 (1.4)	82 (37.4)	36 (16.4)	8 (3.7)	86 (39.3)	4 (1.8)	219 (100.0)

Unlike what we saw for sons, parents' education does raise occupational aspirations for the daughters. Thus the largest proportion of parents who choose farming for the daughters have no formal education (56.4%) and the smallest proportion who do are those with secondary education (11.1%), while those with primary education are in between (26.5%). On the other hand, of those choosing white collar employment for their daughters, the largest proportion are parents with secondary education (51.9%), next those with primary education (48.0%), and then those with no formal education (26.6%).

The occupational aspirations of parents for their children are best understood in the context of the occupation preferences of the students themselves.

(d) *Reference Persons*

If occupational preferences for their children indicate what future parents see for them, then the reference persons and groups they choose are also very helpful in ascertaining the same.

Of the 190 parents who responded to this question, contemporary leaders receive the highest number of first choices among reference persons (53.7%), especially at Dhundalwadi (87.5%) and the ashram schools (85.7%), though less so at the mission schools (41.8%) and Thakkarbapa (54.1%). Historical persons are next with 29.5 per cent first choices. They score very low in Dhundalwadi (0.0%) and in ashram schools (14.3%) but highest in the mission schools (32.7%) and the Thakkarbapa (32.4%). School and institutional personnel score the lowest number of first choices overall (16.8%), very low in all, but moderately in Thakkarbapa (13.5) per cent and high in mission schools (25.5%).

TABLE 4.87: Reference Persons for Parents by School of Child

N (%)	School						
	MS	TB	DW	DC	AS	ZP	ALL
Historical persons:	32 (32.7)	12 (32.4)	0 (0.0)	6 (30.0)	2 (14.3)	4 (30.8)	56 (29.5)
Contemp. leaders	41 (41.8)	20 (54.1)	7 (87.5)	13 (65.0)	12 (85.7)	9 (69.2)	102 (53.7)
School, institu-tional personal	25 (25.5)	5 (13.5)	1 (12.5)	1 (5.0)	0 (0.0)	0 (0.0)	32 (16.8)
Total	98 (51.6)	37 (19.5)	8 (4.2)	20 (10.5)	14 (7.4)	13 (6.8)	190 (100.0)

It would seem then that reference persons of mission school parents are the most balanced across the three categories, with some leaning to contemporary leaders and an encouragingly higher preference for school and institutional personnel in comparison with others. The reference persons for these other parents are heavily tilted towards contemporary leaders and away from school personnel.

TABLE 4.88: Reference Group for Parents by School of Child

N (%)	School						
	MS	TB	DW	DC	AS	ZP	ALL
Farmers	10 (9.0)	12 (25.0)	0 (0.0)	4 (14.8)	0 (0.0)	2 (8.3)	28 (11.0)
White Collar workers	10 (9.0)	1 (2.1)	2 (11.8)	2 (7.4)	1 (3.6)	3 (12.5)	19 (7.5)
Businessmen	27 (24.3)	12 (25.0)	6 (35.3)	12 (44.4)	23 (82.1)	15 (62.5)	95 (37.3)
Landlords	13 (11.7)	5 (10.4)	8 (47.1)	4 (14.8)	3 (10.7)	2 (8.3)	35 (13.7)
Politicians	3 (2.7)	4 (8.3)	0 (0.0)	1 (3.7)	1 (3.6)	0 (0.0)	9 (3.5)
Social Workers and Mission school personnel	48 (43.2)	14 (29.2)	1 (5.9)	4 (14.8)	0 (0.0)	2 (8.3)	69 (27.1)
Total	111 (43.5)	48 (18.8)	17 (6.7)	27 (10.6)	28 (11.0)	24 (9.4)	255 (100.0)

(e) *Reference Groups*

Occupational groups were rated by the parents in terms of the most progressive/advanced one. Businessmen received the highest number of first ratings (37.3%) though so few choose this as the preferred occupation for their children, while white collar employment received a rather low score (7.5%) in spite of being the most preferred occupation for them. Politicians as a group score the lowest (3.5%) though as individual leaders they had scored the highest. Social workers and mission personnel do second best (27.1%) with landlords and farmers somewhat equal (13.7% and 11.0% respectively).

A schoolwise breakdown shows that in mission schools, mission personnel and social workers score the highest (43.2%) with businessmen next (24.3%). The same is true of Thakkarbapa: social workers 29.9 percent; businessmen 25.0 per cent. At Dapchari, the ashram, and zilla parishad schools the businessmen score highest (44.4%, 82.1% and 62.5% respectively). At Dhundalwadi it is the landlords who are the highest (47.1%) and the businessmen next (35.3%). In all the schools the politicians as a group are considered to be the least progressive/advanced, except in the zilla parishad ones where they are second lowest.

(5) The Parents and the School

(a) *Parental Choice of School*

Parental concern for education is reflected in the factors that influence their choice of school for their children.

The most important factor affecting this choice is the academic standard of the school (affecting 86.6% of parents), next the cost of education (affecting 83.2%), followed by the convenience of location (affecting 67.6%). The least important factor in the choice of school is non-admittance elsewhere. Evidently these schools are not overcrowded. The importance of special facilities for adivasis or care for religious instruction must be seen in the context of the breakdown by caste and religion.

A schoolwise breakdown shows that academic standards are most important for mission schools and Dhundalwadi, affecting 94.6 per cent and 94.1 per cent of parents respectively. The lower cost of education most affects the parents at ashram schools and least affects these at Dapchari (79.3% and 70.0% respectively). So too does convenience of location affect Dapchari parents the most (93.3%) per cent and mission school parents the least (54.4%) Special facilities for adivasis is the most influential factor at ashram schools (affecting 96.6% of parents) and is least influential at Dapchari (affecting 56.7%). Special care for religious instructions is lowest at Dapchari (affecting 6.7%) while it is most effective for the mission schools, affecting 75.0 per cent of parents though not as high as the special facilities for adivasis which affects 83.0 per cent of parents. Non-admittance elsewhere is the least influential factor at mission schools (affecting 5.4%) and ashram ones (affecting 6.9%) while at Thakkarbapa this factor is highest (affecting 22.0%). Thus, Thakkarbapa would seem to take more rejects from elsewhere while mission and ashram schools are more likely to be the first choice of parents.

TABLE 4.89: Parents' Choice of School: Schoolwise Breakdown

Reason for choosing sch. N saying "yes"(%)	School						
	MS	TB	DW	DC	AS	ZP	ALL
1. Close to the home	61 (54.4)	37 (74.0)	12 (70.6)	28 (93.3)	20 (69.0)	19 (79.2)	177 (67.6)
2. Less costly education	96 (85.71	38 (76.0)	15 (88.2)	22 (73.3)	26 (89.7)	21 (87.5)	218 (83.2)
3. Best for study	106 (94.6)	40 (80.0)	16 (94.1)	21 (70.0)	23 (79.3)	21 (87.5)	227 (86.6)
4. Special facilities for Adivasis	93 (83.0)	39 (78.0)	15 (88.2)	17 (56.7)	28 (96.6)	18 (75.0)	210 (80.2)
5. Special care for religious instruction	84 (75.0)	22 (44.0)	4 (23.5)	2 (6.7)	14 (48.3)	9 (37.5)	135 (51.5)
6. Not admitted elsewhere	6 (5.4)	11 (22.0)	2 (11.8)	3 (10.0)	2 (6.9)	3 (12.5)	27 (10.3)

A castewise breakdown of parental choice of school seems to indicate that adivasis make a more positive choice for the school than non-adivasis. Thus academic standards, especial facilities for schedule tribes, the lower cost of education affect their choice more than they affect that of non-adivasis. The percentage of parents choosing the school for these reasons is 90.3 to 64.9, 88.1 to 32.4, and 86.8 to 62.2 per cent respectively.

TABLE 4.90: Parental Choice of School: Castewise breakdown

N (%)	Reasons for choosing school					
	Close to the home	Less costly educa- tion	Best for study	Special facilities for Adi- vasis	Special care for religious instruction	Not admitted elsewhere
Caste						
Adi- vasi	145 (63.9)	197 (86.8)	205 (90.3)	200 (88.1)	131 (57.8)	26 (11.5)
Non- Adi- vasi	33 (89.2)	23 (62.2)	24 (64.9)	12 (32.4)	6 (16.2)	2 (5.4)
Both	178 (67.4)	220 (83.3)	229 (86.7)	212 (80.3)	137 (51.2)	28 (10.6)

TABLE 4.91: Parental Choice of School: Religionwise Breakdown

N (%)	Reason for choosing school					
	Close to the home	Less costly educat- ion	Best for study	Special facilities for Adi- vasis	Special care for religious instruction	Not admitted elsewhere
Religion						
Chri- stian	62 (53.4)	98 (84.5)	106 (91.4)	102 (87.9)	99 (85.3)	14 (12.1)
Non- Chri- stian	116 (78.4)	122 (82.4)	123 (83.1)	110 (74.3)	38 (25.7)	14 (9.5)
Both	178 (67.4)	220 (83.3)	229 (86.7)	212 (80.3)	137 (51.9)	28 (10.6)

Regarding especial care for religious instruction adivasi parents are more affected than by this non-adivasi ones, 57.8 to 16.2 per cent. But this is because of the Christians in mission schools. Non-adivasi parents are more affected by school location, 89.2 to 63.9 per cent, and less affected by non-admittance in the school of their first choice, 5.4 to 11.5 per cent.

(b) *Parental Contact with School*

A most crucial aspect of the school-community link is through the parents. Their contact with the school was measured along three dimensions on a 0 to 2 range of frequency: attendance at meetings for parents (50 per cent do so rarely, 19 per cent do so often) enquiring after their children's studies (65 per cent do so rarely, only 7 per cent often); helping the school when needed (76 per cent rarely, 6 per cent often)

These three dimensions were combined into an additive scale with range 0 to 6 to give a single measure for parent-to-school contact. A schoolwise breakdown shows Dapchari to have the highest, while Dhundalwadi and the zilla parishad schools have the lowest parent-to-school contact, probably because adivasi parents have much less school contact than non-adivasi ones. Differences on the basis of religion are very marginal.

TABLE 4.92: Parental to School Contact by School: Caste and Religion (Range 0-6)

	School						
	MS	TB	DW	DC	AS	ZP	ALL
Score	3.26	3.32	3.06	4.00	3.17	3.08	3.32
(N)	(112)	(50)	(17)	(30)	(29)	(24)	(262)

	Caste:		Religion:	
	Adivasi	Non-Adivasi	Christian	Non-Christian
Score	3.19	4.11	3.30	3.33
(N)	(227)	(37)	(114)	(148)

Parental contact with the school can be looked at from the perspective of parents reaching out to the school, as above, or *vice versa*, as below. This was done on three dimensions again; whether the school communicated its need for assistance from the parents (49 per cent said it did rarely, 16 per cent said often), whether it enquired after their real needs (77 per cent said rarely, 4 per cent often), and whether it asked for their suggestions (86 per cent said rarely, only 2 per cent often). Once again combining these three dimensions into a scale of range 0 to 6 to measure school-to-parent contact, we find that this measure is complementary to the earlier parent-to-school one. Thus Dapchari has the highest contact, ashram and the zilla parishad schools the lowest contact, adivasis less than non-adivasis, and Christians just marginally more than non-Christians.

TABLE 4.93: School-to-Parent Contact by School, Caste and Religion (Range = 0-6 N=262)

	School						
	MS	TB	DW	DC	AS	ZP	ALL
Score:	3.26	3.22	3.06	3.37	3.03	3.04	3.21
	Caste:			Religion:			
	Adivasi	Non-Adivasi		Christian	Non-Christian		
Score	3.18	3.35		3.31	3.31		

The initiative in this relationship between school and parent would seem to come mostly from the school. But what needs to be probed further is whether the emphasis is on bringing the parents to the school by involving them in the school and with their children in it, or whether it is on taking the school to the parents, by reaching out to their needs and suggestions. In other words, whether the thrust of the school-community relationship is more centripetal or centrifugal, since in some measure it must be both.

(c) *Parental Satisfaction with the School*

In comparison to other schools the parents seem quite satisfied with the one their own children go to. Only 13 per cent are dissatisfied with the students, 8 per cent with the teachers and the same with the facilities. But 30 per cent are not satisfied with the other parents in the school and 61 per cent are not so with the villagers' help to the school. Overall then, they are more satisfied with the school than with themselves, an interesting point of self-criticism.

Combining all these internal and external aspects of the school into a consolidated measure of satisfaction of range 0 to 10 we find that mission school parents are the most satisfied with their schools and Dhundalwadi and Dapchari the least, adivasis are more satisfied than non-adivasis, and Christians more than non-Christians.

TABLE 4.94: Parental Satisfaction with the School (Range 0-10 N=262)

School						
MS	TB	DW	DC	AS	ZP	ALL
5.79	5.56	4.76	4.77	5.00	5.00	5.40
Caste:			Religion:			
Adivasis	Non-Adivasi			Christian	Non-Christian	
5.51	4.7			5.97	4.96	

(6) The Parents and the Community

(a) *Parental Participation in the Village*

If an important part of the school's contact with the village community is through the parents, then their participation in the community is of considerable consequence too. This participation was operationalized at several levels; personal assistance, village meetings and festivals, leadership, political awareness and social action.

Personal assistance comprised aspects like writing letters or application forms for others, advising them on education and employment, helping them with government officials, settling family disputes. These were combined into a scale of range 0 to 5. Parents from Thakkarbapa and the mission Schools are most helpful to others in these matters, those from Dhundalwadi and the ashram Schools are the least, adivasis and Christians just marginally more than the others.

TABLE 4.95: Personal Assistance of Parents by School, Caste and Religion (Range=0-5 N=262)

School						
MS	TB	DW	DC	AS	ZP	ALL
4.31	4.50	3.82	4.20	4.07	4.13	4.26
Caste:			Religion:			
Adivasi	Non-Adivasi			Christian	Non-Christian	
4.26	4.22			4.38	4.17	

Involvement in village meetings was measured on a scale of 0 to 5 in terms of attendance and active participation. Here Dapchari and mission school parents score the highest, Dhundalwadi and ashram schools the lowest, adivasis less and Christians more than others.

TABLE 4.96: Parents' Involvement in Village Meetings by School, Caste and Religion (Range = 0-5 N = 262)

School						
MS	TB	DW	DC	AS	ZP	ALL
2.89	2.25	2.34	2.90	2.28	2.58	2.68

Caste:		Religion:	
Adivasi	Non-Adivasi	Christian	Non-Christian
2.63	2.97	2.98	2.45

Involvement in village festivals was scaled the same way, mission Schools and Thakkarbapa score the highest, Dhundalwadi the lowest, adivasi and Christians more than the others.

TABLE 4.97: Parents' Involvement in Village Festivals by School Caste and Religion (Range = 0-5 N = 262)

School						
MS	TB	DW	DC	AS	ZP	ALL
301	2.84	2.29	2.47	2.48	2.58	2.77

Caste:		Religion:	
Adivasi	Non-Adivasi	Christian	Non-Christian
2.79	2.59	3.16	2.47

Village leadership was measured on two counts: presiding over village meetings and holding public office. On a scale of range 0-5, except for Dhundalwadi parents who score the lowest, the other differences are very marginal.

The measurement of political awareness covered two aspects: voting in the elections and participating in political demonstrations, on a range of 0 to 5, Thakkarbapa parents score the highest, Dhundalwadi ones the lowest. Caste and religious differences were quite marginal.

TABLE 4.98: Parents' Village Leadership by School, Caste and Religion (Range=0-5 N=262)

School						
MS	TB	DW	DC	AS	ZP	ALL
2.82	2.76	2.71	2.80	2.86	2.88	2.82

Caste:		Religion:	
Adivasi	Non-Adivasi	Christian	Non-Christian
2.82	2.84	2.84	2.81

TABLE 4.99: Parents' Political Awareness by School, Caste and Religion (Range=0-5 N=262)

School						
MS	TB	DW	DC	AS	ZP	ALL
3.70	3.76	3.18	3.67	3.52	3.75	3.66

Caste:		Religion:	
Adivasi	Non-Adivasi	Christian	Non-Christian
3.64	3.68	3.72	3.54

Finally, involvement in social action was measured on a 0 to 5 scale in terms of belonging to a social action group and taking an active part in it. Here Dapchari parents score the highest, Dhundalwadi the lowest again, adivasis just a little lower, Christians a little higher.

TABLE 4.100: Parents' Involvement in Social Action by School Caste and Religion (Range=0-5 N=262)

School						
MS	TB	DW	DC	AS	ZP	ALL
1.85	2.10	1.53	2.20	1.72	1.75	1.89

Caste:		Religion:	
Adivasi	Non-Adivasi	Christian	Non-Christian
1.86	2.05	2.02	1.79

All six measures of village participation above were combined in a single consolidated one of range 0 to 30 for further analysis. Since differences on each measure separately were rather small, this consolidated measure would hopefully show greater variation and allow more incisive analysis. Dhundalwadi parents have the lowest level of participation, mission school ones the highest. Christian parents are higher than non-Christians ones but caste differences are very small.

TABLE 4.101: Parents Social Participation by School, Caste and Religion (Range = 0-30 N = 262)

School						
MS	TB	DW	DC	AS	ZP	ALL
18.62	18.48	15.76	18.23	16.93	17.67	18.09

Caste		Religion:	
Adivasi	Non-Adivasi	Christian	Non-Christian
18.01	18.35	19.20	17.13

(b) *Village Support for the School:*

We have been looking at the school-to-community relationship through the intermediary link of the parents. We can now examine the community-to-school relationship in terms of the support it gives the school in particular and education in general. Obviously the two aspects are complementary but each is distinct and likely to yield new information.

The two aspects of village support mentioned above were combined to give a scale of range 0 to 4. Mission schools and Dapchari have the most support from their local communities, Dhundalwadi and ashram Schools the least. Adivasis report less community support, but religionwise there are very marginal differences.

(c) *Relationship between School and Community*

We have till now considered three aspects of the relationship between the school and the local community:

(1) the involvement of parents in the school
(2) the outreach of the school to the parents
(3) the support of the community for the school

TABLE 4.102: Village support for the School, by School, Caste and Religion (Range=0-4 N=262)

School						
MS	TB	DW	DC	AS	ZP	ALL
2.21	2.08	1.94	2.20	2.00	2.04	2.13

Caste:		Religion:	
Adivasi	Non-Adivasi	Christian	Non-Christian
2.067	2.51	2.11	2.14

All these can be combined to describe the relationship in a more stable and comprehensive manner. This would summarize information on all three aspects by consolidating them into an additive scale with a range from 0 to 16. On this measure Dapchari had the most positive relationship with the local community, followed by the mission schools. Dhundalwadi has the least positive one. Non-adivasis report a rather more positive relationship and Christians a somewhat more positive one than the others.

(7) Conclusion

This has been a descriptive presentation of the data on the parents in the sample. A more analytical treatment must still be made, and a parent-child pairwise grouping which would allow a more fine-tuned analysis.

TABLE 4.103: School-community Relationship by School, Caste and Religion (Range=0-16 N=262)

School						
MS	TB	DW	DC	AS	ZP	ALL
8.73	8.62	8.06	9.57	8.21	8.17	8.65

Caste:		Religion:	
Adivasi	Non-Adivasi	Christian	Non-Christian
8.43	9.97	8.72	8.60

3. THE TEACHERS

(1) The Sample

The teachers interviewed for this study were selected from the schools where the students and parents had been interviewed earlier. One teacher for each standard was selected, generally the class teacher was chosen. Since only primary school students from the seventh standard were included in the student sample, only teachers from the three mission schools that had seven standards should have been included. However, since a more intensive study and follow up of these schools was planned, all eleven mission schools were included. The sample therefore covered 113 teachers from 19 schools grouped into 6 categories.

TABLE 4.104: Distribution of Teacher Sample

Standard taught	School						
	MS	TB	DW	DC	AS	ZP	ALL
1-4	41	5	4		6	7	63
5-7	12	2	3	4	6	9	36
8-10	1	7		3	3		14
Both	54	14	7	7	15	16	113

(2) The Teachers' Socio-economic Background

(a) *Caste*

Just less than half the teachers (46.9%) are adivasis, but they all come from the government run and especially from mission schools, and mostly from the first four standards there. The other privately run ones do not have a single adivasi teacher in the sample.

(b) *Sex*

Female teachers are less represented in the sample (only 24.8%). They are the least in ashram schools (6.7%) where residence is required. Further they are less represented in the higher standards than the lower ones (14.0 to 33.3%)

TABLE 4.105: Percentage of Adivasi Teachers by School and Standard

N (%)	School						
	MS	TB	DW	DC	AS	ZP	ALL
Adivasi	40 (74.1)	0 (0.0)	0 (0.0)	0 (0.0)	7 (46.7)	6 (37.6)	53 (46.9)
	Standard:						
	1 - 4		5 - 10		ALL		
Adivasi	39 (61.9)		14 (28.0)		53		

TABLE 4.106: Percentage of Female Teachers by School and Standard Taught

N	School						
(%)	MS	TB	DW	DC	AS	ZP	ALL
	15 (27.8)	5 (35.7)	3 (42.9)	1 (14.3)	1 (6.7)	3 (18.8)	28 (24.8)
N	Standard:						
(%)	1 - 4		5 - 10		ALL		
	21 (33.3)		7 (14.0)		28 (24.8)		

(c) *Religion*

The Christian teachers in the sample have quite obviously been recruited by the mission Schools where 79.6 per cent of their teachers are Christian. Since these schools have mostly primary teachers we find more Christian teachers in standards 1 to 4 as well.

TABLE 4.107: Percentage of Christian Teachers by School and Standard Taught

	School						
	MS	TB	DW	DC	AS	ZP	ALL
N	43	0	0	0	0	1	44
(%)	(79.6)	(0.0)	(0.0)	(0.0)	(0.0)	(6.3)	(38.9)

	Standard:		
	1 - 4	5 - 10	ALL
N	33	11	44
(%)	(25.4)	(22.0)	(38.9)

(d) *Age*

The teachers' age ranges from 19 to 57 years, with a median age of 29 years. The oldest teachers are found in the zilla parishad schools, the youngest at Dhundalwadi (35.6 years and 28.1 years). Lower primary teachers are slightly younger than middle and high school ones (29.6 years and 30.2 years) as are non-Christian to Christian teachers (29.3 to 30.8 years). More marked are differences between male and female teachers (30.7 to 26.3 years) and adivasi to non-adivasi ones (31.1 to 28.7 years).

TABLE 4.108: Teacher's Age by School

	School						
	MS	TB	DW	DC	AS	ZP	ALL
Age (yrs)	28.64	28.07	25.14	30.71	29.53	35.56	29.56
(N)	(54)	(14)	(7)	(7)	(15)	(16)	(113)

(e) *Family Size*

Family size was considered in terms of the number of dependents the teacher supported. The average size was 5.7 dependents, ranging from none to as many as 20. But then these could not possibly be fully but only partially dependent on the teacher's salaries. There must be other sources of family income from land and labour. Mission schools have the largest number of dependents and Dapchari the least (6.5 and 3.7). Lower primary teachers have more dependents than middle and secondary ones (6.1 to 5.3) males more than females (6.1 to 4.3), adivasis more than non-adivasis (7.9 to 5.6) and Christians more than non-Christians (7.8 to 5.1).

TABLE 4.109: Number of Dependents on Teachers by School

	School						
	MS	TB	DW	DC	AS	ZP	ALL
No.	6.51	4.46	4.86	3.71	5.6	6.0	5.74

(f) *Father's Occupation*

To ascertain the economic class background of these teachers, their father's occupation was asked. The most common occupation was farming with 61.1 per cent of the fathers in it. There was only one daily wage labourer. Somewhere inbetween were those whose fathers both farmed their own land and hired their labour out as well (13.3%). Among those with regular employment the most frequent one was office work (11.5%) followed by unskilled labour (7.1%), with very few in skilled labour (1.8%).

Almost a quarter (24.8%) of the teachers' fathers did not live on the land, and of these almost half (11.5%) were white collar workers. Of the three quarters (74.3%) who lived on the land, only a fifth were daily wage labourers for at least part of their income (15.2%).

Since teaching is a white collar occupation, these teachers are clearly an upwardly mobile group in respect to the earlier generation: 11.5 of fathers to 100 per cent of sons in high status white collar employment. Moreover in comparison to the parents of their students, the teachers are clearly of a higher occupational status as a group, as also with the earlier generation of the two groups, i.e., fathers' of teachers being of higher status than fathers of the students' parents.

TABLE 4.110: Occupation of Teacher's Father by School

N (%) Occupations	School						
	MS	TB	DW	DC	AS	ZP	ALL
Landless labour (LL)	0 (0.0)	0 (0.0)	0 (0.0)	0 (0.0)	0 (0.0)	1 (6.3)	1 (.9)
LL and farming (L+FA)	5 (9.3)	0 (0.0)	1 (14.3)	1 (14.3)	5 (33.3)	3 (18.8)	15 (13.3)
Farming (FA)	36 (66.7)	11 (78.6)	4 (57.1)	2 (28.6)	8 (53.3)	8 (50.0)	69 (61.1)
Unskilled work (UW)	5 (9.3)	1 (7.1)	1 (14.3)	0 (0.0)	1 (6.7)	0 (0.0)	8 (7.1)
Skilled work (SW)	0 (0.0)	0 (0.0)	0 (0.0)	0 (0.0)	0 (0.0)	2 (12.5)	2 (1.8)
White collar work (WC)	6 (11.1)	1 (7.1)	1 (14.3)	3 (42.9)	1 (6.7)	1 (6.3)	13 (11.5)
Business (BU)	2 (3.7)	1 (7.1)	0 (0.0)	1 (14.3)	0 (0.0)	1 (6.3)	5 (4.4)
Total	54 (47.8)	14 (12.8)	7 (6.2)	7 (6.2)	15 (13.3)	16 (14.2)	113 (100.0)

TABLE 4.111: Occupation of Teacher's Fathers by Standard Taught

N (%) Standard taught	Occupation							
	LL	LL&FA	FA	UW	SW	WC	BU	ALL
1-4	1 (1.6)	4 (6.3)	44 (69.8)	3 (4.8)	1 (1.6)	7 (11.1)	3 (4.8)	63 (55.8)
5-10	0 (0.0)	11 (22.0)	25 (50.5)	5 (10.0)	1 (2.0)	6 (12.0)	2 (4.0)	50 (44.2)
Both	1 (.9)	15 (13.3)	69 (61.1)	8 (7.1)	2 (1.8)	13 (11.5)	5 (4.4)	113 (100.0)

In terms of their father's occupation, teachers in the lower primary differ from the others on three counts. There were fewer farmers among them (50.0 to 69.8%), and more employed regularly at unskilled work (10.0 to 4.8%). Otherwise the differences are minimal, and generally those teaching in the higher standards do not seem to have had fathers with a higher occupational status than those in the lower ones.

(g) *Father's Education*

The educational level of the teachers' fathers is decidedly more positive than the students' parents or their fathers. The 29.2 per cent with no formal education are well below the national illiteracy average. About two-thirds (63.7%) have had a primary education, but only 4.4 per cent a secondary one, and just 2.7 per cent had gone beyond that. Once again, since the minimum qualifications for teachers are a post SSC, Dip. Ed., it would seem that the teachers are a very upwardly mobile group educationally as well as occupationally.

Educational levels can be scored on a 5-point scale from no formal education to SSC and beyond. A comparison between such scores shows that ashram schools teachers have the least educated fathers (1.87) and Dapchari High School the best educated ones (3.34).

TABLE 4.112: Educational Level of Teacher's Father by School (Range = 1-5)

N (%) Education level	School						
	MS	TB	DW	DC	AS	ZP	ALL
1. No formal ed.	21 (38.9)	0 (0.0)	1 (14.3)	0 (0.0)	7 (46.7)	4 (25.0)	33 (29.3)
2. Std. 1-4	17 (31.5)	7 (50.0)	3 (42.9)	1 (14.3)	3 (20.0)	6 (37.5)	37 (32.7)
3. Std. 5-7	15 (27.8)	5 (35.8)	3 (42.9)	4 (57.1)	5 (33.3)	3 (18.8)	35 (31.0)
4. Std.8-SSC	1 (1.9)	1 (7.1)	0 (0.0)	0 (0.0)	0 (0.0)	3 (18.8)	5 (4.4)
5. SSC+	0 (0.0)	1 (7.1)	0 (0.0)	2 (28.6)	0 (0.0)	0 (0.0)	3 (2.7)
Total	54 (47.8)	14 (12.4)	7 (6.2)	7 (6.2)	15 (13.3)	16 (14.2)	113 (110.0)
Educational level score:	1.93	2.71	2.29	3.34	1.87	2.31	2.19

The teachers in the lower standards tend to have fathers who had a lower level of education than those in the higher ones. Thus 68.3 per cent of the teachers whose fathers had a 4th standard education or less, teach in the lower standards, to 54.0 per cent in the higher standards. Moreover, while 31.8 per cent of teachers whose fathers had a 5th standard of higher education, teach in the lower standards, 46.0 do in the higher ones.

TABLE 4.113: Educational Level of Teacher's Father by Standard Taught (Range = 1-5)

Educational level	4 std. or less	5 std. or more	Total	Educational level score
Std.taught				
1 - 4	43 (68.3)	20 (31.8)	63 (55.8)	2.05
5 - 10	27 (61.9)	23 (38.1)	50 (100.0)	2.36

(h) *Mothers' Education*

TABLE 4.114: Educational Level of Teacher's Mother by School (Range 1-5)

N (%) Education level	School MS	TB	DW	DC	AS	ZP	ALL
1. Non formal ed.	44 (81.5)	6 (42.9)	3 (42.9)	1 (14.1)	13 (86.7)	11 (68.8)	78 (69.0)
2. Std. 1-4	4 (7.4)	5 (35.7)	3 (42.9)	4 (57)	1 (6.7)	4 (25.0)	21 (18.6)
3. Std. 5-7	5 (9.3)	2 (14.3)	1 (14.3)	0 (0.0)	1 (6.7)	1 (6.3)	10 (8.8)
4. Std. 8-SSC	1 (1.9)	0 (0.0)	0 (0.0)	1 (14.3)	0 (0.0)	0 (0.0)	2 (1.8)
5. SSC+	0 (0.0)	1 (7.1)	0 (0.0)	1 (14.3)	0 (0.0)	0 (0.0)	2 (1.8)
Total	54 (47.8)	14 (12.4)	7 (6.2)	7 (13.3)	15 (13.3)	16 (14.2)	113 (100.0)
Educational level score	1.31	1.93	1.71	2.57	1.20	1.38	1.49

The level of education of the teachers' mothers is decidedly lower than that of their fathers. More than thrice as many have had no formal education (69.0 to 29.2%), only a third as many have had a primary education (27.4 to 63.7%), and just half as many an education beyond that (3.6 to 7.1%). As with the fathers here too Dapchari high School teachers had the best (2.57) and the ashram schools the least educated mothers (1.20). The difference in educational level between the two parents is .70 or almost three quarters of a level.

(i) *Teachers' Parental Education*

Adding up the educational level scores for fathers' and mothers' we get a score for the parental educational level. This gives us a broader based and more stable score for further analysis. Here too the earlier differences between schools is confirmed: Dapchari the highest, ashram schools the lowest. Moreover, male adivasis and Christian teachers have less educated parents.

TABLE 4.115: Educational Level Score of Teachers' Parents by School, Sex, Caste and Religion (Range=2-10)

N	School						
(%)	MS	TB	DW	DC	AS	ZP	ALL
Score	3.24 (54)	4.46 (14)	4.00 (7)	6.00 (7)	3.07 (15)	3.69 (16)	3.67 (113)

	Sex		Caste	
Score	Male	Female	Adivasi	Non-adivasi
	3.42 (85)	4.43 (28)	2.75 (53)	4.48 (60)

Religion	
Christian	Non-Christian
3.36 (44)	3.37 (69)

(3) The Teachers' Occupational Characteristics of Teachers

One's performance at work is not only a question of one's qualification for it but rather very much a function of one's of reasons for selection, that brought the persons to the job, the chances of improvement that keep him there, or the willingness to change that might move him out. The teachers' commitment to their profession was studied with reference to these three crucial dimensions.

(a) *Occupational Selection*

The most important reason for choosing teaching as an occupation was because they liked teaching (not important for 8 per cent, very much so for 44 per cent). The next being the regular income it brought (not important for 36 per cent very important for 10 per cent), and the social recognition too. It was a first choice occupation for 79 per cent of the teachers, a last choice one for less than one per cent and the most convenient one for just 12 per cent.

If the first three reasons can be categorized as positive choices and the last three as negative ones, then the difference between the two sets could serve as a rough indicator of occupational commitment at the point of entering in on it. A schoolwise breakdown shows Dhundalwadi teachers to have the most positive reason for their choice of occupation (3.29), mission ones the least (1.39).

TABLE 4.116: Occupational Selection by School (Range = 16 to +6, N = 113)

	School						
	MS	TB	DW	DC	AS	ZP	ALL
Score (%)	1.39	2.00	3.29	.86	1.6	2.44	1.72

(b) *Occupational Advancement*

The perception of improving one's prospects in an occupation could be used to indicate one's commitments in it. Asked whether improving one's possibilities on the job in terms of promotion or social recognition were minimal, depended on luck, or on effort, once again Dhundalwadi teachers report their chances as the best (1.71) and mission ones the least (1.30).

TABLE 4.117: Occupational Selection by School (Range = -6 to +6, N=113)

	School						
	MS	TB	DW	DC	AS	ZP	ALL
Score	1.30	1.43	1.71	1.14	1.67	1.63	1.42
(N)	(54)	(14)	(7)	(7)	(15)	(16)	(113)

(c) *Occupational Change*

The openness of a person to occupational change is a negative indicator of his commitment to staying on in it. Here teachers were asked about their willingness to such change, 97 per cent said they would stay in the occupation even if they had to change jobs, 11 per cent would not want to change jobs, 17 per cent would change jobs for the same pay, and 23 per cent would for better pay. It would seem then that teachers are not very open to changing their occupation, or even their present appointments.

A scale of openness to occupational change can be computed by subtracting their commitment to the occupation, from their willingness to change jobs. On a range of -2 to +6, the Dapchari teachers are the most open to change (1.00), zilla parishad ones the most closed to it (-1.13) on an overall average of -.42.

TABLE 4.118: Occupational Change by School (Range = -2 to +6, N=113)

	School						
	MS	TB	DW	DC	AS	ZP	ALL
Score	-.57	-.43	-.43	1.00	.27	-1.13	-.42

(d) *Occupational Stability*

The resistance of these teachers to occupational change noted above should be confirmed by the occupational stability they show. The number of years a teacher has spent in the profession, in a particular school, or with the institution running them would be an indicator of stability Thus we find that teachers are on an average longer in their profession (6.69 years) than with their institution (6.04 years) and are the least time in their present school (3.28 years).

A schoolwise breakdown shows that Dhundalwadi with the youngest teachers has the lowest average for years in teaching (3.71 years) while the zilla parishad ones, with the oldest teachers have, the highest (11.90 years). The difference between years in teaching and years with the institution are small: the highest is the zilla parishad school (1.75 years) indicating that teachers move there after teaching elsewhere, and actually negative in the ashram schools (-.14 years) because some teachers there seem to have begun with non-teaching appointments i.e. boarding masters. The difference between years with the institution and in their present school are larger than the early difference between years in teaching and with the institution. This points to a greater mobility of teachers from school to school within the same institution, than from one institution to another. The difference seems highest for zilla parishad schools (5.49 years), Dapchari (3.43 years) and mission schools (3.35 years) and lowest for the others: ashram schools (1.27 years), Dhundalwadi (.15 years), Thakkarbapa (0.0 years).

Finally, adivasi teachers seem to be longer in the profession and with their institution than non-adivasis (8.46 to 5.60 years and 8.46 to 4.40 years respectively) as do Christians over non-Christians (8.92 to 5.91 years and 8.57 to 5.14 years respectively).

TABLE 4.119: Occupational Stability by School, Standard Taught, Sex, Caste, Religion (N=113)

No.of years in	School						
	MS	TB	DW	DC	AS	ZP	ALL
1. Teaching	6.49	4.93	3.71	7.00	4.75	11.90	6.69
2. The institution	6.08	4.29	2.86	5.57	4.89	10.15	6.04
3. The school	2.73	4.29	2.71	2.14	3.62	4.86	3.28
4. 1 and 2	.41	.64	.85	1.43	-.14	1.75	.65
5. 2 and 3	3.35	0.0	.15	3.43	1.27	5.49	2.76

(e) *Academic Qualifications*

The minimum qualification for a teacher in the primary school is a diploma in education (Dip. Ed.) after the SSC. For the high school it is a post graduate degree in education, (B.Ed.). Some of the older teachers who were already confirmed teachers when these minimum qualifications came into force were allowed to carry on. Thus 7 teachers had not done their SSC. Of the 106 who had, 17 per cent got a first, 77 per cent a second and 10 per cent a pass class. Of the qualified teachers, 86 had done a Dip. Ed., 4 per cent with a first, 15 with a second class, and 12 a B.Ed., 2 with a first, 8 with a second class.

(f) *Location of Degree Taken.*

There is a lack of facilities for teacher training in the area and so either those interested in the profession must go outside to qualify or teachers from outside must be recruited. Thus, we find that 33 per cent of the teachers did their SSC in the neighbouring talukas, like Dahanu and Palghar, 32 per cent did it within Thane district and the rest outside the district. So too with the Dip. Ed., 19 per cent did the degree in the neighboring talukas, and 57 per cent within the district. For the B.A. only 6 teachers did the degree in the neighboring area, and 6 within the district, while for the B.Ed., all 12 did it outside the district.

TABLE 4.120: Place and Degree Obtained

N (%)	Place			Total
	1 Neighbouring talukas	2 Within the District	3 Outside the District	
SSC	35 (33.0)	34 (32.1)	69 (34.9)	106 (100.0)
Dip.Ed.	16 (18.6)	49 (57.0)	21 (24.4)	86 (100.0)
B.A.	6 (31.6)	6 (31.6)	7 (36.8)	19 (100.0)
B.Ed	0 (0.0)	0 (0.0)	12 (100.0)	12 (100.0)

(g) *Teacher Qualifications*

Teacher qualifications can be scaled by multiplicative scale combining the two; dimensions of degree and class, weighted as below, giving a scale of range 0 to 30:

Degree obtained:		Class Obtained:
SSC	=1	1st class = 3
Dip.Ed.	=2	2nd class = 2
B.A.	=3	3rd class = 1
B.Ed.	=4	

On this scale the minimum score for a qualified primary school teacher would be '7' (i.e. a 3rd class up to the Dip. Ed.), and for a secondary school one '10' (i.e. a 3rd class up to the B.Ed.). A schoolwise breakdown shows the two full fledged high schools Dapchari and Thakkarbapa having the best qualified teachers, (10.71 and 10.21), while the primary schools have the less qualified ones, e.g., Dhundalwadi (6.29). Adivasi and Christian teachers are more qualified, as are females over males (7.83 to 7.18), non-adivasis over adivasis (8.59 to 5.93) and non-Christians over Christians (7.77 to 6.66).

The qualifications of the teachers should not be confused with their quality as teachers, but they do represent an important academic input for school.

TABLE 4.121: Teachers Qualifications by School, Sex, Caste and Religion (Range = 0-30)

	School						
	MS	TB	DW	DC	AS	ZP	ALL
Score	6.76	10.21	6.29	10.71	6.47	6.56	7.34
(N)	(54)	(14)	(7)	(7)	(15)	(16)	(113)

	Sex		Caste		Religion	
	Male	Female	Adivasi	Non-adivasi	Christian	Non-Christian
Score:	7.18	7.83	5.93	8.59	6.66	7.77
(N)	(85)	(28)	(53)	(60)	(44)	(69)

The overall level of teacher qualifications does indeed leave room for improvement, but when asked if they would like to study further, the teachers who were already well qualified were the ones more likely to want to study, i.e., the ones from Thakkarbapa and Dapchari, and the ones teaching in the higher standards.

TABLE 4.122: Percentage of Teachers Wanting to, Study Further by, School and Standard Taught

	School						
%	MS	TB	DW	DC	AS	ZP	ALL
(N)	(29)	(11)	(2)	(3)	(4)	(9)	(60)
	Standard taught						
	STd.1-4			5-10			Total
%	41.3			68.0			53.1
(N)	(26)			(34)			(60)

(h) *The Time Distribution of Teachers*

One of the most incisive ways of studying an institution is to look at how the personnel there spend their time. This is a very practical way of showing up the actual priorities of the persons concerned. Here our concern is with the teachers.

(i) *In-school Time Distribution*

The proportion of their time spent in various chores at school was averaged over two estimates made by them: hours spent on a typical day at school, and the percentage of time spent over an ordinary school term. This was checked against information elicited on the hours spent at school, the time of leaving home and returning, and the commuting time.

The average number of hours a teacher spent at school were 6.68, the highest at the mission schools (7.19), the lowest at Dapchari 5.80.

TABLE 4.123: In-School Hours, by School

	School						
	MS	TB	DW	DC	AS	ZP	ALL
Average hours spent	7.19	6.54	6.46	5.80	6.10	6.09	6.68

Most of the teachers' time at school is spent on classroom teaching including preparation, classes, corrections (67.80%). The rest of their time is distributed between administrative work (10.41%) extra-curricular activities (12.05%) and outside class on school work or with students (9.31%).

A schoolwise breakdown shows small differences in teaching time with Dapchari teachers spending 70.44 and Dhundalwadi ones 63.65 per cent on it. Ashram school teachers put in the most time on administration (11.43%) Dapchari and Thakkarbapa the least (8.24% and 8.15%). Outside class Dhundalwadi teachers spend most time with their students and on school work (2.49%) and mission ones the least (8.00%).

TABLE 4.124: Teachers in School Time Distribution by School (N=113)

Percent time spent on	School						
	MS	TB	DW	DC	AS	ZP	ALL
1. Teaching	68.26	68.07	63.65	70.44	66.49	67.92	67.80
2. Administration	10.8	8 8.24	10.83	8.15	11.43	10.58	10.41
3. Extra curricular activities	11.96	13.86	13.04	10.24	12.72	10.48	12.05
4. Outside class on school work & students	8.00	9.83	12.49	11.18	9.36	11.03	9.31
Total	99.1	100.0	100.01	100.01	100.0	100.01	99.57

(j) *Out-of-School Time*

Outside school the teachers' time distribution was estimated across three categories. Most of their time was spent with their families (54.99%), next on school work and students (30.96%), and least with village affairs (14.05%). A schoolwise breakdown shows that mission school teachers spend most time with their families (61.74%) and Dhundalwadi ones the least (27.86%). The opposite is true for time on school work and students, Dhundalwadi teachers with 60.71 per cent, mission ones 22.31 per cent. And on the village matters

Thakkarbapa teachers put in the least time (7.14%), ashram school ones the most (17.13%).

TABLE 4.125: Teacher Out-of-school Time Distribution by School (N = 113)

	Percent time spent on	School						
		MS	TB	DW	DC	AS	ZP	ALL
1.	Family matters	61.74	44.79	27.86	44.71	51.67	60.63	54.99
2.	School work and students	22.31	48.07	60.71	39.57	31.20	28.13	30.96
3.	Village matters	15.94	7.14	11.43	15.71	17.13	11.25	14.05
	Total	99.99	100.0	100.0	99.99	100.00	100.01	100.0

(4) The Teachers in School

A positive perception of one's students is a crucial factor in a sound pedagogy. A teacher cannot really communicate constructively with his students, much less motivate them to learning, if he himself has little faith in their potential to learn.

(a) *Teachers' Perception of Students*

The teachers in this sample do not have much of a negative attitude towards their students, since 68 per cent say their students are interested in their studies and only 13 per cent say they are not. On a scale of 0 to 2, the Dhundalwadi teachers score their students the highest (2.00), Thakkarbapa the lowest (1.00), with the overall average of 1.53.

TABLE 4.126: Teacher's Perception of Student Interest in their Studies by School (Range = 0-2)

	School						
	MS	TB	DW	DC	AS	ZP	ALL
Score	1.52	1.00	2.00	1.29	1.60	1.88	1.53
(N)	(54)	(14)	(7)	(7)	(15)	(16)	(113)

The teachers' perception of their adivasi students is also positive; comparing them to non-adivasis, 15 per cent say they are as good, 75 per cent, as good if helped; and only 10 per cent say they are not as good. On a 1 to 3 scale, the zilla parishad teachers have the most favourable perception of adivasi students (2.38) and Dapchari the least (1.71), with the overall average of 2.04.

TABLE 4.127: Teachers' Rating of Adivasi Students by School (Range = 1-3)

	School						
	MS	TB	DW	DC	AS	ZP	ALL
Score	1.94	2.21	2.14	1.71	1.93	2.38	2.04
(N)	(47)	(14)	(7)	(7)	(14)	(16)	(105)

(b) *The Teachers' Academic Initiative*

With an overall positive appreciation of their students, we can expect some personal initiative in teaching from the teacher. Thus 63 per cent use teaching aids often, 38 per cent sometimes, while (65.5) per cent give their students tests frequently, 26 per cent sometimes. Scaling these on a 1 to 2 range, the most frequent teacher initiative is giving tests (1.54), the least is making teaching aids (1.23). Perhaps this is because so many teachers think the tests are useful, (53 per cent very useful and 45 per cent useful)

TABLE 4.128: Teachers Initiative in Class (N = 113, Range = 1-2)

N (%)	Seldom	Sometimes	Often	Total	Score
Use of aids	12 (10.6)	38 (33.6)	63 (55.8)	113 (100.0)	1.45
Making aids	25 (22.1)	37 (32.7)	51 (45.1)	113 (100.0)	1.23
Giving tests	13 (11.5)	26 (23.0)	74 (65.5)	113 (100.0)	1.54

An important indicator of teacher initiative outside the class is how he responds to absentee students. If the student was absent for a week or two, 41 per cent of the teachers say they would visit his home, 58 per cent would enquire after him. If the student was absent for a month or two, 53 per cent would visit his home, 58 per cent would send a message through the headmaster, 10 per cent would enquire after the student.

Yet another indicator of a teacher's initiative is the special attention and care he gives to the slow learners and the gifted among his students. Here 72 per cent say they specially prepare the better students to do well in the district level examinations, and 83 per cent take extra care to bring those lagging behind to the level of the class, while 40 per cent have prepared students for scholarship examinations over the last three years.

This, however, is often not a matter of teacher initiative but of imposition by the headmaster, so it has been dropped from the additive scale of teacher initiative computed from the 7 items above: the first 5 with a range of 0 to 2 (i.e., use of and making of aids, giving tests, responding to week-long and month-long student absences); the last two with a range of 0 to 1 (i.e., special attention to gifted and slow learners).This scale will hence have a range of 0 to 12.

TABLE 4.129: Teacher Initiative by School, Standard Taught, Sex, Caste and Religion (Range=0-12)

	School						
	MS	TB	DW	DC	AS	ZP	ALL
	7.94	8.79	10.57	9.43	8.33	9.13	8.52
(N)	(54)	(14)	(7)	(7)	(15)	(16)	(113)
	Standard taught			Sex			
	1-4	5-10		Male	Female		
Score	8.30	8.80		8.53	8.50		
(N)	(63)	(50)		(85)	(28)		
	Caste			Religion			
	Adivasi	Non-adivasi		Christian	Non-Christian		
Score	8.02	8.96		7.88	8.93		
(N)	(53)	(60)		(44)	(69)		

A schoolwise breakdown of teacher initiative found the highest initiative reported at Dhundalwadi, (10.57), the lowest at the mission schools (7.94), on an average of 8.52. This may be because the sample of teachers selected at the non-mission schools was biased to include the better teachers, while all the mission school teachers were included, even those from the first to the sixth standards. A separating out of these teachers might make for a more valid comparison. It could of course be that the teachers reporting on their own initiative have exaggerated, but that must be verified by more careful on-the-spot observation before it can be accepted.

The differences between teachers in the lower and the higher standards is minimal (8.30 to 8.86) and the one between male and female teachers even more so (8.53 to 8.50). However, non-adivasi (8.96) to adivasi (8.02) and non-Christian teachers (8.93) to Christians (7.88) show more initiative, which may be the reason why mission schools with more adivasi and Christian teachers score lower than the others on teacher initiative. Of course, the quality of this teacher input is not measured by the scale used.

TABLE 4.130: Teacher's Extra-curricular Activities by School, Standard Taught, Sex, Caste, Religion (Range = 0-4, N = 113)

	School						
	MS	TB	DW	DC	AS	ZP	ALL
Score:	3.02	3.29	3.43	3.29	3.20	3.00	3.12
	Standard taught				Sex		
	1-4	5-10			Male	Female	
Score:	3.04	3.22			3.10	3.18	
	Caste				Religion		
	Adivasi	Non-adivasi			Christian	Non-Christian	
Score:	3.10	3.14			3.07	3.15	

(c) *The Teachers' Extra-Curricular Activities*

An important aspect of a child's education are the extra-curricular activities of the school. These are not possible without teacher's co-operation. Though their participation in these is less clearly specified and required than in classroom teaching, yet their level of participation seems quite high. On an annual basis 97 per cent are involved in the school sports day, 89 per cent in some cultural programme, 97 per cent on a school tour, 83 per cent in some other extra-curricular activity. Scaling these four items into a single scale of 0 to 4, we find an average score of 3.12, while differences between schools, standards taught, sex, caste and religion are insignificant. Perhaps these activities should have been scaled on the basis of a term or a month rather than a year.

An indirect but useful indicator of the teachers' involvement in extra-curricular activity is to look at the student response to such activities. This was done on two counts: in terms of number of participants and the enthusiasm of their participation. To the first, 38 per cent report more than half the number of their students participating, 51 per cent about half, and only 12 per cent less than half. To the second, 68 per cent report very enthusiastic participation and 31 per cent a somewhat enthusiastic one. Adding these two indicators of range 0 to 2 into a single one of range 0 to 4, we can make a schoolwise breakdown that shows Dapchari and the zilla parishad schools with the lowest level of student participation in such extra-curricular activities, and Thakkarbapa and Dhundalwadi with the highest. There is some correspondence between the students' reporting on how much time they have for extra-curricular activities and the teachers' reporting on the level of student participation in them. (See Section 1).

TABLE 4.131: Teachers' Reporting of Student Participation in Extra-curricular Activities by School (Range = 0-4, N = 113)

	School						
	MS	TB	DW	DC	AS	ZP	ALL
Score	2.83	3.43	3.43	2.57	2.87	2.63	2.90

(5) In-Service Supervision and Training

The role of the supervisor in the school system can be constructive or destructive for good teaching, quite independently of the teacher. An effort is made here to sort out what makes for a positive or a negative contribution on the part of the supervisor in the perception of the teacher. This must be complemented later with the perceptions of the supervisors, which have been elicited in more open-ended qualitative interviews.

For the schools in this sample there are two kinds of supervisors. The government-run schools are supervised by an official from the department concerned, i.e., from the block development department for the ashram Schools. For the privately-run schools, although they are under the block education offices (EO), they are effectively supervised by the officials of their own institutions. Since we were concerned with the effective level of supervision in this survey, the supervisors referred to are the respective government officials for the government-run schools and the appointees of the institution concerned for the privately-run ones.

(a) *Frequency and Subject-matter*

Firstly with regard to the frequency of the supervisor's visits, this was averaged over two estimates by the teacher, the frequency per month and per term, to give a single estimate of visits per month on a range of 0 to 4.

A schoolwise breakdown shows that the most frequently visited schools are the zilla parishad and mission schools (2.53 and 2.29 visits per month), the least visited ones are the ashram schools and Dapchari (1.07 visits per month each), the overall average being 1.94 visits per month.

TABLE 4.132: Frequency of Supervision by School (Range = 0-4)

	School						
	MS	TB	DW	DC	AS	ZP	ALL
Score (N)	2.29 (54)	1.64 (14)	1.29 (7)	1.07 (7)	1.07 (15)	2.53 (16)	1.94 (113)

Coming to the subject matter dealt with at these visits of the supervisor, on a 0 to 2 scale, the most frequently discussed subjects are academic matters (1.71) and discipline (1.42); less frequently discussed are administrative matters(1.14) and school facilities (.98), and least frequently personal and social topics (.63 each).

We can collapse the six topics listed above into three pairs to a frequency range of 0 to 4 for each. The most frequently discussed topics are academic matters (3.13), next administrative ones, (2.12), and then personal-social ones (1.26). A schoolwise breakdown of these combined topics shows that academic matters are the most frequent supervision topics at Dhundalwadi (3.71) and Thakkarbapa (3.57), and least at mission schools (2.98) and zilla parishad ones (3.06). Administrative matters are most discussed at Dhundalwadi (3.86) and ashram schools (3.13), least Dapchari (1.71) and mission ones (1.59). Personal and social matters are most discussed at Dhundalwadi (2.29) and ashram schools (1.80) and least at Thakkarbapa (1.00) and mission schools (.98)

TABLE 4.133: Subject-matter of Supervisor's Visits by School (Range = 0-4, N = 113)

Subject matter	School						
	MS	TB	DW	DC	AS	ZP	ALL
1. Academic	2.98	3.57	3.71	2.86	3.20	3.06	3.13
2. Adminis-trative	1.59	2.21	3.86	1.71	3.13	2.31	2.12
3. Personal-Social	.98	1.00	2.29	1.43	1.80	1.38	1.26

(b) *Characteristics of Supervision*

A more critical aspect of the supervisor's visits than mere frequency or subject-matter is their purpose, in the perception of the teachers. On a 0 to 2 scale, generally the teachers see these visits as more to inspire (1.28) and help (1.61) than to check (1.80) and evaluate (1.07). Subtracting the last two measures from the first two ones, we have a scale (range -4 to +4) of how supportive the teachers see their supervisors to be. A schoolwise breakdown shows mission schools' supervisors to be by far the most supportive (.93), while the least are government supervisors at zilla parishad schools (-.50) and ashram ones (-.47).

TABLE 4.134: Supervisor Supportiveness (Range = -4 to +4, N = 113)

	School						
	MS	TB	DW	DC	AS	ZP	ALL
Score	.93	-.14	-.14	.14	-.47	-.50	.29

On a scale of 0 to 2, Thakkarbapa (1.21) and Dapchari (1.14) have the most demanding supervisors, while Dhundalwadi (.57) has the least, with an average of .86. Similarly with regard to how useful the supervision is to their work as teachers, the average score is 2.62 with little difference across schools; for how useful in personal lives, it is 1.06. Adding these up into a 0 to 4 scale of usefulness of supervision, we find that zilla parishad schools (2.69) and mission ones (2.63) find it the most useful, ashram schools (2.20) and Thakkarbapa (2.50) the least useful.

With regard to continuing this supervision, 90 per cent said yes, 53 per cent wanted it continued with their present supervisor, 20 per cent wanted him changed. A scale of commitment to the present teacher supervisor was devised by scoring an affirmative to continuing supervision as one point, and to continuing it with the same supervisor as two. On this 0 to 3 scale, Dapchari (1.29) and mission schools (1.22) are the most committed to continuing supervision, zilla parishad schools (.69) and Thakkarbapa (.86) the least, with the average score at 1.06.

TABLE 4.135: Supervisor Characteristics by School (N=113, Range= 0-2)

Characteristics	School							
	MS	TB	DW	DC	AS	ZP	ALL	Range
1. How demanding	.69	1.21	.57	1.14	.93	1.06	.86	(0-2)
2. How useful	2.63	2.50	2.43	2.71	2.20	2.69	2.62	(0-4)
3. Continue	1.22	.86	1.14	1.29	.93	.69	1.06	(0-3)

Since the private-run schools were subject to two kinds of supervision, by their own institutions and by the government, these teachers were asked to compare the two on a 3-point scale, from no difference, to the institution's supervision being better than the government ones. A single measure was formed from five points for comparison, i.e., frequency of visits, topics discussed, purpose of the supervision, how demanding it was, and how useful. On a scale of 5 to 15 the mission schools (10.52) were the most positive about their own supervisors in comparison to the government ones, next Dapchari (8.71), then Thakkarbapa and Dhundalwadi (7.43 each), the overall average score being 9.60.

(c) *Seminars and Meetings*

Seminars, workshops and other such meetings constitute an important aspect of the teachers' in-service training. Sometimes these are organized on an inter-school basis by the sponsoring institutions, or even at the taluka level by the department of education. An attempt was made to study how these meetings contributed to teacher improvement.

(d) *Frequency and Subject-matter*

Regarding the frequency of these meetings, 38 per cent of the teachers attended them less than once a month, 57 per cent about monthly and only 5 per cent more often than that. With an overall average of .67, on a scale of 0 to 2, government school teachers attended them most frequently (.87) followed by mission schools (.65) and other private ones (.50).

The subject-matter of these meetings was categorized as was done earlier for the school supervision. Once again on a 0 to 4 scale, the most frequent topics were academic matters 3.13 followed by administrative matters (2.30), and then personal and social ones (1.24).

A schoolwise breakdown (Table 4.136) shows that academic topics are most frequent at Dhundalwadi teachers' meetings (4.00) and least frequent at Thakkarbapa (2.79), administrative matters are most frequent to Dhundalwadi (3.57) and least at ashram schools (2.00), personal and social ones are most frequent at Dhundalwadi (2.14), least at the mission schools (.80).

TABLE 4.136: Subject-matter of Teachers' Meetings by School (N = 113, Range = 0-4)

Subject matter	School						
	MS	TB	DW	DC	AS	ZP	ALL
1. Academic matters	2.93	2.79	4.00	3.43	3.13	3.57	3.13
2. Administrative "	2.13	2.14	3.57	2.29	2.00	2.75	2.30
3. Personal/social "	.80	1.43	2.14	1.57	1.47	1.82	1.24

(e) *Characteristics of Teacher Meetings*

The purpose of these meetings is rather positively perceived (on a scale of 0 to 2) as being more to inspire (1.28) and help (1.19) than to evaluate (.95) and check (.943). Computing a score of supportiveness for these meetings by subtracting the last two from the first two items above we have a scale of range -4 to +4, on which the overall average is .57.

A schoolwise breakdown shows mission schools to be the most supportive at such teacher meetings (.96) and Dhundalwadi to be the least (-.29) (Table 4.137). Asked how useful they found these meetings (on a 0 to 2 scale), ashram school teachers find them the most useful (1.89), mission ones the least (1.22).

TABLE 4.137: Characteristic of Teacher Meetings by School (N=113, Range= 0-2)

Characteristics of meetings	Schools							
	MS	TB	DW	DC	AS	ZP	ALL	Range
1. Suppor-tiveness	.96	.36	-.29	.29	.13	.38	.57	(-4to+4)
2. Usefulness	1.22	1.57	1.71	1.29	1.89	1.57	1.44	(0-2)

(6) School-Community Relationship

The school teacher's participation in the village is one more crucial aspect of the school-community focus of this study. Here the variables used to estimate parental participation were used with the teachers. Only with regard to helping others, the item referring to accompanying people to government offices was dropped, since this would not easily be possible for teachers, who are bound by school hours.

(a) *Teachers' Involvement in the Community*

Thus personal assistance to others covered 3 items, each on a 0 to 2 scale: writing letters, etc., advising on education and employment, settling family disputes etc. A schoolwise breakdown on this 0 to 6 scale showed Dhundalwadi teachers to score the highest (2.00) and

Thakkarbapa ones the lowest (.79). Except for political awareness, which had a range of 1 to 7, the rest of the ranges were 0 to 4.

On local community meetings measured on frequency and involvement, Dhundalwadi and Dapchari score the highest (1.57 each), mission schools the lowest (.93). For participation in village festivals similarly measured, Dapchari is the highest (2.14) and Thakkarbapa the lowest (.57) (Table 4.138). On village leadership in terms of presiding at meetings and local offices held, Dhundalwadi is second highest (2.29), ashram schools the lowest(1.80). On political awareness measured on the basis of voting and participating in demonstrations ashram schools score highest (2.40), Dhundalwadi lowest (1.14). For social action comprised of membership and involvement in an organization, zilla parishad schools score highest (2.25), mission schools the lowest (.91).Adding all these scores up into a composite one on social participation, (range 0 to 29), we find the highest level at zilla parishad schools (10.82), Dapchari (10.57), Dhundalwadi (10.15) and ashram schools (10.06). The lowest are at mission schools (7.68) and Thakkarbapa (7.78).

TABLE 4.138: Teacher Participation in Local Village Community by School (N=113)

Kind of Participation	School							
	MS	TB	DW	DC	AS	ZP	ALL	Range
1. Personal assistance	.94	.79	2.00	.86	1.60	2.44	1.28	(0-6)
2. Village meetings	.93	1.14	1.57	1.57	1.00	1.25	1.09	(0-4)
3. Village festivals	1.74	.57	1.86	2.14	1.93	1.31	1.59	(0-4)
4. Village leadership	1.94	1.86	2.29	2.00	1.80	1.88	1.93	(0-4)
5. Political awareness	1.22	1.71	1.14	2.00	2.40	1.69	1.55	(1-7)
6. Social action	.91	1.71	1.29	2.00	1.33	2.25	1.35	(0-4)
7. Social	7.68	7.78	10.15	10.57	10.06	10.82	8.79	(1-29)

(b) *Community Support for the School*

The teachers' participation in the village represents the school-to-community link. Their perception of the village support for the school represents the community-to-school link. As earlier, this was measured in terms of support for the education of their children in general and for the school in particular. On a 0 to 4 scale, the most supportive local communities as reported by the teachers were the ashram schools and the zilla parishad ones (2.13 each), the least supportive being the mission schools (1.48) and Thakkarbapa (1.57).

TABLE 4.139: Community Support by School (Range=0-4)

	School						
	MS	TB	DW	DC	AS	ZP	ALL
Score	1.48	1.57	1.71	1.86	2.13	2.13	1.71
(N)	(54)	(14)	(7)	(7)	(15)	(16)	(113)

(c) *Relationship to School Constituents*

To study how the teachers related to the various categories of people in and outside the school, i.e., students, parents, teacher colleagues, supervisors, and village level workers, they were asked to grade on a 0 to 2 scale the level of demands, expectations, support and appreciation they experienced from each of the five school constituents.

In general the level of demands is low (.26), that of expectations high (1.23), the level of support lower (1.06) than that of appreciation (1.15). More particularly, the supervisors were the most demanding (.58), parents (.08) and village workers (.12) the least. Students and supervisors had the highest expectations of them (1.58 each), parents (1.13) and village workers (.52) the lowest. Colleagues (1.47) and students (1.45) were the most supportive, parents (1.64) and village workers (1.34) the least. Students (1.49) were the most appreciative, village workers the least (.56).

The scores on demands and expectations were added up to indicate the level of exaction experienced by the teachers, the ones on support and appreciation added up to indicate helpfulness, experienced by them, the range on both being 0 to 4. The difference between the score on helpfulness and that on exaction indicated the level of encouragement of the teacher, with a range of -4 to +4.

In general the teachers find these groups that they relate with more helpful (2.21) than exacting (1.49) and overall feel somewhat encouraged (.72). The teachers found their supervisors to be the most exacting (2.16), the village workers (.64) and parents (1.21) the least. The students were the most helpful (2.94), village workers (.90) and parents (1.74) the least. The colleagues were the most encouraging (1.20) followed by the students (1.07), with the other groups scoring rather low: supervisors .58, parents .53, village workers .26.

It would then seem that the intra-institutional relationships of the teachers (i.e, with supervisors, students, colleagues) are at a higher level than the extra-institutional ones (i.e, with parents and village workers), and there surely is room for improvement in this.

TABLE 4.140: Teacher Relationships with School Constituents (N=113)

Level of	Constituents						
	Students	Parents	Teachers	Supervisors	Village workers	Av. score	Range
1. Demands	.29	.08	.23	.58	.12	.26	(0-2)
2. Expectations	1.58	1.13	1.32	1.58	.52	1.23	(0-2)
3 Support	1.45	.64	1.47	1.41	.34	1.06	(0-2)
4. Appreciation	1.49	1.10	1.28	1.33	.56	1.15	(0-2)
5. Exaction (1+2)	1.87	1.21	1.55	2.16	.64	1.49	(0-4)
6. Helpfulness (3+4)	2.94	1.74	2.75	2.74	.90	2.21	(0-4)
7. Encouragement	1.07	.53	1.20	.58	.26	.72	(6-5) (-4to+4)

(d) *Differences between Schools*

A schoolwise breakdown of teacher encouragement from the different constituents was made. With regard to feeling encouraged by students, ashram schools were the highest (1.60), mission schools the lowest (.81). With regard to encouragement from parents, it was highest at Dapchari (1.29) and lowest at mission schools (.26). Colleague and supervisor encouragement was highest at Dapchari

(2.00 and 1.29) and lowest at the ashram schools (.80 and .00). Similarly, for encouragement from village level workers, Dapchari and Dhundalwadi are highest (.43 each) and ashram schools lowest (.00). On the overall average score of .73 across the 5 categories, Dapchari scores the highest (1.34) followed by Dhundalwadi (.94) and zilla parishad schools (.80), while lowest scores are for ashram schools (.65), mission ones (.65) and Thakkarbapa (.64) (Table 4.141).

TABLE 4.141: Teacher Encouragement from School Constituents by School (Range = -4 to +4)

Constituents	School						
	MS	TB	DW	DC	AS	ZP	ALL
(N)	(54)	(14)	(7)	(7)	(15)	(16)	(113)
1. Students	.81	1.21	1.57	1.57	1.60	.88	1.07
2. Parents	.26	.43	1.29	1.14	.87	.63	.53
3. Colleagues	1.09	1.29	1.14	2.00	.80	1.56	1.20
4. Supervisors	.81	.07	1.29	.29	.00	.63	.58
5. Village workers	.28	.21	.43	.43	.00	.31	.26
6. Overall average	.65	.64	.94	1.29	.65	.80	.73

(e) *Teacher Satisfaction with their School*

Any realistic estimate of one's satisfaction is always relative to one's expectations. Given the other schools as a reference point for their expectations, the teachers seem rather satisfied with their own schools in comparison to the others. Only seven per cent are not satisfied with their students, three per cent are not with the teachers, and with their supervisors. However, 19 per cent are not satisfied with school facilities, 27 per cent with the parents, and 32 per cent with the village support.

On the other hand, teachers very satisfied with the above groups are as follows: 43 per cent with their supervisors, 31 per cent with school facilities, but only 10 per cent with the parents, and 7 per cent with the village support.

These are comparative evaluations and so should not be exaggerated. But it does seem that the teachers are most satisfied with school-connected persons like their students, colleagues and supervisors and rather dissatisfied with those less involved in the school like the parents and the village. There is a correspondence between teacher satisfaction here and parental satisfaction on the same aspects studied earlier. (See Part 2 (5) The Parents and the School, pp. 100-105).

Adding these various aspects into a single scale of range 0 to 12, a schoolwise breakdown shows Dhundalwadi with the highest teacher satisfaction (9.71) and Thakkarbapa with the lowest (6.50) on an overall average of 6.92.

TABLE 4.142: Teacher Satisfaction by School (Range = 0-12)

	School						
	MS	TB	DW	DC	AS	ZP	ALL
Score	6.78	6.50	9.71	6.43	7.13	6.56	6.92

(7) Conclusion

The overall profile of the teachers presented here is rather positive. The students seem to confirm this too. The weakest aspect of their role performance is their relationship to the local community in which the school is located. This is corroborated by the parents as well.

The analysis presented here is, of course, based on information provided by the teachers themselves. It must be complemented with other sources of data from the internal and external constituents of the school, and areas of congruence and conflict sorted out.

4. INSTITUTIONAL GOALS

(1) Perceptions and Goals

Institutional goals and purposes are complex and difficult to objectify. What has been attempted here is to use the perceptions of the teachers to put together an institutional profile of the objectives and activities of their schools. While these perceptions cannot necessarily claim to be objective, they do constitute "a definition of the situation" from the inside on the part of these teachers, and can be a valuable complement to the other data at hand.

The institutional goals were articulated in a set of propositions describing objectives and activities of the school. The teacher was required to respond to each goal at two levels on a scale of 1 to 3: how important the goal is for his school and how important it *ought* to be. The first pointed to what was *characteristic* of the school, the second to what would be *preferred*. The difference between the two perceptions would indicate an area of *satisfaction* if the difference was *small*, or an area for *improvement* if it was *large*. The importance given a particular goal was estimated in terms of the time and money allocated to it by the school.

All together there were 28 goals articulated, 11 pertaining to students, 7 to teachers, and 10 to the school. These are listed below. (The figures in brackets represent the goal ranks: 'I' for the "is" level, 'O' for the 'ought' one).

(a) *Students*

1. To teach students to *think independently*, i.e. to enable them to criticize what they have learnt and not merely repeat it by rote. (I=15, O=4)
2. To develop sound *moral values* and convictions in students, i.e., to able them to make decisions on a moral basis and follow them through. (I=14, O=19)
3. To *train* students to express and control their *emotions*, i.e., not to merely repress their feelings or be led by them, not to go by feelings of like/dislike, of fear/anxiety etc. (I=16, O=23)
4. To *produce* students who will be *leaders* for their people, i.e., to play an active role in working for the good of the people. (I=9, O=8)
5. To *teach* students their *religion*, i.e., Christianity to Christians, Hinduism to Hindus, etc.. (I=25, O=26)
6. To persuade students to *change* their own *religion*, i.e., from Hinduism to Christianity and *vice versa*. (I=28, O=28)
7. To have special facilities for *backward students*, i.e., special classes or programme for socially, economically, or otherwise disadvantage students. (I=11, O=13)
8. To have special facilities for *gifted students*, i.e., special classes or programmes for students who are more capable,

intellectually and otherwise. (I=17, O=16)

9. To give a *job-oriented education*, i.e., a bias in the school to make students more employable. (I=23, O=22)
10. To develop *self-respect* in students, i.e., to appreciate their own culture and have self-confidence. (I=12, O=6)
11. To have an *all-round development* of students, i.e., of head and heart or body and mind: intellectual, moral, emotional, social. (I=1, O=1)

(b) *Teachers*

1. To keep *teachers happy* and satisfied in their job, i.e., a feeling of well-being and fulfilment in their teaching. (I=20, O=14)
2. To *keep teachers committed* and motivated in their job. (I=19, O=18)
3. To *involve teachers in decisions* of the management, i.e., not merely inform them once decisions are made but to elicit their opinion to arrive at one. (I=22, O=15)
4. To *consult teachers* regarding the running of the school, i.e., not merely expect them to carry out orders but invite suggestions, listen to problems about the implementation. (I=17, O=11)
5. To encourage *teachers* to be *innovative* in their teaching, i.e., providing ideas and support to carry them through. (I=21, O=21)
6. To *reward teachers* for extra work and *initiative*, i.e., a reward monetary or otherwise showing appreciation. (I=26, O=25)
7. To get all to work as a *unified team* in the school, i.e., the teachers of the school and the supervisors as well. (I=11, O=13)

(c) *School*

1. Have a proper *extra-curricular programme*, i.e., games, handicraft, drama, dance, etc.. (I=19, O=18)
2. Have *good discipline*, i.e., habits or regularity, punctuality, orderliness, etc.. (I=7, O=10)
3. Have *efficient management*, i.e., good supervision, smooth administration. (I=7, O=10)

TABLE 4.143: Most Characteristic Goals

Institutional goal		Mean score	(N)	rank on "is"	pertaining to category of:
1. *For All Schools*					
S.11.	All round student devt.	2.46*	(112)	1	students
I-2	Good discipline	2.46*	(112)	2	institution
I-7	Good results	2.42*	(110)	3	institution
I-4	Institutional	2.28	(111)	4	institution
S-7	Help backward	2.24	(102)	5	students
2. *For Mission Schools*					
S-11	All round student deve-lopment	2.39*	(54)	1	students
I-7	Good results	2.23*	(52)	2	institution
I-2	Good discipline	2.21*	(53)	3	institution
I-4	Institutional prestige	2.09	(53)	4	institution
3. *For Other Private Schools*					
I-2	Good discipline	2.79*	(28)	1	institution
S-11	All-round student	2.68*	(28)	2	students
		development.			
I-7	Good results	2.67*	(27)	3	institution
S-10	Develop students	2.464	(28)	4	students
S-7	Help backward	2.462	(26)	5	students
T-7	Work as a team	2.462	(26)	5	teachers
4. *For Government Schools*					
I-2	Good discipline	2.61*	(31)	1	institution
I-7	Good results	2.52*	(31)	2	institution
S-11	All-round student development	2.40	(30)	3	students
T-7	Work as a team	2.29	(31)	4	teachers
T-1	Keep teachers happy	2.20	(30)	5	teachers

4. Have high *institutional prestige*, i.e., to be among the best

schools in the area. (I=4, O=5)

5. Help *students to adjust* to school, i.e., helping them to fit into the school timetables and programmes. (I=8, O=12)
6. Try to *adapt teaching* to the students, i.e., changing school timetables and programmes to meet students needs. (I=13, O=17)
7. Get *good results* in the public exams, i.e., high percentage of passes and marks. (I=3, O=3)
8. Be a centre for *community services* and programmes, i.e., serving its cultural and educational needs. (I=24, O=24)
9. Give preference to *poor students* in admission. (I=6, O=7)
10. Give *preference* to students of a certain *caste* or community in admissions, i.e., to Christians in Christian schools or Hindus in Hindu ones, etc.. (I=27, O=27)

(2) **The Analysis**

In the analysis here the teachers were broken down into three categories: mission schools, other private schools, and government schools. (The asterisk in the tables in this Part 4, 4.143-4.148, indicates the goals which were more than one standard deviation from the mean score of the goals at that level. The differences between levels are similarly indicated).

(a) *Characteristic Goals*

Student-centred goals are very prominent among the most characteristic goals of these schools. The order of priority among these goals varies little, and the basic picture of the student they are trying to turn out is the same: all-round student development, good discipline, good examination results. Other private schools add to this, developing the student's self-respect, and helping backward students. The most characteristic institution-centred goals show some differences, mission schools being more concerned with prestige and efficiency, which are task-oriented goals. Other private schools value teamwork, and government ones value both teamwork and keeping teachers happy. These are support-goals.

Among the least characteristic goals, three are common to all three categories: religious conversion, caste/community preference in admissions and rewarding teachers for extra work/initiative. Besides these, mission schools are least characteristic in helping gifted students and involving their teachers in management decisions.

Other private schools too do not give importance to involving teachers in decision-making, nor to teaching students their own religion. government schools similarly do not teach students their religion, nor are they centres for community services.

TABLE 4.144: Least Characteristic Goals

Institutional		Mean score	(N)	rank on "is"	category pertaining to
1. *For All Schools*					
S-6	Change students' Religion	1.11*	(96)	28	students
1-10	Caste/community preference in admissions	1.37	(100)	27	institution
T-6	Reward teachers for extra work/ initiative	1.58*	(106)	26	teachers
S-5	teach students their own religion	1.61	(108)	25	students
I-9	be centre for Community services	1.86	(108)	24	institution
2. *For Mission Schools*					
S-6	Change students' religion	1.19*	(42)	28	student
T-6	Reward teachers for extra work/ initiative	1.40*	(48)	27	students
I-10	Caste/community preference in admissions	1.41*	(49)	26	institution
S-8	Help gifted students	1.67	(48)	25	students
T-3	Involve teachers	1.70	(50)	24	teachers
3. *For Other Private Schools*					
S-6	Change students' religion	1.04*	(26)	28	students
S-5	Teach students their own religion	1.46*	(24)	27	students
I-10	Caste/community preference in admissions	1.52*	(23)	26	institution
T-6	Reward teachers for extra work/ initiative	1.86*	(27)	25	teachers

(Contd.)

Contd.

Institutional		Mean score	(N)	rank on "is"	category pertaining to
T-3	Involve teachers in management decisions	2.04	(28)	24	teachers
T-4	Consult teachers on running of decisions	2.04	(28)	24	teachers
4. *For Governmental Schools*					
S-6	Change students' religion	1.04*	(28)	28	students
I-10	Caste/community preference in admission	1.18*	(28)	27	institution
T-6	Reward teachers for extra work/ initiative	1.65*	(31)	26	teachers
I-8	Be centre for community services	1.68*	(31)	25	institution
S-5	Teach students their own religion	1.20*	(28)	24	students

(b) *Preferred Goals*

Coming to the level of preferred goals, once again among the most preferred ones are student-centred goals, very similar to those which were most characteristic as well. For mission schools these were: all-round student development, good discipline, and producing leaders. For other private schools, all 4 of the most characteristic goals appear to be the most preferred as well: all-round development, discipline, examination results, students' self-respect. For government schools the first 3, and teaching students independent thinking, are the most preferred student-centred goals. The other preferred goals for mission schools concern teachers, consulting them and involving them in decision-making. For other private and government schools institutional prestige is a preferred goal.

TABLE 4.145: Preferred Goals

Institutional goal		Mean score	(N)	rank on "is"	category pertaining to:
1. *For All Schools*					
S-11	All-round student	1.73*	(111)	1	students
I-2	Good discipline	2.592	(113)	2	institution
I-7	Good results	2.589	(112)	3	institutions
S-1	Teach students	2.50	(112)	4	students
I-5	Institutional	2.49	(111)	5	institution
2. *For Mission Schools*					
S-11	All-round student development	2.68	(53)	1	students
I-2	Good discipline	2.43	(54)	2	institution
S-4	Produce leaders	2.40	(53)	3	students
T-3	Involve teachers in management decisions	2.33	(49)	4	teachers
T-4	Consult teachers on running of school	2.29	(49)	5	teachers
3. *For Other Private Schools*					
S-11	All-round student development	2.86	(28)	1	students
I-7	Good results	2.82	(28)	2	institution
I-2	Good discipline	2.82	(28)	3	institution
I-4	Institutional prestige	2.79	(28)	5	institution
T-4	Consult teachers on running of school	2.71	(28)	5	teachers
S-10	Develop students' self-respect	2.71	(28)	5	students
4. *For Government Schools*					
S-11	All-round student development	2.70	(30)	1	students
I-2	Good discipline	2.68	(31)	2	institution
S-1	Teach students independent thinking	2.63	(30)	3	students
I-4	Institutional prestige	2.61	(31)	4	institution
I-7	Good results	2.57	(30)	5	institution

TABLE 4.146: Least Preferred Goals

Institutional goal		Mean score	(N)	Rank on "is"	Category pertaining to:
1. *For All Schools*					
S-6	Change students' religion	1.08*	(92)	28	students
I-10	Caste/community preference in admissions	1.44*	(105)	27	institution
S-5	Teach students their own religion	1.87	(102)	26	students
T-6	Reward teachers for extra work/ initiative	2.04	(102)	25	teachers
I-8	Be centre for community services	2.23	(105)	24	institution
2. *For Mission Schools*					
S-6	Change students' religion	1.11*	(38)	28	students
I-10	Caste/community preference in admission	1.52*	(50)	27	institution
T-6	reward teachers for extra work/ initiative	1.81*	(43)	26	teachers
I-8	Be centre for community services	2.09	(47)	25	institution
T-2	Keep teachers motivated	2.10	(48)	24	teachers
3. *For Other Private Schools*					
S-6	Change students' religion	1.04*	(26)	28	students
I-10	Caste/community preference in admissions	1.54*	(26)	27	institution
S-5	Teach students their own religion	1.64*	(25)	26	students
T-6	Reward teachers for extra work/ initiative	2.32	(28)	25	teachers
S-3	Students emotional development	2.39	(28)	24	students

(*Contd.*)

Contd.

Institutional goal		Mean score	(N)	Rank on "is"	Category pertaining to:
4. *For Government Schools*					
S-6	Change students' religion	1.07*	(31)	28	students
I-10	Caste/community preference in admissions	1.21*	(29)	27	institution
S-5	Teach students their own religion	1.46*	(28)	26	students
T-6	Reward teachers for extra work/ initiative	2.10	(31)	25	teachers
T-3	Involve teachers in management	2.17	(29)	24	teachers

The same five least characteristic goals now reappear as least preferred ones, making the correspondence between the two complete. Religious conversion, caste/community preference, and rewarding teachers' extra work are least preferred in all three types of schools. For mission schools, being a community centre and motivating teachers rank low. For other private schools, religious instruction and the students' emotional development rank low. In government schools, the students' religious instruction and the teachers' involvement in decision-making are rated as low preferences.

(c) *Area of Satisfaction*

The difference between the "ought" level of a goal and the "is" level, i.e., between the preferred importance to be given and the actual importance given, is a good indicator of whether the goal is over-emphasized, satisfactory or to be improved: the mean on the "ought" being smaller, about the same, or larger than the one on the "is", respectively. There were no important areas of over-emphasis in these findings, but there were areas of satisfaction and improvement.

TABLE 4.147: Areas of Satisfactory Priorities

Institutional goal		difference b/w "ought" and "is"	rank of difference	category pertaining to
1. *For All Schools*				
S-6	Change students' religion	-.028*	28	students
I-10	Caste/community preference in admissions	.068*	27	institution
I-7	Good results	.171*	26	institution
S-9	Job-oriented education	.177*	25	students
I-2	Good discipline	.127*	28	institution
2. *For Mission Schools*				
S-6	Change students' religion	-.085*	28	students
I-10	Caste/community preference in admissions	.112*	27	institution
I-2	Good discipline	.218	26	institution
I-7	Good results	.251	25	institution
I-3	Efficient management	.258	24	institution
3. *For Other Private Schools*				
I-1	Proper extra-curricular programmes	-.037*	28	institution
S-6	Change students' religion	.000*	27	students
I-10	Caste/community preference in admissions	.017*	26	institution
I-2	Good discipline	.036*	25	institution
I-9	Preference to poor students in admissions	.096	24	institution

(*Contd.*)

Contd.

Institutional goal		difference b/w "ought" and "is"	rank of difference	category pertaining to
4. *For Government Schools*				
S-6	Change students' religion	.036	28	students
I-7	Good results	.051*	27	institution
I-2	Good discipline	.065*	26	institution
S-2	Develop students' moral values	.069*	25	students
I-5	Help students	.097	24	institution

The two most consistent areas of satisfaction for all 3 categories of schools were: religious conversion and good discipline. The first is a low priority goal, the second a high priority one. For mission schools good examination results and efficient management were also areas of satisfaction and high priority goals, caste/community preference in admissions was a low priority area of satisfaction, as were extra-curricular programmes and preference to poor students in admissions. For government schools, good examination results was a high priority area of satisfaction, as were developing students' moral values and helping them to adjust to school.

(d) *Areas for Improvement*

TABLE 4.148: Areas for Improved Priorities

Institutional goal		difference b/w "ought" & "is"	Rank of difference	Category pertaining to
1. *For All Schools*				
T-3	Involve teachers in management decisions	.516	1	teachers
T-6	Consult teachers for extra work/ initiative	.454*	2	teachers
T-4	Consult teachers on running of schools	.426*	3	teachers

(*Contd.*)

Contd.

Institutional goal		difference b/w "ought" & "is"	Rank of difference	Category pertaining to
S-1	Teach students independent thinking	.418*	4	students
T-1	Keep teachers happy in their work	.406*	5	teachers
2. *For Mission Schools*				
T-7	Work as a team	.873*	1	teachers
T-3	Involve teachers in management decisions	.627*	2	teachers
S-1	Teach students independent thinking	.526	3	students
S-8	Help gifted students	.506	4	students
S-10	Develop students' self-respect	.461	5	students
3. *For Other Private Schools*				
T-4	Consult teachers on running of school	.679*	1	teachers
T-3	Involve teachers in management decisions	.643*	2	teachers
T-6	Reward teachers for extra work/initiative	.470*	3	teachers
S-9	Job-oriented education	.436*	4	students
T-1	Keep teachers happy in their work	.429*	5	teachers
4. *For Government Schools*				
I-8	Be centre for community services	.523*	1	institution
S-9	Job-oriented education	.459*	2	students
T-6	Reward teachers for extra work/ initiative	.452*	3	teachers
T-2	Keep teachers motivated	.419*	4	teachers
S-10	Develop students' self-respect	.400*	5	students

Overall areas for improvement concerned mostly teacher-centred goals: involving them in decision-making, rewarding them for extra work, consulting them, keeping them happy. The only student-centred area of improvement was teaching them to think independently. However, besides involving teachers in decision-making, teamwork appeared as an area for improvement, and besides independent thinking for students, helping gifted students and developing self-respect were also seen as needing improvement. For other private schools the areas for teacher-centred goal improvement were the same as the overall pattern, but job-oriented education replaced independent thinking as an area for improvement. For government schools, involving teachers in decision-making does not appear as an area for improvement. Rewarding them for extra work and motivation does. Similarly independent thinking is not seen as needing improvement, job-oriented education and developing self-respect are. So too is the school as a community service centre in need of improvement.

(e) *The School Profile*

The profile of the school that emerges from this lengthy analysis can now be sketched. These schools are not strikingly dissimilar across the three categories analyzed, nor are their actual and preferred goals very differently perceived.

At both the levels of the 'is' and the 'ought', student-centred goals predominate, generally adding up to a broad, well rounded education. The area of religious, caste and communal preference, whether in teaching or admission, is decidedly not favored. But neither is the school seen as a community centre.

There are both high and low priorities among these goals that are perceived as satisfactory. Thus no change can be immediately expected from the high emphasis given to student performance in terms of examination results and discipline; nor, for that matter with regard to the present discounting of religious, caste and communal preferences. The areas for improvement pertain mostly to the teachers, generally with more motivated and responsible participation in the running of the school.

The broad outlines of the school profile are now apparent. The schools are very much focussed on their students and are content to be so. It is not a narrow focus on examinations and discipline only but goes beyond to a more rounded development including qualities like self-respect, independent thinking and leadership. The teachers represent the most important area for improvement, especially with regard to involving them in the running of the school as partners rather than employees. For this a certain devolution of authority with effective supervision will be needed. Institution-centred goals are not the most prominent for these schools. And here too institutional prestige is balanced by helping less privileged students. However, in their relationship to the village community, the schools, while wanting to stand apart from religious, caste and communal preferences, do not reach out to become community or service centres either.

(3) **Conclusion**

In conclusion what needs to be stressed here is that this profile is based on teacher perceptions. They are useful and important sources of analysis and understanding but they cannot be the sole basis for a critical study. These perceptions are most helpful not in the absolute scores they are quantified in, but in the internal comparisons and orders of priorities they yield. The attempt here has been to do precisely this and the analysis is useful to the extent it has succeeded in doing so.

5

AN ANALYTICAL DISCUSSION

The lengthy tabulation of the data made in the previous chapter constitutes a descriptive presentation that is a necessary first step in the analysis. But it would be rather superficial and flat without a further analysis that cuts deeper into the data and carries the discussion an important step further. To simplify and make intelligible the statistical analyses used, the tables are reproduced in the appendix and the significant findings are discussed and put together here together with the data presented in chapter IV. Since the text is based on, and explains the tables, the two cannot be logically separated. It is only done here for convenience. However, some familiarity with the tables in the appendix will make this text more intelligible and convincing.

The discussion is presented in four parts. The first three follow the divisions of the previous chapter: students, parents, and teachers. The last presents and discusses the findings on the matched pairs of students and parents. An attempt is made to bring the various aspects of the discussion together in more comprehensive profiles and conclusions. But a more complete interpretation will be made in the next chapter in the light of the qualitative data as well.

1. THE STUDENTS

(1) The Analysis of Variance

(a) *All Students*

A three-way analysis of variance was done on the students sample using the following as independent variables:

(1) the student's school (i.e. MS, TB, etc.)

(2) his village (i.e. whether with a mission school, MSV, or without, NMSV)
(3) his religion (i.e. non-Christian or Christian)

The table in the appendix (p. 193) presents the significant statistical results. These help to confirm and extend the presentation of the data already made in chapter 5. Taken together they do help to indicate the broad lines of a comparative student profile.

The Dapchari high school, with the least proportion of adivasis and the highest percentage of white collar and non-farm workers among the parents, has students significantly different from the more typical adivasi high schools. The Dapchari students have better educated parents, more support for school-going, are more aware of government facilities for scheduled tribes in education and employment, have less difficulties with their classroom subjects even though their teachers are less available for help, and yet they like their school less.

The two more typical adivasi high schools are markedly different. Thakkarbapa and the ashram schools are almost entirely adivasi and non-Christian, with 80 to 90 per cent of the parents in farming. The parents' education is the lowest, support for school-going poor, and the students have difficulty in following the class.

The differences between the primary schools, Dhundalwadi and the zilla parishad ones, with 95 per cent and 80 per cent adivasi respectively, are similar but not so marked.

The profile of the mission school is somewhere in between. The adivasis' enrolment in the primary schools is low, while in the secondary, it is 100 per cent. This is due to the location of the schools, the primary school in Talasari drawing on the non-adivasis of the town, and the secondary one, in isolated Uplat Patipada, committed by policy to serving the adivasis. For these students parental education, school-going support, and coping with class subject-matter are not very different from the others. However, they seem less aware of governmental assistance in education and employment for scheduled tribes.

(b) *Adivasi Students*

What the analysis above points to is the expected divide between adivasis and non-adivasis in the sample. For a closer look at the adivasi students, a further step in the analysis of variance was taken, using as independent variables:

(1) religion (Christian and non-Christian)
(2) standard in school (i.e. primary and secondary)
(3) boarding (i.e. boarder or not)

The significant statistical results are presented in the appendix (p. 193). Here the findings and their implications are discussed together with the data presented in chapter 5.

Among these adivasi students, the primary school ones consider 'work experience' to be less useful than the secondary school ones. Moreover, the primary school boarding is better liked.

The boarders come from a poorer socio-economic family background than non-boarders though they like the school better. The Christian adivasis have more female students among them than the non-Christians, and better educated parents, with more agricultural assets. However, they consider 'work experience' less useful, read less, and are less aware of government concessions to scheduled tribes. The occupational preferences of these students is indicative. The two more commonly preferred occupations are farming and teaching, chosen by about 50 per cent and 60 per cent respectively.

Christians are more likely to choose farming in the primary school, 52 per cent to 43, but there is a drop of 16 percentage points from the primary to the secondary school students. For non-Christians there is an increase of 7 percentage points. Teaching is a popular choice with both groups and at both levels, as is medicine. But the first is surely a more realistic aspiration than the second.

Manual work is chosen by about a third, evenly for both religious groups. For Christians there is a slight drop of 3 percentage points from the primary to the secondary school, while for non-Christians a drop of 13 such points. Business and other non-manual work is chosen by a very small percentage in both groups and at both levels.

With reference to their fathers' occupations, adivasi Christian boys choose it more frequently than non-Christians at the primary level, 70 to 52 per cent. But at the secondary level it is about the same, 44 to 40 per cent. The drop from the primary to secondary level is 26 percentage points for Christians to 12 for non-Christians.

The pattern of decrease in the occupational preference of Christian adivasi students from the primary to the secondary level stands out enough to warrant an explanation. This is especially so with regard to farming, where it moves in a direction opposite to that for non-Christian adivasis. Does education distance the Christian student from farming and is this due to the influence of the school or the parents?

(2) The Regression Analysis

To refine and extend the analysis further, multiple regression was used in two stages: for the sample as a whole, and then for the adivasi students only. The statistical details are presented in the appendix III (pp. 196-200). Here the main findings are collated.

The desire to continue their education rather than accept immediate employment is higher for students in the higher standards and with better educated families. But for adivasi students, the family's agricultural assets are significant here and not their education.

Three occupational preferences were studied, farming, teaching, and medicine, as the most popular choices. For all three, support for the choice was significant.

Not unexpectedly, farming was chosen more by boys than girls, more by adivasis than others, less by Christians than others, more by those having scholastic difficulties. Being a boarder and having better educated parents negatively affects the preference for teaching, perhaps because these students are more ambitious. For adivasis, teaching is chosen more by boys than by girls. Medicine is chosen more by boys and less often by those in the higher standards.

With regard to the awareness of educational and occupational concessions for tribals, students in the higher standards are more aware of these, those with better educated parents less aware, as also are the Christians. Those with greater agricultural assets have more awareness, as also those supported in their occupational choice. It would seem then that economic class has a positive effect on such awareness, while quite anomalously, educational background correlates negatively with it. Could this be explained by the upward mobility of the first generation learners, ready to take advantage of opportunities their parents did not have?

Liking the school is negatively related to scholastic difficulties of the student, which in turn are greater for adivasis, and among these greater for those with less educated parents. Finding enough time to study is also positively affected by parental education, while reading is less among the Christians and in the lower standards. For adivasis, participation in village programmes is more prevalent with boarders and primary school children.

(3) The Students' Profile

Some striking features emerge from this rather convoluted description. Thus the widespread significance of the occupational support that the student perceives, which positively affects his occupational preferences, his awareness of concessions to tribals, and his participation in village programmes. It would seem that such support focuses and motivates the student very significantly.

The negative effect of family educational background on a preference for teaching, and for adivasis on preference for medicine as well, as also on awareness of government concessions to tribals, all these do not quite disappear when the sample is limited to adivasis. This does seem to demand further study on more qualitative lines. It could be that educated parents do ambition more than teaching for their children but are realistic about their chances for the medical profession. But then why does family educational background have a negative correlation with awareness of scheduled tribe concessions? Here it would seem, as suggested earlier, that the upward mobility of first generation learners, economically supported by the agricultural assets, comes into play.

2. THE PARENTS

(1) The Analysis of Variance

(a) *All Parents*

As with the students, the descriptive analysis of the frequency distributions and cross-tabulations was extended with a three-way analysis of variance using three independent variables for the samples of parents as well:

(1) school of their child (MS, TB, etc.)
(2) religion of the parent (non-Christian or Christian)

(3) village of residence (whether with a mission school or not)

The relevant statistical tables are presented in the appendix (p. 194). Here the findings are discussed with the data presented earlier.

The comparative profile of the parents from the different schools is quite compatible with the one of the corresponding students, namely the differences between the schools with a higher percentage of adivasis and those with a lower one.

Thus for the high schools, at the Dapchari school the parents are better educated, even had better educated fathers, and have more contact with the towns and the school than the parents of Thakkarbapa, and are more markedly so than the parents of the ashram schools. However they are less committed to the education of their children than the Thakkarbapa parents but no more so than the ashram school ones. This seems strange, though it could mean that they are more realistic about education as a potential channel of upward mobility, having had more experience of it themselves, and having access to other such channels as well. It could also mean that their children's education up to high school level is so taken for granted, as it were, that it did not require the same level of affirmation of their commitment to it as it did for the others. The ashram schools give their students so much government-sponsored financial support that the parental commitment need hardly come into play.

The pattern of difference is the same at the primary level between the zilla parishad and the Dhundalwadi schools, though it is less marked here, just as the difference in the proportion of adivasi versus non-adivasi enrolment is less marked too. The mission school parents, as expected, come in between these two poles, though their contact with the town is the highest.

Coming now to the Christians, they are less educated, more agriculturally based, and have larger families than the non-Christians. But they are more committed to the education of their children, more socially aware, more involved in village meetings and celebrations, have more contact with, and are more supportive of, the school than the others. Once again these differences on the basis of religion overlap with those of caste, since most Christians here are adivasis.

(b) *Adivasi Parents*

Hence, separating out the adivasi parents, a two-way analysis of variance was done to refine the differences further, using as independent variables:

(1) parents' religion (Christian, non-Christian)
(2) child's school [mission school (MS), other private schools (OP), and government ones (GS)].

The statistical tables are presented in the appendix (p. 194).

Here the earlier difference between Christians and others is accentuated. Socio-economically, the Christians are better off. They are more aware of educational benefits and are more committed to educating their children. They participate more in village activities, have greater contact with, involvement in, and appreciation of, their children's school.

On the other hand, mission school parents have greater contact with the town, are more appreciative of the benefits of education, and like their children's school better than the parents of either government schools or other private ones.

It is apparent, then, that the effect of religion on school contact, involvement and the community-school connection is significant while the school effect on these is not.

(2) **The Regression Analysis**

To confirm these conclusions a regression analysis was done, using, among others, the type of school as an independent variable, dichotomized between mission schools and others. As with the students, the regression was done in two stages: one for the sample of parents as a whole, and one again for the adivasis separately. The regression tables are presented in appendix III (pp. 200-204).

Interestingly, the school effect fails to show significance, while religion, i.e., being Christian, does over a wide range of variables. Thus Christian parents are more committed to educating their children, more appreciative of the benefits of education, and also participate more in village activities .

For the adivasi parents, in the sample analyzed separately, religion was even more significant in the range of its effects. Here, the respondent's being Christian positively affected variables like commitment to the children's education and participation in village activities, as above. Besides these, the other variables affected were the perception of educational benefits and the community-school connection.

For the adivasi parents the link to the child's school is weaker than that to their community. The community-school connection too is weaker for them than for non-adivasis, since here both the level of school contact and parental involvement are lower. However, they participate more in community activities than non-adivasis, since they are more rural than urban-based. No wonder then that except for the Christians among them these adivasis are less committed to educating their children and less appreciative of the benefits of education, though they do appreciate their child's school more than non-adivasis, perhaps because they have little to compare it to.

(3) The Parents' Profile

More generally, then, a profile of the parent can be put together from the regression analysis. Better educated parents participate more in village activities and have more contact with the school. Those with larger agricultural assets perceive less the benefits of education and participate more in the village. Those with a higher socio-economic status are more committed to education and have less contact with the school, though the ones with more urban contact have more school contact as well.

Parents who perceive education as beneficial have more school contact, a stronger community-school connection, and appreciate their child's school more than the others.

Parents with a higher participation in village activities have more contact with the school and a stronger community-school connection.

In villages seen as supportive of education, educational benefits are perceived better, and educational commitment runs higher, as also participation in village activities and the community-school connection.

(4) Conclusion

More specifically, with regard to the individual variables the findings of the regression analysis can be presented to confirm the earlier conclusions.

Thus the benefits of education are perceived less by adivasis than others, more by Christians than non-Christians, more by those with smaller agricultural assets and more by those in villages more supportive of education. The commitment to educating one's children is similarly weaker among adivasis, stronger among Christians and those in villages more supportive of education, as also stronger among those with a higher socio-economic status.

The school's contact with the parents is higher for non-adivasi parents, for those more participative in village activities, for those with more contact with the town, and for those who perceive the benefits of education more. The parents' involvement in the school increases with their participation in the village and their contact with the town.

Moreover, adivasi Christians and parents more committed to educating their children are more appreciative of their child's school.

The community-school connection is strengthened by participation in the village and its support for education by the perception of educational benefits and by the non-adivasis.

When the regression analysis is done for the adivasi parents separately, the pattern is repeated though, not unexpectedly, variables on which the adivasis show lesser variation tend to drop out of the regression equation, just as ones showing greater variation tend to enter into it.

Thus for the adivasi parents, appreciation of educational benefits and agricultural assets have no significant effect, while for commitment to education these have a negative one, though socio-economic status is more positively correlated to such an appreciation of education.

For their participation in village activities, the only differences for the adivasis from the sample as a whole is that socio-economic status seems to sum up, and so it replaces the effects of educational level and agricultural assets.

For the school's contact with these adivasi parents, the only difference here is that the perception of educational benefits, rather than the level of education, has a positive effect, this being a more discriminating variable among the poorly educated adivasis. For parental involvement in the school the earlier pattern is repeated, except that contact with the town becomes a less discriminating variable among the adivasis and has no significant effect.

Among the adivasis, appreciation for their child's school is affected a little differently than for the sample as a whole. The perception of educational benefits has a positive effect in both instances, and participation in village activities and its support for education becomes significant for the adivasis' appreciation of the school. The effect of religion would seem to be indirect through its effect on village participation.

With regard to the community-school connection among adivasis, as remarked earlier, religion has a positive effect. The effect of education for the adivasi seems to differ from that of the whole sample, since it is represented by two variables here: the perception of educational benefits with a positive effect as earlier, and the level of the parents' education with a negative one. The effect of participation in the village and its support for education, which was significant in the sample, is here indirect, through the parents' appreciation of the school.

So also with regard to the community-school connection, the analysis is somewhat different for adivasis when separated out of the sample. As remarked earlier, for Christians the connection is stronger, as for those more appreciative of their child's school and the benefits of education. But unfortunately it is weaker for the better educated parents! Could it be that the reference group for these is beyond the village and its school?

3. THE TEACHERS

(1) The Analysis of Variance

The analysis of variance of the sample of teachers was a five-way one with the following independent variables:

(1) school type: (mission, MS; other private, OP; and government, GS)
(2) primary and secondary standards (1-4, and 5-10)
(3) sex (male, female)
(4) caste (non-adivasi, adivasi)
(5) religion (non-Christian, Christian)

The statistical tables for this analysis are presented in the appendix (p.195). The findings are discussed together with the earlier data. The type of school was collapsed from 6 into 3 categories since the sample of teachers was smaller, (N = 113).

In comparison to the mission and other private school teachers, the ones in government schools are most senior in terms of age and years of service, but they are the least qualified. At school they put in longer hours than mission school teachers, though less than other private school ones. Similarly at home they spend more time on school matters and less on family affairs than the mission school teachers but not more than the others. The frequency of their supervisors' visits is midway between the others, but they find these the least supportive, least satisfying, and are least willing to continue with them. Nor do they find the teachers' meetings supportive. They find the village most supportive, and they participate more than the other teachers in village activities in terms of personal and social involvement and political awareness. Perhaps this is because they are often required to do so by the government.

Other private schools have teachers who are the least senior in age and service, but the best qualified. They put in the longest working hours at school, and at home spend the most time on school matters and the least on family affairs compared to the others. For them the frequency of supervisory visits is the least, and the support and satisfaction these give, as also their willingness to continue with them, are more than that for the government teachers but less than that for the mission ones. So also their participation in village activities and the village support for education is less than for government schools but more than for mission ones. Neither do they find the teachers meetings supportive.

With regard to seniority and qualifications, the mission schools come out in between the others. However, at school these teachers put in the shortest working hours, and at home the most time with family affairs. They have the highest frequency of inspections, which they find the most supportive and satisfying, and are the most willing to have them continued. Moreover, they find the teachers' meetings the most supportive. But their participation in the village and its support for education is the least.

(2) Comparative Profiles

From these three profiles an interesting comparison between the mission schools and the others emerges. Mission schools are highest on administrative inputs in terms of supervision and its positive results, as also the supportive meetings of teachers held. But they are lowest on the teachers' inputs, e.g., their qualifications, the hours of work put in at school, the time given to school matters at home, their participation in the village activities in personal, social and political terms, and their village's support for education. This raises the question as to which inputs are the more strategic.

The Christian teachers, compared to the others, are more senior in age and service, have larger families, spend more time on village and community matters and at home. However, they still participate less in village activities. They are not negative about their supervisors but do not find the teachers' meetings useful. Moreover, they are less positive about improving their prospects on the job.

Adivasi teachers are less qualified than others, and have less educated parents. They feel less encouraged by their students, but are appreciative of their supervisors and want them to continue.

Compared to the men, women teachers are younger, have fewer dependents, are more positive about their adivasi students. At school they put in fewer hours, at home they spend more time on their family affairs and less on village and community matters. They are more open to a change of job.

The primary school teachers, in comparison to the secondary ones, are less qualified, but they find their students more interested in learning than the secondary school teachers. However, the primary teachers perceive less village support for education than the secondary ones.

(3) **The Regression Analysis**

Once again, as for the others, for the teachers too a regression analysis was done. The appendix (pp. 204-208) carries the statistical tables, while the findings are described here.

With regard to their time distribution, at home, primary school teachers spend more time with their families, adivasi teachers less time on school matters. Christians spend more time with their families, and less on school matters, but more on village and community matters.

Women spend less time on such village matters and are more open to a change of job than male teachers.

With regard to supervision, Christian teachers find this to be more supportive, and those who have made a positive choice for teaching rather than a negative one or one by default find it more useful. Not unexpectedly, such teachers and Christians as well feel encouraged by their supervisors.

Teachers' meetings are found to be supportive by the less qualified teachers, and by those where the village is supportive of education.

Teaching initiative comes from senior teachers and those spending more time on school matters at home, but Christian teachers show less initiative.

The teachers who spend less time with their families, have better qualifications but less desire to study further, are more appreciative of teachers meetings, these are the ones who feel encouraged by their students.

Teachers more appreciative of their schools are those who have made a positive rather, than a negative, choice for their vocation, feel encouraged by their students, find supervision useful and are younger.

When the regression was done for the adivasi teachers alone, the basic patterns are somewhat repeated with a few new wrinkles. Thus with regard to time distribution, women seem to spend more time with their families and religion does not seem to make a significant difference here. Teachers with a better educational background are less appreciative or perhaps more critical of their school. They feel more supported by their supervisors, but less encouraged by their students and colleagues. Senior teachers and less qualified ones also feel less colleague encouragement.

(4) **Conclusion**

In general then it would seem that senior teachers show more initiative but are more critical of their schools. Those with better qualifications feel more encouraged by their students but are less appreciative of teachers' meetings. Those who have made a positive choice for the teaching vocation are positive towards supervision and their school. Christian teachers feel encouraged by their students and supervisors, and yet, at home they spend less time on school and more on village and community matters than the others.

4. THE MATCHED PAIRS

(1) The Analysis

To refine the analysis of the data on students and parents, a sample of matched pairs was constructed, each student matched with his or her parent, to give a total of 234 pairs. This would enable the analysis to isolate the effect of parents on their children more accurately.

First a series of cross-tabulations of parental characteristics against characteristics of their children was run. The appendix carries the appropriate tables (pp. 209-210). Here the findings are presented descriptively.

With regard to continuing their education in spite of the offer of immediate employment: students with better educated parents and better employed ones, i.e., white collar and skilled labour, are most likely to want to continue beyond their high school. With regard to following their parents' occupations: boys with fathers in unskilled labour, or who are daily wage earners, are the least likely to do so. However, the level of parents' education does not affect this choice of their sons. Farmer parents are most likely to have children preferring farming as an occupation but better educated parents do not.

Parental occupation has an uneven influence on the child's preference for the teaching profession, and parental educational level, strangely, has a negative one. This would indicate that the effect of the school is what makes the difference here.

An analysis of variance was done on some student characteristics using two parental ones as independent variables:

(1) Parental occupation (DW, FA, UN, SW, WC, BU)
(2) Parental educational level (no schooling, std 1-4, 5-8, 8-10, 10th std and above)

The statistical results are not presented in the appendix, since they were not specially pertinent. However, some of the findings are discussed here.

Parents with higher status occupations have children who feel more supported in their school-going. Better educated parents have children who read more, and are more aware of governmental concessions to tribals in education and employment.

The characteristics not significantly influenced bv either factor were: difficulties in following the class, participation in extra-curricular activities, the perception of the usefulness of work experience, the accessibility of teacher assistance in the difficulties, and appreciation of their school and boarding. It would seem that these characteristics are more concerned with the school and the teacher than the family background of the child.

The regression analysis (appendix pp. 211-213) did refine the earlier student and parent profiles as discussed below.

(2) **The Students**

Students who find, or make enough time for, study outside school hours have parents more committed to their education. Similarly, the students who would rather continue their education further than drop out for some immediate employment have parents with a higher socio-economic background, tend to be Christians, and from the higher standards in school.

With regard to occupational aspirations, farming is preferred by students with Christian parents of lower socio-economic status but with high agricultural assets. They tend to be boys, and in the primary school. Teaching is preferred by Christian students and by those with better educated parents, and medicine by boys with better educated parents, but where the school-village linkage is weaker. Moreover, students in boarding find more support for their occupational choices.

Students who feel more supported in going to school have parents of a higher socio-economic status, and who come from villages seen as supportive of the school.

When it comes to reading habits, Christian students and primary school ones read less, as do those with parents of a higher socio-economic status, but not those with better educated parents.

Boarders and adivasis find it more difficult to follow the class. Participation in village programmes is higher for boarders and boys. The students' awareness of educational and employment assistance from the government for tribals is lower among Christians and those in primary school, as also among those with parents from the higher socio-economic group and villages where educational support is seen to be low.

(3) The Parents

Christian parents appear to be supportive of farming and teaching as occupational preferences for their children. But Christian students are less aware of educational and employment concessions to tribals by the government. They do not prefer farming more than others, but they read less and are not keen to continue their school studies if immediate employment is offered. Is this once again because the pastoral work of the mission with Christian parents, in orienting them to the education of the children, is more positive than the school effect on their children? The drop in the preference for farming from the primary to the secondary, for Christian students, must be explained in this context.

Better educated parents seem to influence their children to read more and prefer white collar occupations like teaching and medicine; those more committed to educating their children have wards who find enough time to study outside school hours and are less likely to discontinue their school studies for immediate employment. The effect of parental education on the middle class aspirations and academic habits of their children is evident.

Parents with a higher socio-economic status have children who feel supported by them in their schooling and would not want to discontinue their studies for a job offer now. However the students with such parents prefer farming less, read less and are less aware of government concessions to scheduled tribes in education and employment. The effect of parental socio-economic status then is somewhat ambiguous. They are supportive of their children's education in a general way, but do not help them to be more aware of the opportunities for tribals or encourage them to read. The fact that most better-off parents among the adivasis will have larger agricultural assets, and among non-adivasis they will be in business, may have something to do with this.

6

CONCLUSION

1. Introduction

This concluding discussion of the significant findings of the study will attempt to bring the statistical and non-statistical data together, by interpreting the quantitative findings in the light of the qualitative feedback. Indeed, the interaction between these two levels of analysis was coextensive and concurrent with the participatory methodology chosen for this study.

The findings of this study as presented in the earlier chapters are not entirely surprising and the conclusions they lead to will not be completely new. Certainly they are pertinent to the local situation from which they derive and are most helpful for any follow-up at this level. Indeed, a series of workshops with teachers, discussions with village leaders, meetings with parents, and deliberations with administrators were planned and executed as part of the effort to carry forward this participatory study into collaborative action.

An adequate account of this process would go well beyond the limitations of this monograph, for it would involve a fairly extensive documentation of the follow-up process which was carried through for almost two years. It would perhaps not be an entirely inappropriate extension of the presentation here, though it would make it somewhat long drawn out and diffused. Hence it does seem better to document the follow-up separately so as to do justice to both: neither over-extending the discussion here nor truncating documentation on the follow-up.

For there are larger issues that have emerged in this discourse that do have relevance to wider contexts and which must be illumined within the discursive framework sketched in the earlier chapters of this book. But first these issues must be identified, elaborated and critically examined before any useful or insightful conclusions can be drawn out of the discussion.

The discussion must be read in the context of the two concerns with which the study began, as mentioned earlier in the study design:

1. the impact of the schools on the students and how it can be adapted to their culture,
2. the influence of the school on the village and how it can be adjusted to needs of the community.

Since these two concerns cannot conveniently be isolated from each other, the discussion will not separate them either but cover the two together. Such a comprehensive rather than a segmented approach will be more intelligible and better serve the discussion.

The more generalized aspects of this investigation regarding the social context of elementary and tribal education in the Indian arena, discussed in an earlier chapter, will not be repeated here. But the discussion there is the necessary background to the conclusions arrived at here. For while conclusions drawn from a particular study have a certain specificity, when placed in a broader context their more universal significance can be better perceived.

2. Student and Family

The effect of family background on the children's education is confirmed at various levels of analysis and for diverse sub-groups studied. This takes the discussion back to where it started: the relationship of society and education.

A better economic status and higher educational levels of the parents make for a more positive integration of the students in the school system, as indicated on several counts, especially in terms of parental support for, and the child's coping ability with schooling. On both counts the adivasis are disadvantaged: the parents in society and the children at school. The Christian adivasis are somewhat better off than the non-Christian ones, in that they have slightly greater agricultural assets and a significantly higher level of awareness regarding education. But what exactly is the causal relationship here remains to be sorted out. The role of mission in this can hardly be gainsaid.

3. Mission and School

A further analytical refinement showed that the mission input through its socio-religious work, i.e., the 'religion effect' was clearly significant while the 'school effect', i.e., the inputs through schools, was not so. In other words Christian parents were more concientized in regard to education than non-Christian ones regardless of what school their children went to. For the adivasis here community interventions do effect the level of educational involvement.

The difference among the schools clearly reflects the composition of their students; in terms of parental support, classroom performance and occupational preferences, adivasi students score less than non-adivasis. However, though mission schools tend to have a higher than the average percent of adivasis, specially at the secondary level, their students score better than average on these same measures. Certainly this must reflect something of the 'school effect' in terms of effective inputs made.

Looking at these more closely across the various school types, the mission schools were distinguished with the highest level of administrative inputs in terms of an effectively positive supervision and supportively encouraging meetings of teachers, while direct teacher inputs were the lowest in regard to qualifications, work-time, and community participation. In other words, whether the mission school inputs bear directly on the institution or indirectly on it through the teachers and their students, in either case they seem to centre on the school and reach out less through these persons to the community.

Thus while school interventions do affect the students, this is not significant on their parents. And surely it is these parents that must be a vital link of the school to the community. This raises the question of the school-community linkage more pertinently.

4. School and Community

There were two aspects of the school-community linkage which were studied:

1. the linkage from the side of the school to the community in terms of the teachers' social participation, and the schools' contact with parents; and

2. the linkage from the side of the community to the school in terms of village support and parental inputs for the school.

A correspondence between these two aspects can be expected and together they should give a more inclusive picture. Moreover, teachers' participation and village support were indicated by the teachers, while school contact and parental inputs were reported by the parents, so that teacher and parent perspectives are included on both sides of the linkage to give a broader based measure.

The teachers' social participation in government run schools is the highest, but the parental contact with these schools is the lowest. This anomaly can be explained because the teachers' participation in the community is generally a required involvement in governmental schemes which do not directly involve the parents.

With the mission schools, on the other hand, their teachers' social participation is the least, yet their schools' contact with the parents and the parents' with the school is the highest. What is then apparent here is that not all the school-to-community linkages need be through the teachers. Further the response of the parents seems to depend on the type of contact made by the school, and, at least for mission schools, on the other direct interventions of the mission with the Christian adivasi community. This is the 'religion effect' discussed earlier,[1] and a closer look at it might yield far reaching conclusions.

5. Religion and Education

The Christians, especially the adivasis among them, are the group most in contact with the mission and most influenced by it. This group scores better than non-Christian adivasis on all the following measures: commitment to educating their children, participation in village activities; contact with, involvement in, and appreciation of their children's school. The community-to-school linkage is stronger too for the Christians, but weaker for the adivasis in general. This needs some explanation.

As the earlier historical outline of the mission has shown, its contact with the adivasis was never exclusively religious. Almost as soon as it began, it reached out into social, educational and medical work, which were increasingly secularized as the mission's own perspectives evolved. Its confrontation with the local communist party, and their resistance to any intervention that might threaten the party's base eventually led the mission to take a non-confrontationist and less aggressively interventionist approach, and so formal school education, which suited these conditions rather well, became a priority area from the late 70s on.

As was seen in the historical outline of the Talasari mission,[2] it has, like many others elsewhere, moved from the 'evangelical' inspiration of an older more conservative theology, to more service-oriented one, inspired by the newer liberation theology. No wonder, then, Christian adivasis who have surely been the main beneficiaries are so positive about education and school.

But then why is the community-to-school connection slightly weaker for the better educated adivasis whereas it should expectedly be naturally even stronger? In other words, if better educated adivasis are less involved in their schools is it because they depend less on them? And yet they would be the ones with most to contribute, so it would seem to be in the interest of the school to reach out to them.

The school-to-community relationship, then, needs to be discussed as well. Earlier it was pointed out that the parental involvement in the school depended on the type of teacher investment in the community. A more personal and social involvement in the village by the teachers, rather than a merely bureaucratic one required by their job, evoked in return a positive response to the school from the parents. Moreover, the schools' contact with the parents is higher for non-adivasis.

It would seem, then, that the bridge between the tribal community and the formal school is made less by the school reaching out to the community than vice versa. And it is the mission efforts with these people that have made the difference for their Christians. There is less of a complementary effort on the part of the school to reach out to the tribal community, mission schools not excepted.

6. Identity and Change

Now if a reciprocal relationship is posted between society and education, between community and school, as was done in the theoretical framework sketched earlier,[3] then interventions on both sides could be mutually reinforcing and be so much the more effective. However, it is the community on the margin that is forced to adjust to the mainstream, rather than *vice versa*. For the adivasi tribals this means more than just a loss of educational effectiveness. It implies the loss of tribal identity and the consequent alienation implicit therein. This warrants some explanation.

The mission effort does indeed conscientize the tribals to education and helps to integrate them into the system. This makes up for the socio-economic and other disadvantages they experience by reducing the opportunity cost of education for them. Surely this is a positive achievement.

However, even if this be facilitated by a well meaning agency, a one-sided or a lopsided reaching out by the tribal community and the adivasi parents to a school system, that does not sufficiently reciprocate this by reaching out in turn to them, can only mean that the community is adapting and adjusting to the school rather than *vice versa*. Eventually, this must have an alienating effect on tribal identity.

One can argue that tribal identity must inevitably be compromised with, or even sacrificed for, modern development. However, the national policy evolved is to integrate the tribals into the national mainstream keeping their distinctiveness; not to assimilate them into it, so it is lost; or segregate them from it, so they are left behind. Certainly the loss of tribal identity will not be their loss alone, it would be a national impoverishment as well. Unfortunately, as is all too obvious, bureaucratic practice has not measured up to this high-minded national policy.

But even if such 'noble' considerations were discounted, the *de facto* one-sided adaptation pointed out earlier will more probably lead to tribal segregation and elimination rather than to their assimilation. For a loss of identity and the consequent alienation of a people is more likely to lead to hostile protest or regressive withdrawal rather than to a mass movement for something as forward looking as education.

As the open forest diminishes under increasing population pressure, there is nowhere to withdraw. Protest is left as the only alternative. These have been mostly suppressed or diffused but even when they do achieve a measure of redress and reprieve, the need for education still remains as urgent as before and the tribals still as distanced from it.

A mass movement for education remains the most necessary means for a breakthrough in education for these systematically disadvantaged people. This has been underscored repeatedly in the

Indian context. There must be a two-fold approach to precipitate such a movement;

(1) mobilizing the community for education and not merely adapting it to the school;
(2) reorienting the methodology and content of education to the socio-cultural circumstances of the community and not just adopting techniques and skills, the syllabus and the text books from an alien milieu.

For
"We are more likely to obtain the best results only if we combine the various approaches and techniques suitably. The backdrop of a mass movement is in any case inescapable. But against it, we may combine the selective and mass campaign approaches".[4]

Both these aspects have been elaborated at great length in the relevant literature on the subject, and referred to elsewhere in this study. At the national and state levels, several initiatives have been taken to conscientize disadvantaged communities and mobilize them through non-formal education, adult literacy campaigns and the like by governmental and non-governmental organizations. There have also been innovative efforts at these levels to reorient the school syllabus and pedagogy to meet the needs of diverse groups. But the results have not quite been commensurate with efforts in terms of achieving a breakthrough that can be replicated elsewhere.

What perhaps is more pertinent here is a micro-level focus on school-community relationships which could make for the beginnings of a down-up approach to educational change. This of course is not to dismiss top-down initiatives for various other changes at the macro-level of society and the state. However, restricting this discourse within the realistic constraints of this study will make its conclusions so much the closer to the ground and hence better founded, and so all the more convincing.

7. Isolation and Integration

The alienating effect of education on the tribals must be tackled in the context of the four-fold isolation described earlier in this study[5] which will bear repetition here: "the community as a whole, the school within the community, the pupil within the class room and the teacher within the education system".[6] This is not an exhaustive list. Other contexts and alienations can be mentioned the psychological, the religious, etc., but they would be well beyond the scope of this study. Here each of the four isolations will be treated within the constraints pertinent to the area under study.

(1) *The Community within Society*

The isolation of the tribal community from the mainstream of society is a much larger issue in which education, as an agency of socialization is one important dimension. Only a few manage to take advantage of education and these are readily coopted to "bourgeois values," of the system which "thereby curbs their potential for radical expression"[7] and distances them from the others in the community left behind. Preoccupation with this 'tiny minority' is misplaced when the real concern should be brought to bear on "the vast numbers of SC and ST children who stop going to school long before the carrot of a middle class job can appear before them."[8] Formal education has not served to integrate this larger community of tribals into the mainstream of national society.

In bringing to world attention the failures and shortfalls of the formal system, UNESCO's International Education Commission in 1972[9] emphatically urged the meed for non-formal models' of education and alternative routes to development. In fact, "that the formal education system made only a limited contribution to development and that the potential of non-formal education was much greater," was a discovery "more due to development planners than educators as such".[10] Conscientization of the underprivileged through such initiatives has proved to be a very effective way of mobilizing them towards a mass movement which is the one hope of their finding a 'place in the sun' and an equitable integration into society.

The Anthropological Survey of India in 1976 identified as many as 36 on-going tribal movements.

> "Behind all these movements lie the tribals interminable search for identity and his urge to secure a better deal for himself. . . . Like peasant movements the tribal movements at this stage of social formation are bound to remain local, limited, restricted to

dominant tribe or a group of tribes. This however does not minimize their importance, or detract from the issues they seek to highlight".[11]

In the area under study there have been no lack of such movements in the past motivated by political parties, or at present inspired by non-party political groups. These

> "by mobilizing around adivasi cultural identity on economic issues . . . offer a perspective for resolving the contradictions, between and at these levels, faced by formalized adivasi education. Above all, they create a climate of critical social awareness and political action which generates a felt need for literacy-numerary and functionality, in a more relevant formalized educational programme".[12]

However, insofar as such efforts set in motion an 'alternate hegemony' they are bound to be challenged and opposed by the powers in the *status quo*, political and educational. This in fact has happened in the case of the Warlis as mentioned in the historical sketch earlier.[13] Most formal education here both by governmental and non-governmental agencies seems to adopt a 'welfarist approach' inspired by humanitarian concerns and reaching only a minority of the adivasis. In the final analysis

> "Voluntary effort in institutional education in the region may be seen, in effect, as a more efficient instrument than that of the state, for the social reproduction of the relations of production along the lines of the state sponsored strategy of development".[14]

This strategy is precisely what has left the vast tribal majority behind in the mainstream of development and still on the margins of society.

Actually, there has been some realization of this in the mission with the advent of the social apostolate and specially of liberation theology. And although it has stayed by and large out of direct confrontation with political powers and parties, it has sought viable alternatives in less contestational, non-formal ventures, e.g., with women groups (mahila mandals) and legal aid, in areas of health and income generation projects. Such initiatives are but a small though pertinent attempt towards concientizing the local adivasi community and eventually building up a people's mass movement towards integration into the wider society around in more equitable ways.

(2) *The School within the Community*

The strategies of non-formal education can not only help to effectively bridge the distance between a marginal community and the mainstream, it also can create a critical social awareness and a felt need to take advantage of the formal system. The school in its turn must then reach out to the community in complementary ways so that there is a twofold approach to the integration of the school within the community: both from the side of the community and from that of the school. This would imply a model for a 'community school' which would be a 'community centre' as well.

If the strategies for non-formal education are centered in, and facilitated by the school, then the school can become a centre integrated into the community. Non-formal education in turn, while bringing the community into the school, would itself be strengthened by its support from the infrastructural facilities and the goodwill of the school. The school too benefits from such an association. For the "education of adults not only facilitates their active large scale participation in social development programmes but also accelerates the process of education of children in the community".[15] While there are differences between formal and non-formal education

> "in their sponsorship and institutional arrangements and often in their educational objectives-and the groups they serve . . . there is no sharp dividing line between them. Moreover, their differences occasionally merge in 'hybrid' programs combining the significant features of both".[16]

Certainly, breaking down the rather artificial divide between formal and non-formal education could mean a breakthrough in both.

Besides being a centre for adult education, a community-school must also "use the resources of the community as the core of the curriculum, relating the major content of the curriculum to what is happening and can be studied in the community".[17] This would mean that "the teachers are full participating members of the community, with the children, and carry out projects of community development".[18] Given the centralized control of the school system, this may not always be easy, but with some determination and creativity, parts of the curriculum can be adapted in the desired direction, e.g., work-experience and environmental studies, not to mention other co- and extra-curricular activities.

The involvement of the school in the community will of course depend on the teachers and school administrators being active members in the community. For until more formalized links are put in place, such informal ones will have to do. Eventually, a more structured relationship can be evolved through parent-teacher associations (PTAs) and advisory school boards. But if the integration is to be at the community-school level then a centralized state level administration is surely not the appropriate mechanism for this.

Reviewing *Educational Administration in the Zilla Parishads in Maharashtra,* N.R. Inamdar concludes that the only alternative to the present inadequate system, is not to turn primary education to the state government, but "the creation of independent and autonomous School Boards".[19] To be relevant, such local self-government for the community school must be a democratization in terms of participatory power that can exercise a coordinated control effectively and not become fragmented and dissipated into factions and vested interests.

Autonomous local school boards cannot be implemented without the proper legislation, which may as yet be a long way off. But the need for decentralization in many areas and at several levels is increasingly felt and accepted. However, there are steps that can be taken already now that need not wait for this process of decentralization to catch up with primary education among the tribals. Thus PTAs and advisory boards, community consultations and village meetings, can even now provide the alternative structures which can later better prepare the way for a more formal local autonomy when it is officially granted.

Though a few schools in this area are taking some steps in this direction, there is still a long way to go.

(3) *The Pupil within the Classroom*

If the school is integrated into the community, then the integration of the pupils in the classroom will bring them closer to the community. If, however, the school itself is regarded as alien to the community milieu, then surely its students too will be similarly regarded; whereas a community which supports and is proud of their school will be all the more accepting and encouraging of its students. There are classroom initiatives which can very well contribute in this direction.

The integration of students in the classroom must necessarily be around a relevant curricular programme or it will only further alienate them. But the understanding of relevance itself may be problematic. Relevance can be considered from several perspectives. Here it is taken in the limited "sense of relating the design of basic schooling to the life and work of the wider community".[20] The clash of perspectives, not to mention interests between policy-makers and clients, as also between the various categories of clients, finally leaves the disadvantaged and the marginalized outside the ambit of the narrow understanding of relevance that eventually comes to prevail.

This relevance is operationalized in the centralized curriculum, which must select and organize knowledge. No wonder then government sponsored text books become an "instrument of alienation" in the present educational culture,[21] and the marginalized go unrepresented or even misrepresented there.[22] This not only affects the self-perception of the marginalized themselves, but also the perception the other students have of them. It cannot make for an equitable integration in the classroom.

The problem of relevance in education is not solved by

> "preparing young people to enter the 'traditional' sector of the economy, to remain as members of their home community and as participants alongside their parents in manual work and peasant agriculture. Pupils and parents, however, have continued to see education as providing a ladder to prosperity, as an escape route from the subsistence economy. It is for this reason that they have been willing to make sacrifices to maintain their children in school".[23]

Their choice against rural and manual labour is not likely to change as long as "the differentials in earnings, security, styles of living and status which exists between them and non-manual employment in the modern sector"[24] remain as steep and stark as it is at present. Hence "instead of 'ruralizing' the education provided for the farming community, the education of the whole nation should be based on the requirements of an evolving society".[25]

The fundamental question that curriculum design must ask is this: what is worth teaching? This of course cannot be separated from "our perception of the kind of society and people we are, and to our vision of the kind of society we want to be"[26]. Obviously there are very different such perceptions in a pluralist and diverse society such as India, and so a decentralized curriculum might have a better chance at more local levels. Not that this will eliminate all contestation, but here at least there is a greater possibility of giving the voiceless a voice in a matter that impinges on them so crucially even when they do not always realize it.

Perhaps an extreme example of the need for change in the classroom would be the very medium of instruction there. In spite of policy recommendations to teach at least the first two years of primary school in the mother-tongue of the child, this has not been done for most tribal languages. In fact, the Census figures indicate a fast decline in the Warli language speakers, with many reporting the state language, Marathi, as their mother-tongue even though the reality at home is otherwise. Clearly this "destruction of mother tongues represents a situation of language imperialism, wherein the major, the dominant and the standard wears the badge of privilege and acts as the passport to rank, status and wealth".[27] This cannot but be alienating though addressing this issue would require long term efforts for a major breakthrough at the macro-level.

But there are more immediate initiatives that can be adopted even now. These will open the system to greater flexibility later. Work experience is already provided for in the Talasari area. This can be imaginatively used to "add a necessary dimension to the experience of growing up",[28] and be of community service as well, thus bringing students through their class curriculum, to be more integrated with the village community. When this is designed around local crafts and production-related skill, as Gandhi's basic education proposed, then it helps to legitimize relevant subaltern knowledge and skills by the

> "allocation of a substantive place in the school curriculum to systems of knowledge developed by and associated with the oppressed groups of Indian society, namely artisans, peasants and cleaners. It was no less than a proposal for a revolution in the sociology of school knowledge".[29]

Relating the class curriculum thus to the natural and social environment can have far reaching consequences challenging "the prevailing hierarchy of the different monopolies of knowledge in our caste society".[30] For at present it is this implicit dynamic in curriculum construction which is directly related to "the failure of education to reach the oppressed groups in our society".[31] And it is not just the curriculum alone that can be used to reverse this "quiet, civilized dynamic of dominance".[32] There are a host of co-and extra-curricular activities as well which are left to the creativity and initiative of the local school administration even now.

There are some examples of such initiatives in this area, but they need to be strengthened and multiplied if they are to make a breakthrough here.

(4) *The Teacher within the Education System*

The teachers' integrative role has been referred to earlier in several contexts, with regard to the community, the school, the classroom. Here the discussion will be more concerned with the teachers and the education system, not at the macro-level but at the local one.

Already the Director of Public Education for the Bombay Presidency in his Annual Report of 1884-85 wrote: "Experience elsewhere has shown that the Brahmin schoolmaster fails as a teacher of backward tribes; our first need, therefore, is for teachers, and teachers belonging to the hill or forest tribes would be the best instruments".[33] Such a preferential recruitment policy does prevail only in the mission schools with almost three quarters of the teachers being adivasis, somewhat for the ashram schools with about half, much less for the zilla parishad ones without a third, and none at all for the other private schools in this study. Adivasi teachers would be better suited to integrate the school and community, especially if they are resident in the village in which they teach school.

Non-tribal teachers are at a disadvantage with regard to the language and culture of their pupils in school, and need some kind of "special training and orientation".[34] The Dhebar Commission wrote this into policy in 1961:

> "A teacher in tribal areas must have a thorough knowledge of tribal life and culture. He must speak the tribal language. Only so he can be in a position to act as tribal friend, philosopher and guide to the tribals."[35]

This would be a first step. For they could still be isolated within the educational system in far flung villages, and so support structures, communication channels and in-service training programmes must be planned. There is some measure of this in the area, specially for the mission schools, more recently as a follow-up to this study. As mentioned earlier, these would best be the subject of a separate work.

Without adequate training in the necessary skills and the proper support from the institutions, most creative innovations are bound to fail or be dismissed as too idealistic even before tried. What is needed is

> "the progressive build-up of committed personal through the normative-re-educative strategy . . . to shelter the work of these innovators and permit diffusion of their work based on 'contagion' of the re-educative spirit and the rational-empirical appreciation of their work".[36]

This must mean a greater initiative and control over the pedagogic process by the teachers.

Unfortunately, in the present system, "the teacher is a subordinate officer. He is not expected to have a voice, only expertise".[37] This helps neither institutional decentralization, nor teacher motivation. A good place to start both is the curriculum. First, by including the teachers in the process of curriculum deliberation so as to give them greater initiative in and control over it. Indeed, "this is where the problem of curriculum encounters its greatest challenge in the culture of education in India".[38] Second, "to decentralize the curriculum-making process and hand down, not ready made curricula, but the skills of curriculum-construction to all elementary school teachers".[39] Such involvement will of course demand a higher level of teacher motivation.

Unfortunately, poor teacher-motivation is not a difficulty to be wished away. "But this inertia might be lessened if teachers could see a positive return for themselves to the efforts required to gain mastery of a new range of educational activities".[40] It may well be difficult to structure incentives for the teaching force as a whole to generate positive attitudes and motivation for the teachers as a body. Larger bodies have greater inertia! It is less difficult, however, to devise incentive structures that may provide a stimulus for teachers with a special interest or talent to make a breakthrough and then allow a multiplier effect to carry it into the school system.

For the concern here is not to have the teachers so identified with the system that they replicate it willy-nilly in their school, regardless of its effects on the students, but to make them ready, willing and able to creatively adapt and adjust it to local needs. This is certainly a priority for tribal areas and the one studied here is no exception.

8. **Implementation Strategies**

It would be extremely naïve to suppose that the initiatives and innovations being recommended in this study will not meet with resistance. For they will inevitably threaten those vested interests in society, the local community, the school system that will have something to loose; just as they will challenge the inertia by parents, teachers and students who are resistant to change. Indeed,

> "While it is comparatively easy to introduce educational reforms that support the existing social structure, it is extremely difficult, if not impossible, to implement radical educational reforms which threaten the existing social structure or run counter to its imperatives".[41]

In the Indian context a 'big offensive' in education, or revolutionary change in society seems very improbable. Lack of political will and populist policies have made this nation a 'soft state' as Gunnar Myrdal[42] characterized it long ago. But what has not been achieved in one giant leap at the national level can at least be begun in smaller steps at the local one. This precisely has been the emphasis of the recommendations here, which have focused on the community-school relationship. But to succeed they must be put together in a carefully planned strategy for implementation.

In a six-nation review of 'the management of relevance innovation' in School and Community in the Third World, Sinclair and Lilis, study six different approaches taken in them and offer three possible strategies for consideration, each a step-wise one, not a precipitate 'great leap forward', but with the potential for a basic transformation of the system if consistently and tenaciously pursued without compromise.

"The first is thus the stepwise development of a subpopulation of innovating institutions".[43] A group of schools, mission or otherwise, under a single coordinating management represents the best possibility for this approach. However, if these can play the role of 'model schools' their impact on the school system is multiplied. Already, the high school at Uplat Patilpada has been asked to function as such a resource for the neighboring schools.

"The second model offered for considerations is that of universal adoption of a relevant orientation but with a two-tier system permitting stepwise development of high-quality programmes in an expanding group of selected innovative schools".[44] This strategy seems better suited to a larger system of schools such as the government ones in the area. But if there is any selection for innovation among these schools, it happens less by 'plan' than by 'accident', e.g., a particularly dedicated teacher or headmaster or specially involved village community. Examples of this abound.

Finally, "a third strategy involves the omission of any special relevance programme but the attempt to reorient the existing curriculum towards activity methods and local relevance".[45] An agency managing just a single school, or too few to make the previous two strategies viable, would find this most convenient to their situation. But it is the one that can be dissipated most easily, as has been evidenced before in this area, and elsewhere.

None of these strategies are guaranteed to succeed, but they are pointed in the right direction. In the final analysis, education is 'an arena of struggle' in society, and an unequal one at that, in which like other such struggles, the weak are driven to the wall, unless something positive is done to even out their handicap and integrate them more equitably in the system. For tribals specially, a more collaborative and supportive climate is needed, or they will be eliminated by the unequal and unfair competition. Indeed, they have a cooperative clan culture in which competition is still quite foreign. How then can they survive in the competitive marketplace that Indian society is rushing head long into? A question that could turn out to be tragically rhetorical!

For educationists and social planners have destroyed individual and group autonomy among the tribals, and

> "by imposing the outside view of development, they have been disabled, deprived and exploited. . . . Radical alternatives to the mainstream by way of strengthening their social and economic autonomy can only save them from total ruination".[46]

Education, formal and non-formal, conscientization and vocationalization will certainly have a crucial role to play, if these tribals are to be able to use and create the autonomy they need, to integrate into society without sacrificing their identity or dignity.

However, ultimately it is not for the outsider to decide how exactly such autonomy must be used by these people. That would amount to truncating it prematurely, or even taking it back before it is given. Hopefully, granted the space and opportunity that autonomy will provide, they themselves will generate their own indigenous 'organic intellectuals', to use Gramsci's term, who will light the torch for their people into the future.

NOTES

1. Cf. Ch. V, pp. 162-163.
2. Cf. Ch. III above.
3. Cf. Ch. II above.
4. Citizens for Democracy, *Education for Our People*. Allied Pub., Bombay, 1978, p. 29.
5. Cf. C. II, p. 25.
6. Rathnaiah, op. cit., p. 9.
7. K. Kumar, "Educational Experience of Scheduled Castes and Tribes," op. cit., p. 1572.
8. Ibid.
9. *Learning to be: The World of Education Today and Tomorrow*, Unesco, Paris, 1972, and Sterling, Delhi, 1973.
10. Cf. J.P. Naik, *Some Perspectives on Non-Formal Education*. Allied Pub., Bombay, 1977, p. 19.
11. K.S. Singh, "Transformation of Tribal Society," op. cit., p. 1344.
12. Denzil Saldanha, "Socialization of Critical Thought: Responses to Illiteracy among the Adivasis in Thane District," *Economic and Political Weekly*, Vol. XXIV, No. 30, 29 July 1990, p. PE 61.
13. Cf. Ch. 3 above.
14. D. Saldanha, op. cit., p. PE 60.
15. Rathnaiah, op. cit., p. 191.
16. Coombs and Ahmed, op. cit., p. 9.
17. M.E. Sinclair and Kevin Lilis, *School and Community in the Third World*, Croom Helm, London, 1980, p. 33.
18. Ibid. p. 34.
19. N.R. Inamdar, *Educational Administration in the Zilla Parishads in Maharashtra: A Pilot Study*, Popular Prakashan, Bombay, 1974, p. 247.
20. Sinclair and Lilis, op. cit. p. 21.
21. K. Kumar, "Textbooks and Educational Culture", *Economic and Political Weekly*, Vol. XXI, No. 30, 26 Jul. 1986, p. 1310.

22. Cf. K. Kumar, "Educational Experience of Scheduled Castes and Tribes," op cit., pp. 1567-68 for an illustrative instance of tantricism and tribals.
23. Sinclair and Lilis op. cit., p. 149.
24. Ibid. p. 85.
25. Louis Malassis, *The Rural World: Education and Development*. Unesco, London, 1976, p. 22.
26. K. Kumar, "Curriculum, Psychology and Society," *Economic and Political Weekly*, Vol. XXII, No. 12, 21 March 1987, p. 506.
27. D.P. Pattanayak, op. cit., p. xiii.
28. Sinclair and Lilis, op. cit., p. 32.
29. K. Kumar, "Curriculum, Psychology and Society," op. cit., p. 509.
30. Ibid.
31. Ibid. p. 510.
32. Ibid.
33. Cited by N.R. Paranis in, *The History and Survey of Education in Thane District*. op. cit., p. 299.
34. E.V. Rathnaiah, op. cit., p. 156.
35. *Report of the Scheduled Areas and Scheduled Tribes Commission*, op. cit., p. 229.
36. Sinclair and Lilis, op. cit., p. 112.
37. K. Kumar, "Curriculum, Psychology and Society", op. cit., p. 510.
38. Ibid.
39. Citizens for Democracy, *Education for Our People*, op. cit., p. 35.
40. Ibid. p. 157.
41. Citizens for Democracy, *Education for Our People*, op. cit., p. 16.
42. Cf. Gunnar Myrdal, *Asian Drama: An Inquiry into the Poverty of Nations*, Pantheon Books, New York, 1968.
43. Sinclair and Lilis, op. cit., p. 164.
44. Ibid.
45. Ibid.
46. D.P. Pattanayak, op. cit., pp. 91-92.

APPENDICES

APPENDIX I

Index of Variables

Variable No.	Code name	Description
1. *For Students*		
2	SCHTYP	Type of school attended
3	STD	Standard studying in
4	VIL	Village of residence
6	AGE	Students age in years
7	SEX	Sex of student
8	CAST	Caste of student
9	REL	Religion of student
11	BOARD	Boarding at school or not
19	FAEDUC	Father's education level
20	MOEDUC	Mother's education level
21	FAOCC	Father's occupation
27	DIFCLAS	Difficulty in following teacher in class
33	STUDYHRS	Hours of studying
34	FAIL4	No. of subjects failed in 4th std.
35	FAIL7	No. of subjects failed in 7th std.
47	EXCHHRS	Hours: for extra-curricular activities
51	EDAMB	Aspiration to pursue education
52	OCCAMB1	Aspiration of son to follow father's occupation
54	FARAMB	Aspiration to be a farmer
58	TEACAMB	Aspiration to be a teacher
62	DOCAMB	Aspiration to be a doctor
99	VILPRO	Participation in village programmes
113	ECOPROD	Family's economic status
119	FAMED	Parents' educational level
125	SCHSUP	Support for student's schooling
128	CLASDIF	Difficulty in following the class
136	READ	Strength of reading habit
141	EXCU	Involvement in extra-curricular activities
149	WKEXUS	Usefulness of work-experience
165	OCCSUP	Support for occupational aspirations
185	SOLDIF	Frequency of teacher solving difficulties

(*Contd.*)

Contd.

Variable No.	Code name	Description
191	STAWA	Awareness of scheduled tribe benefits
193	LIKSCH	Satisfaction with the school
196	LKBOA	Satisfaction with the boarding
2. *Parents* (Household Head)		
2	VIL	Village of residence
5	SCHTYPS	Type of school attended by child
6	SCHTYPP	Type of school attended by parent
7	AGE	Age in years
8	SEX	Sex of household head
10	CAST	Caste of parent, household head
12	REL	Religion of parent, household head
13	CHNO	No. of children
28	EDUC	Education of parent
29	FAEDUC	Education of parent's father
30	OCC	Occupation of parent
31	FAOCC	Occupation of parent's father
32	WIOCC	Occupation of wife
57	READ	Strength of reading habit
129	EDMOB	Educational mobility
130	OCCMOB	Occupational mobility
133	ECOPROD	Economic status
139	ECOCON	Economic consumption level
140	SES	Socio-economic status
142	TOWNVIS	Urban contact
150	FAMBEN	Educational benefits for the family
151	ECOBEN	Economic benefits of education
152	INDBEN	Educational benefits for the individual
153	SOCBEN	Social benefits of education
154	EDBEN	Overall benefits of education
156	EDCOM	Commitment to education
157	SOCAWA	Social awareness
172	VILSUP	Village support for the school
173	HELPOT	Involvement in assisting others
177	VILMEET	Involvement in village meetings
179	VILFEST	Involvement in village festivals
181	VILLEAD	Involvement in village leadership
183	POLAWA	Political awareness
186	SOCACT	Social action involvement
187	SOCPART	Overall social participation
196	PASCHCON	Parental contact with the school
200	PASCHINP	Parental input for the school

(*Contd.*)

Contd.

Variable No.	Code name	Description
203	SCHCOM	The School Compared to others
204	VILSCHON	Village-school relation/connection

3. *For Teachers*

Variable No.	Code name	Description
2	SCHTYP	Type of school attended
4	TESTD	Standard Taught
5	TEYRS	Years of teaching
7	INSYRS	Year of teaching in this institution
18	STUDYMO	Motivation to study further
19	AGE	Age in years
20	SEX	Sex of teacher
22	CAST	Caste of teacher
24	REL	Religion of teacher
25	DEPNO	No. of dependents
28	FAEDUC	Father's education level
29	MOEDUC	Mother's education level
30	FAOCC	Father's occupation
42	STUINT	Perceived student interest
43	ADICOM	Comparative ability of adivasi students
75	SCHWKHRS	Hours per day working for the school
84	FAMTI	Percentage of time with family outside school hours
85	SCHTI	Percentage of time for school outside school hours
86	VILTI	Percentage of time for village outside school hours
99	SUPDEM	Supervisor demands
110	TEMEET	Frequency of teachers' meetings
121	MEETUSE	Usefulness of teachers' meetings
122	VILEDSUP	Village support for schooling
145	JOBIMP	Job improvement prospects
309	TEAQUA	Teachers' qualifications
328	FAED	Parents' educational level
332	TEAINI	Teachers' initiative
336	TEAEXCU	Involvement in extra-curricular activities
340	STUEXCU	Students' involvement in extra- curricular activities
355	STUENCO	Encouragement from students
356	PAENCO	Encouragement from the parents
357	COLENCO	Encouragement from their colleagues
358	SUPENCO	Encouragement from their supervisors
359	SWENCO	Encouragement from social workers
380	TETI	Overall per cent time on teaching
381	ADTI	Overall per cent time on administration
382	EXTI	Overall per cent time on extra-curricular activities
383	STTI	Overall per cent time on students

(*Contd.*)

Contd.

Variable No.	Code name	Description
387	SUPFRE	Frequency of supervision
389	SSUDACC	Supervisor discussion on academic matters
391	SSUBAC	Supervisor discussion on administration
393	SSUBPS	Supervisor discussion on personal and social matters
395	SUPSUP	Supervisor supportiveness
400	SUPUSE	Usefulness of supervision
403	SUPCON	Supervisor's continuance
405	SUPCOM	Supervisor comparison
411	MSUBAC	Teachers' meetings on academic matters
413	MSUBAD	Teachers' meetings on administrative matters
415	MSUBAD	Teachers' meetings on personal/social matters
420	MEETSUP	Supportiveness of teacher meetings
423	HELPOT	Involvement in assisting others
426	VILMEET	Involvement in village meetings
428	VILFEST	Involvement in village festivals
430	VILLEAD	Involvement in village leadership
432	POLAWA	Political awareness
435	SOCACT	Involvement in social action
436	SOCPART	Overall social participation
437	VILEDSUP	Village support for the school
438	SCHCOM	The school compared to others
446	JOBCHOI	Job choice of teaching
453	JOBCHA	Job change from teaching

APPENDIX II

TABLE 1: Analysis of Variance: Students (N = 313)

Main Effects				Independent Variables: (significance), deviation from grande mean:												
Dependent Variables:	(sig)	Grande X	(Range)	2 SCHTYP: (sig)	MS=1	TB=2	DW=3	DC=4	AS=5	ZP=6	4 *VIL*: (sig)	MSV=1	NMSV=2.	9 *REL*: (sig)	NC=1	C=2.
6 AGE	(.000)	14.55	(years)	(.000)	-.73	1.48	-1.95	-.02	.94	-.59				(.001)	-.03	.06
19 FAEDUC	(.000)	2.17	(1 - 5)	(.000)	.13	-.10	-.82	.85	-.63	-.32	(.017)	.18	-.18			
27 DIFCLAS	(.000)	2.26	(1 - 3)	(.000)	-.07	-.08	-.16	.31	-.03	.10	(.000)	-.06	.05	(.058)	.06	-.12
33 STUDYHRS	(.000)	.78	(0 - 2)	(.000)	.06	.01	-.33	.15	-.11	-.18	(.000)	-.01	.01			
47 EXCUHRS	(.003)	.52	(0 - 1)	(.005)	.11	-.03	.08	-.12	-.21	.12						
51 EDAMB	(.001)	2.51	(1 - 3)	(.001)	-.14	.18	.19	.14	-.08	-.11						
99 VILPRO	(.028)	1.22	(0 - 2)	(.009)	.07	-.09	.43	-.17	-.04	-.02						
113 ECOPROD	(.000)	1.72	(0 - 4)	(.009)	.12	-.01	.18	-.49	.03	.28				(.001)	-.14	.29
119 FAMED	(.000)	3.62	(2 -10)	(.000)	.18	-.20	-1.28	1.48	-1.08	-.47	(.007)	.11	-.10	(.015)	.06	-.11
128 CLASDIF	(.000)	.83	(0 - 4)	(.000)	.07	-.38	.77	-.43	.46	.13				(.000)	-.08	.16
136 READ	(.000)	6.04	(3 - 9)	(.000)	-.46	-.01	-.34	.52	.45	.60						
149 WKEXUS	(.000)	1.15	(0 - 2)	(.000)	-.23	.32	.10	.09	.20	-.39						
165 OCCSUP	(.002)	2.36	(0 - 4)	(.003)	.04	.33	.09	-.60	.19	-.24						
185 SOLDIF	(.009)	4.55	(0 - 8)	(.002)	.12	-.04	.70	-.70	.45	-.39						
191 STAWA	(.000)	1.15	(0 - 2)	(.000)	-.26	.37	-.35	.46	.46	-.11						
193 LIKSCH	(.024)	3.69	(0 - 6)	(.010)	.09	.03	.61	-.25	-.11	-.25				(.012)	.06	-.11

TABLE 2: Analysis of Variance: Parents (N = 264)

Main Effects				Independent Variables: (significance), deviation from grande mean:												
Dependent Variables:	(sig)	Grande X	(Range)	2 SCHTYP: (sig)	MS=1	TB=2	DW=	DC=4	AS=5	ZP=6	4 VIL: (sig)	MSV=1	NMSV=2.	9 REL (sig)	NC=1	C=2.
13 CHND	(.000)	5.32		(.072)										(.000)	-.75	.97
57 READ	(.005)	1.35	(0 - 2)	(.005)	.08	.09	-.23	.08	-.32	-.15						
28 EDUC	(.000)	2.06	(1 - 5)	(.000)	.15	.08	-.88	.51	-.64	-.10						
29 FAEDUC	(.000)	1.28	(1 - 5)	(.000)	-.01	.12	-.28	.48	-.25	-.28				(.007)	.08	-.11
129 EDMOB	(.050)	.77	(-4 4)	(.084)	.16	-.03	-.60	.03	-.40	.18						
133 ECOPROD	(.001)	1.76	(0 - 4)	(.083)	.09	.04	.18	-.60	.03	.07				(.001)	-.20	.25
139 ECOCON	(.000)	1.47	(-3 6)	(.003)	.17	.31	-1.06	.13	-.58	-.14				(.005)	.09	-.09
142 TOWNVIS	(.003)	10.33	(0 -18)	(.001)	.99	-.27	-1.39	.11	-1.98	-.83						
152 INDBEN	(.001)	2.34	(0 - 4)	(.059)	.08	.22	-.16	-.21	-.20	-.21						
154 EDBEN	(.009)	2.13	(-4 4)											(.064)	-.44	.57
156 EDCOM	(.000)	5.23	(0 - 8)	(.006)	.32	.67	-1.53	0.0	-.54	-1.15				(.003)	-.44	.57
157 SOCAWA	(.001)	5.83	(-4 12)											(.026)	-.63	.82
172 VILSUP	(.000)	2.13	(0 - 4)	(.002)	.08	-.05	-.19	.07	-.09	-.13	(.050)	.05	-.07	(.003)	.01	-.02
177 VILMEET	(.005)	2.68	(0 - 5)											(.004)	-.23	.30
179 VILFEST	(.001)	2.77	(0 - 5)											(.001)	-.30	.39
186 SOCACT	(.028)	1.89	(0 - 5)	(.041)	-.04	.21	-.36	.31	-.17	-.14				(.009)	-.10	.13
187 SOCPART	(.001)	18.09	(0 -30)											(.001)	-.86	1.11
196 PASCHCON	(.000)	3.32	(0 - 6)	(.000)	-.06	0.0	-.26	.68	-.14	-.23						
200 PASCHINP	(.037)	3.21	(0 - 6)											(.022)	-.08	.10
203 SCHCOMP	(.000)	5.40	(0 -10)											(.000)	-.44	.57
204 VILSCHON	(.000)	8.65	(0 -16)	(.000)	.08	.03	-.59	.91	.45	-.49						

TABLE 3: Analysis of Variance: Teachers (N = 113)

Main Effects				Independent Variables: (significance), deviation from grande mean:												
Dependent Variables:				2 SCHTYP:	MS = 1	TB = 2	DW = 3	DC = 4	AS = 5	ZP = 6	4 VIL:	MSV = 1	NMSV = 2.	9 REL:	NC = 1	C = 2.
	(sig)	Grande X	(Range)	(sig)							(sig)			(sig)		
5 TEYRS	(.010)	6.99	(1 -30)	(.006)	.21	-2.02	1.45							(.002)	-1.08	1.93
7 INSYRS	(.000)	6.37	(1 -30)	(.003)	.55	-2.33	1.24							(.001)	-1.23	2.20
19 AGE	(.002)	29.83	(22 -68)	(.001)	-.79	-1.91	2.81			(.061)	.88	-3.24		(.003)	-.55	.98
25 DEPNO	(.001)	5.74	(0 -20)							(.059)	.39	-1.42		(.030)	-.57	1.02
75 SCHWKHRS	(.020)	7.57	(1 -15)	(.093)	-.72	.89	.29			(.079)	.16	-.50				
84 FAMTIM	(.000)	55.18	(0 -100)	(.000)	7.67	-14.65	1.65	(.059)	-1.75	5.32						
85 SCHTIM	(.000)	30.70	(0 -100)	(.000)	-10.27	18.41	-1.10									
86 VILTIM	(.000)	14.12	(0 -100)							(.001)	2.15	-6.55		(.093)	-2.12	3.32
121 MEETUSE	(.006)	1.43	(0 - 2)											(.030)	.20	-.32
309 TEAQUA	(.000)	7.34	(4 -37)	(.098)	-.58	2.02	-.82	(.001)	-1.23	1.54	(.060)	-1.41	1.25			
328 FAMED	(.000)	3.26	(2 -10)								(.000)	-.92	.81			
356 PAENCO	(.012)	.53	(-4 +4)	(.002)	-.27	.29	.21	(.011)	.12	-.15				(.061)	.08	-.12
395 SUPSUP	(.002)	.29	(-4 +4)	(.040)	.63	-.36	-.78									
403 SUPCON	(.014)	1.06	(0 - 3)	(.044)	.16	-.03	-.26				(.010)	.28	-.25	(.065)	-.02	.03
405 SUPCOM	(.000)	7.83	(5 -15)	(.000)	2.69	-.08	-4.61				(.062)	1.64	-1.45			
415 MSSUBPS	(.001)	1.24	(0 - 4)	(.014)	-.44	.40	.41			(.039)	-.07	.23	(.046)	-.11	.09	
432 POLAWA	(.004)	1.53	(1 . 7)	(.004)	-.33	.09	.48							(.047)	.09	-.14
436 SOCPART	(.036)	8.79	(1 -29)	(.005)	-1.10	.28	1.66							(.011)	.14	-.22
437 VILEDSUP	(.025)	1.71	(0 - 4)	(.038)	-.23	-.03	.42	(.095)	-.18	.23						

APPENDIX III

Regression Analysis

1. *All Students* (N=313)

TABLE 1: Dependent Variable: 35 FAIL 7
Independent Variables:

	beta (b)	(sign)	Corr.(r)
3 STD	-.35867	(.0000)	-.3712
7 SEX	.26945	(.0012)	.1959

Rsq = .16634 adj Rsq = .16096

TABLE 2: Dep. Var: 51 EDAMB
Indep. Vars.:

	b	(sig)	r
119 FAMED	.22326	(.0001)	.1875
3 STD	.22101	(.0001)	.1849

Rsq = .08274 adj Rsq = .07682 (.0001)

TABLE 3: Dep. Var: 54 FARAMB
Indep. Vars.:

	b	(sig)	r
8 CAST	.14663	(.0147)	.2811
165 OCCSUP	.17132	(.0013)	.2205
128 CLASDIF	.12780	(.0217)	.2252
7 SEX	-.14403	(.0080)	-.2087
9 REL	.13288	(.0195)	.2121

Rsq = .16603 adj Rsq = .15244 (.0000)

TABLE 4: Dep. Var: 58 TEAAMB
Indep. Vars.:

	b	(sig)	r
119 FAMED	-.14459	(.0203)	-.2425
165 OCCSUP	.14849	(.0071)	.1892
11 BOARD	-.15320	(.0132)	-.1532

Rsq = .09966 adj Rsq = .09092 (.0000)

TABLE 5: Dep. Var: 62 DOCAMB
Indep. Vars.:

		b	(sig)	r
7	SEX	-.20355	(.0003)	-.2194
165	OCCUSUP	.15785	(.0047)	.1771
3	STD	-.11514	(.0368)	-.0834

Rsq = .08223 adj Rsq = .07332 (.0368)

TABLE 6: Dep. Var: 99 VILPRO
Indep. Vars.:

		b	(sig)	r
165	OCCUSUP	.14725	(.0091)	.1472

Rsq = .02168 adj Rsq = .01854 (.0091)

TABLE 7: Dep. Var: 191 STAWA
Indep. Vars.:

		b	(sig)	r
3	STD	.26428	(.0000)	.3195
165	OCCSUP	.19975	(.0001)	.2531
119	FAMED	-.15868	(.0030)	-.2384
9	REL	-.14566	(.0062)	-.1253
113	ECOPROD	.10932	(.0402)	.0909

Rsq = .20101 adj Rsq = .18800 (.0000)

TABLE 8: Dep. Var: 193 LIKSCH
Indep. Vars.:

		b	(sig)	r
165	OCCSUP	.22853	(.0000)	.2193
128	CLASDIF	-.14855	(.0072)	-.1344

Rsq = .07008 adj Rsq = .06409 (.0000)

TABLE 9: Dep. Var: 33 STUDYHRS
Indep. Vars.:

	b	(sig)	r
119 FAMED	.18360	(.0006)	.1836

Rsq = .03371 adj Rsq = .03088 (.0006)

TABLE 10: Dep. Var: 128 CLASDIF
Indep. Vars.:

	b	(sig)	r
8 CAST	.32323	(.0000)	.3232

Rsq = .10448 adj Rsq = .10185 (.0000)

TABLE 11: Dep. Var: 136 READ
Indep. Vars.:

	b	(sig)	r
9 REL	-.16453	(.0021)	-.1711
3 STD	.11099	(.0377)	.1207

Rsq = .04155 adj Rsq = .03591 (.0007)

2. *Adivasi Students* (N=276)

TABLE 12: Dep. Var: 33 STUDHRS
Indep. Vars.:

	b	(sig)	r
119 FAMED	.13219	(.0281)	.1322

Rsq =.01747 adj Rsq = .01339 (.0281)

TABLE 13: Dep. Var: 128 CLASDIF
Indep. Vars.:

	b	(sig)	r
119 FAMED	-.12106	(.0445)	-.1211

Rsq = .014565 adj Rsq = .01106 (.0445)

TABLE 14: Dep. Var: 191 STAWA
Indep. Vars.:

		b	(sig)	r
119	FAMED	-.12443	(.0360)	-.2302
3	STD	.19011	(.0009)	.2119
165	OCCSUP	.18967	(.0010)	.2186
9	REL	-.19755	(.0009)	-.2158
136	READ	-.13288	(.0214)	-.0581

Rsq = .16073 adj Rsq = .14519

TABLE 15: Dep. Var: 193 LIKSCH
Indep. Vars.:

		b	(sig)	r
165		.26360	(.0000)	.2636

Rsq = .06948 adj Rsq = .06609

TABLE 16: Dep. Var: EDAMB
Indep. Vars.:

		b	(sig)	r
113	ECOPROD	.13861	(.0210)	.1282
3	STD	.13073	(.0294)	.1197

Rsq = .03342 adj Rsq = .02634 (.0097)

TABLE 17: Dep. Var: 99 VILPRO
Indep.Vars.:

		b	(sig)	r
165	OCCSUP	.13431	(.0245)	.1404
3	STD	-.15475	(.0098)	.1321
11	BOARD	-.12370	(.0396)	.1180

Rsq = .05390 adj Rsq = .04340 (.0017)

TABLE 18: Dep. Var: 54 FARMAMB
Indep.Vars.:

	b	(sig)	r
128 CLASDIF	.20622	(.0004)	.2026
165 OCCSUP	.12574	(.0349)	.2023
7 SEX	-.18169	(.0019)	-.1636
193 LIKSCH	.15275	(.0105)	.1510
125 SCHSUP	.11975	(.0384)	.1017
9 REL	.11510	(.0457)	.0921

Rsq = .14278 adj Rsq = .12366 (.0000)

TABLE 19: Dep. Var: 58 TEAAMB
Indep.Vars.:

	b	(sig)	r
165 OCCUSUP	.16331	(.0062)	.1758
7 SEX	-.13662	(.0219)	.1515

Rsq = .04941 adj Rsq = .04245 (.0010)

TABLE 20: Dep. Var: 62 DOCAMB
Indep.Vars.:

	b	(sig)	r
119 FAMED	-.17633	(.0038)	-.2085
3 STD	-.14733	(.0120)	-.1118
165 OCCSUP	.13441	(.0228)	.1713
7 SEX	-.13294	(.0253)	-.1779

Rsq = .09991 adj Rsq = .08662 (.0000)

3. All Parents (N=264)

TABLE 21: Dep. Var: 154 EDBEN
Indep.Vars.:

	b	(sig)	r
12 REL	.31496	(.0000)	.2989
10 CAST	.25695	(.0001)	.2646
172 VILEDSUP	.17886	(.0036)	.2989
133 ECOPROD	-.14147	(.0188)	.2025

Rsq = .20839 adj Rsq = .19617 (.0060)

TABLE 22: Dep. Var: 156 EDCOM
Indep.Vars.:

	b	(sig)	r
12 REL	.34425	(.0000)	.2672
140 SES	.32295	(.0000)	.4583
10 CASTE	.19538	(.0043)	.2909
172 VILEDSUP	.14892	(.0073)	.2989

Rsq = .33820 adj Rsq = .32793 (.0000)

TABLE 23: Dep. Var: 187 SOCPART
Indep.Vars.:

	b	(sig)	r
28 EDUC	.47817	(.0000)	.4636
172 VILEDSUP	.21890	(.0002)	.2787
10 CAST	.18072	(.0089)	.0291
12 REL	.14716	(.0090)	.2325
133 ECOPROD	.13884	(.0134)	.1707

Rsq = .33535 adj Rsq = .32247 (.0000)

TABLE 23a: Dep. Var: 196 PASCHLON
Indep.Vars.:

	b	(sig)	r
10 CAST	.39036	(.0000)	.4157
187 SOCPART	.35728	(.0000)	.4016
28 EDUC	.25640	(.0038)	.4364
140 SES	.21420	(.0128)	.3266

Rsq = -.34766 adj Rsq = .33759 (.0000)

TABLE 24: Dep. Var: 200 PASCHINP
Indep.Vars.:

	b	(sig)	r
187 SOCPART	.34694	(.0000)	.4231
154 EDBEN	.15243	(.0081)	.2611
142 TOWNVIS	.12245	(.0337)	.2392

Rsq = .21588 adj Rsq = .20683 (.0000)

TABLE 25: Dep. Var: 203 SCHCOM
Indep.Vars.:

	b	(sig)	r
154 EDBEN	.34183	(.0000)	.3249
12 REL	.21561	(.0005)	.3557
10 CAST	-.21502	(.0007)	-.2016

Rsq = .23110 adj Rsq = .22223 (.0000)

TABLE 26: Dep. Var: 204 VILSCHON
Indep.Vars.:

	b	(sig)	r
187 SOCPAT	.86305	(.0000)	.5092
172 VILEDSUP	.29124	(.0000)	.5416
10 CAST	.23180	(.0000)	.4162
154 EDBEN	.11446	(.0163)	.3727
142 TOWNVIS	.09550	(.0468)	.3584

Rsq = .51596 adj Rsq = .50658 (.0000)

4. *Adivasi Parents* (N=227)

TABLE 27: Dep. Var: 154 EDBEN
Indep.Vars.:

	b	(sig)	r
12 REL	.20604	(.0000)	.3315
172 VILEDSUP	.20036	(.0016)	.2528

Rsq = .14878 adj Rsq = .14118 (.0000)

TABLE 28: Dep. Var: 156 EDCOM
Indep.Vars.:

	b	(sig)	r
12 REL	.35739	(.0000)	.4452
140 SES	.34468	(.0000)	.3931
172 VILEDSUP	.13571	(.0176)	.2490
133 ECOPROD	-.13055	(.0348)	.0689

Rsq = .31938 adj Rsq = .30711 (.0000)

TABLE 29: Dep. Var: 187 SOCPART
Indep.Vars.:

	b	(sig)	r
140 SES	.49544	(.0000)	.5614
172 VILEDSUP	.19643	(.0003)	.3031
12 REL	.14683	(.0078)	.2964

Rsq = .38120 adj Rsq = .37288 (.0000)

TABLE 30: Dep. Var: 196 PASCHON
Indep.Vars.:

	b	(sig)	r
187 SOCPART	.25846	(.0006)	.4172
154 EDBEN	.24699	(.0001)	.3409
140 SES	.14590	(.0412)	.3139

Rsq = .23781 adj Rsq = .22756 (.0000)

TABLE 31: Dep. Var: 203 SCHCOM
Indep.Vars.:

	b	(sig)	r
187 SOCPART	.41616	(.0000)	.5547
172 VILEDSUP	.22980	(.0000)	.4120
154 EDBEN	.22163	(.0001)	.4092

Rsq = .41621 adj Rsq = .40835 (.0000)

TABLE 32: Dep. Var: 200 PASCHINP
Indep.Vars.:

	b	(sig)	r
187 SOCPART	.40969	(.0000)	.4591
154 EDBEN	.15892	(.0105)	.2863

Rsq = .23359 adj Rsq = .22675 (.0000)

TABLE 33: Dep. Var: 204 VILSCHON
Indep.Vars.:

	b	(sig)	r
154 EDBEN	.24716	(.0002)	.4220
204 SCHCOM	.26717	(.0001)	.3880
12 REL	.21303	(.0008)	.3465
28 EDUC	-.12362	(.0478)	.0271

Rsq = .27861 adj Rsq = .26561 (.0000)

5. *Teachers* (N=113)

TABLE 34: Dep. Var: 84 FAMTI
Indep.Vars.:

	b	(sig)	r
24 REL	.22355	(.0242)	.4253
4 TESTD	-.22331	(.0244)	-.4235

Rsq = .12938 adj Rsq = .11197 (.0000)

TABLE 35: Dep. Var: 85 SCHTI
Indep.Vars.:

	b	(sig)	r
22 CAST	.27976	(.0077)	.4253
24 REL	-.27576	(.0086)	-.4235

Rsq = .23577 adj Rsq = .22048 (.0000)

TABLE 36: Dep. Var: 86 VILTI
Indep.Vars.:

	b	(sig)	r
20 SEX	-.37121	(.0001)	-.3572
24 REL	.25936	(.0048)	.2392

Rsq = .19463 adj Rsq = .17853 (.0000)

TABLE 37: Dep. Var: 395 SUPSUP
Indep.Vars.:

	b	(sig)	r
24 REL	.32914	(.0007)	.3291

Rsq = .10833   adj Rsq = .09950 (.0007)

TABLE 38: Dep. Var: 400 SUPUSE
Indep.Vars.:

	b	(sig)	r
446 JOBCHOI	.25379	(.0097)	.2538

Rsq = .06441   adj Rsq = .05515 (.0097)

TABLE 39: Dep. Var: 420 MEETSUP
Indep. Vars.:

	b	(sig)	r
309 TEAQUA	-.22479	(.0204)	-.2199
437 VILEDSUP	.31642	(.0338)	.2000

Rsq = .0905   adj Rsq = .07231 (.0328)

TABLE 40: Dep. Var: 355 STUENCO
Indep. Vars.:

	b	(sig)	r
18 STUDYMO	-.32321	(.0017)	-.1975
420 MEETSUP	.27670	(.0050)	-.1902
84 FAMTI	-.25773	(.0083)	.1677
309 TEAQ	.20863	(.0440)	.0812

Rsq = .17617   adj Rsq = .14254 (.0007)

TABLE 41: Dep. Var: 358 SUPENCO
Indep. Vars.:

	b	(sig)	r
400 SUPUSE	.30226	(.0017)	.2874
24 REL	.20939	(.0277)	.1879

Rsq = .12621   adj Rsq = .10873 (.0012)

TABLE 42: Dep. Var: 332 TEAINI
Indep. Vars.:

	b	(sig)	r
85 SCHTI	.35149	(.0003)	.3929
5 TEYRS	.34472	(.0001)	.2320
24 REL	-.24126	(.0120)	-.3175

Rsq = .29468 adj Rsq = .27331 (.0000)

TABLE 43: Dep. Var: 438 SCHCOM
Indep. Vars.:

	b	(sig)	r
355 STUENCO	.24072	(.0104)	.2425
446 JOBCHOI	.22126	(.0216)	.2439
400 SUPUSE	.19405	(.0433)	.2764
5 TEYRS	-.18529	(.0466)	.2764

Rsq = .19089 adj Rsq = .15786 (.0003)

TABLE 44: Dep. Var: 453 JOBCHA
Indep. Vars.:

	b	(sig)	r
20 SEX	-.22367	(.0231)	-.2237

Rsq = .05003 adj Rsq = .04062 (.0231)

6. *Mission School Teachers* (N=54)

TABLE 45: Dep. Var: 84 FAMTI
Indep. Vars.:

	b	(sig)	r
20 SEX	.50144	(.0002)	.4862
4 TESTD	-.34313	(.0084)	-.3208

Rsq = .35388 adj Rsq = .32312 (.0001)

TABLE 46: Dep. Var: 85 SCHTI
Indep. Vars.:

	b	(sig)	r
4 TESTD	.41652	(.0044)	.4165

Rsq = .17348 adj Rsq = .15426 (.0044)

TABLE 47: Dep. Var: 86 VILTI
Indep. Vars.:

	b	(sig)	r
20 SEX	-.47409	(.0010)	.4741

Rsq = .22476 adj Rsq = .20673 (.0010)

TABLE 48: Dep. Var: 395 SUPSUP
Indep. Vars.:

	b	(sig)	r
328 FAMED	.30096	(.0445)	.3001

Rsq = .09058 adj Rsq = .06943 (.0445)

TABLE 49: Dep. Var: 403 SUPCON
Indep. Vars.:

	b	(sig)	r
328 FAMED	-.40681	(.0040)	-.4747
19 AGE	-.33749	(.0091)	-.2143
20 SEX	-.31745	(.0215)	-.4307

Rsq = .40217 adj Rsq = .35842 (.0001)

TABLE 50: Dep. Var: 355 STUENCO
Indeo. Vars.:

	b	(sig)	r
328 FAMED	-.29729	(.0473)	-.2973

Rsq = .08838 adj Rsq = .06718 (.0473)

TABLE 51: DEp. Var: 356 PAENCO
Indep. Vars.:

	b	(sig)	r
4 TESTD	-.30191	(.0438) -.3019	

Rsq = .09115 adj Rsq = .07002 (.0438)

TABLE 52: Dep. Var: 357 COLENCO
Indep. Vars.:

	b	(sig)	r
309 TEAQUA	-.53561	(.0003)	-.4537
328 FAMED	-.31660	(.0176)	-.3221
5 TEYRS	-.31244	(.0288)	-.0399

Rsq = .35746 adj Rsq = .31045 (.0004)

TABLE 53: Dep. Var: 438 SCHCOM
Indep. Vars.:

	b	(sig)	r
328 FAMED	-.33421	(.0248)	-.3342

Rsq = .11169 adj Rsq = .09103 (.0248)

APPENDIX IV

Matched Pairs (N=241)

(NB. The prefixes 'STD' and 'PAR' indicates whether the variable refers to the student of the parent in the pair respectively. The rest of the variable code name follows the corresponding index above)

1. *Cross Tabulations*

TABLE 1: Parent's Education (PAR28EDUC) and Students Educational Ambition (STD51EDAMB)
N (col. per cent)

PAR28EDUC STD51EDAMB	1.No Ed	2.Std 1-4	3.Std 5-7	4.Std 8-10	5.SSC +	7.ALL
1. not continue education	3 (3.1)	1 (1.7)		1 (5.0)		5 (2.1)
2. continue up to SSC	56 (58.3)	27 (45.8)	30 (54.5)	4 (20.0)	1 (9.1)	118 (49.0)
3. continue after SSC	37 (38.5)	31 (52.5)	24 (45.4)	15 (75.0)	10 (90.9)	117 (48.5)
	96 (39.8)	59 (24.5)	55 (22.8)	20 (8.3)	11 (4.6)	241 (100.0)

TABLE 2: Parent's Occupation (PAR30OCC) and Students Educational Ambition (STD51EDAMB)
N (col. per cent)

PAR30OCC STD51EDAMB	1 DW	2 FA	3 USW	4 SW	5 WCW	6 BU	7 ALL
1. not continue education		4 (2.4)				1 (8.3)	5 (2.1)
2. continue to SSC	10 (76.9)	84 (49.4)	9 (64.3)	5 (41.7)	4 (20.0)	6 (50.0)	118 (49.0)
3. continue after SSC	3 (23.1)	82 (48.2)	5 (35.7)	7 (58.3)	16 (80.0)	5 (41.7)	118 (48.5)
	13 (5.4)	170 (70.5)	14 (5.9)	12 (5.0)	20 (8.3)	12 (5.0)	241 (100.0)

TABLE 3: Parent's Occupation (PAR30OCC) and Male Students Occupational Ambition i.e.follow parents occupation) (STD52OCCAMB1)
N (col. per cent)

PAR30OCC STD52OCCAMB1	1 DW	2 FA	3 USW	4 SW	5 WCW	6 BU	7 ALL
1. Yes	4 (40.0)	74 (50.0)	3 (27.3)	4 (44.1)	8 (57.1)	4 (44.4)	97 (48.3)
2. No	6 (60.0)	74 (50.0)	8 (72.7)	5 (55.6)	6 (42.9)	5 (55.6)	104 (51.7)
	10 (5.0)	148 (73.6)	11 (5.5)	9 (4.5)	14 (7.0)	9 (4.5)	201 (100.0)

TABLE 4: Parent's Occupation (PAR30OCC) and Students Choice of Farming (STD54FARAMB)
N (col. per cent)

PAR30OCC STD52FARAMB	1 DW	2 FA	3 USW	4 SW	5 WCW	6 BU	7 ALL
1. Yes	9 (69.2)	80 (48.5)	8 (61.5)	8 (66.6)	16 (76.2)	10 (90.9)	131 (55.7)
2. No	4 (30.8)	85 (51.5)	5 (38.5)	4 (33.3)	5 (23.8)	1 (9.1)	104 (44.3)
	13 (5.5)	165 (70.2)	13 (5.5)	12 (5.1)	21 (8.9)	11 (4.7)	235 (100.0)

TABLE 5: Parent's Occupation (PAR28EDUC)and Students Choice of Farming
N (col. per cent)

PAR28EDUC STD54FARAMB	1.No Ed.	2.Std 1-4	3.Std 5-7	4.Std 8-10	5.SSC +	7.ALL
1. Yes	42 (45.2)	38 (64.4)	27 (51.9)	14 (70.0)	10 (90.9)	131 (55.7)
2. No	51 (54.8)	21 (35.6)	25 (48.1)	6 (30.0)	1 (9.9)	104 (44.3)
	93 (39.6)	59 (25.1)	52 (22.1)	20 (8.5)	11 (4.7)	235 (100.0)

2. *Regression Analysis (Matched Pairs: N=112)*

TABLE 6: Dep. Var: STD 33 STUDY HRS

Indep Vars.	b	r	f	(sig)
PA 156 EDCOM	.16649	.16649	6.871	(.0093)

Rsq = .02772 adj Rsq = .02368 F = 6.871 (.0093)

TABLE 7: Dep. Var: Std 51 EDAMB

Indep Vars.	b	r	f	(sig)
Par 140 SES	.15180	.23286	4.878	(.01)
Std 3 STD	.16536	.19405	7.234	(.0001)
Std 9 REL	-.14314	-.11101	5.210	(.001)
Par 156 EDCOM	.15866	.22005	5.010	(.001)

Rsq = .11824 adj Rsq = .10342 F = 7.97844 (.0000)

TABLE 8: Dep. Var: Std 54 FARMAMB

Indep Vars.	b	r	f	(sig)
Par 12 REL	.19059	.24624	9.483	(.0000)
Par 140 SES	-.20378	-.23379	10.749	(.0000)
Std 3 STD	-.14921	-.15888	6.224	(.001)
Par 133 EDPROD	.12888	.15316	4.271	(.001)
Std 7 SEX	-.11101	-.17428	3.248	(.01)

Rsq = .15737 adj Rsq = .13959 F = 8.8512 (.0000)

TABLE 9: Dep. Var: Std 58 TEAAMB

Indep Vars.	b	r	f	(sig)
Par 28 EDUC	-.19103	-.20122	9.277	(.0000)
Par 12 REL	.14254	.15618	5.165	(.01)

Rsq = .06670 adj Rsq = .05287 F = 7.75477 (.0005)

TABLE 10: Dep. Var: Std 62 DOCAMB

Indep Vars.	b	r	f	(sig)
Std 7 SEX	-.18040	-.20917	8.041	(.0001)
Par 203 SCHCOM	-.15899	-.13010	6.521	(.001)
Par 28 EDUC	-.15887	-.18258	6.166	(.001)

Rsq = .08743 adj Rsq = .07597 F = 7.63230 (.0001)

TABLE 11: Dep. Var: Std 99 VILPRO

Indep Vars.	b	r	f	(sig)
Std 11 BOARD	-.17230	-.14924	7.160	(.001)
Std 7 SEX	.12681	.09549	3.879	(.01)

Rsq = .03782   adj Rsq = .02980   F = 4.71704 (.0098)

TABLE 12: Dep. Var: Std 125 SCHSUP

Indep Vars.	b	r	f	(sig)
Par 140 SES	.21669	.24786	11.735	(.0000)
Par 172 VILSUP	.14778	.19339	5.458	(.01)

Rsq = .08227   adj Rsq = .07463   F = 10.75809 (.0000)

TABLE 13: Dep. Var: Std 128 CLASSDIF

Indep Vars.	b	r	f	(sig)
Std 11 BOARD	-.20824	-.30316	8.561	(.001)
Std 10 CAST	-.18175	-.29050	6.522	(.01)

Rsq = 11.593   adj Rsq = .10856   F = 15.73552 (.0000)

TABLE 14: Dep. Var: Std 136 READSTU

Indep Vars.	b	r	f	(sig)
Std 9 REL	-.21293	-.21365	12.019	(.0000)
Std 3 STD	.16326	.14860	7.028	(.0000)
Par 140 SES	-.30012	-.10421	9.162	(.0000)
Par 28 EDUC	.23727	.00610	5.739	(.001)

Rsq = .10247   adj Rsq = .08739   F = 6.79336 (.0000)

TABLE 15: Dep. Var: Std 165 OCCSUP

Indep Vars.	b	r	f	(sig)
Std 11 BOARD	-.13864	-.13864	4.723	(.0307)

Rsq = .01922   adj Rsq = .01515   F = 4.72282 (.0307)

TABLE 16: Dep. Var: Std STAWA 191

Indep Vars.	b	r	f	(sig)
Std 3 STD	.23626	.24272	14.935	(.0000)
Par 172 VILSUP	-.12723	-.18045	4.147	(.01)
Std 9 REL	-.15304	-.14837	6.375	(.001)
Par 140 SES	-.14460	-.15845	5.411	(.001)

Rsq = .12592 adj Rsq = .11123 F = 8.57164 (.0000)

APPENDIX V

The Questionnaires

1. Questionnaire for Students

Name of the School:

Class:

Read the questions carefully and check the appropriate answer:

I. *Some information about your family*

1. Your name:
2. Father's name:
3. Name of the village where he stays:
4. Name of the hamlet (*Pada*):
5. Your Age:
6. Are you a boy or a girl: (1) Boy __________
   (2) Girl __________
7. Your caste/community: (1) Tribal __________
   (2) Non-Tribal __________
8. Your religion (1) Hindu __________
   (2) Christian __________
   (3) Other __________
9. How many years have you been in this school? __________
10. Are you a boarder? (1) Yes _____
    (2) No _____
11. How do you come to school? (1) Walking ________
    (2) By bus ________
    By truck ________ or some other vehicle
12. Does your family have the following:

	Yes	*No*	*Don't know*
(1) their own land	____	____	____
(2) their own bullocks	____	____	____
(3) a well	____	____	____
(4) a well with a pump	____	____	____
(5) two crops each year	____	____	____
(6) electricity in the house	____	____	____

13. How far was your father educated?
    (1) No formal/school education __________
    (2) First to fourth __________

(3) Fifth to seventh ________
(4) Eight to S.S.C. ________
(5) S.S.C. and more ________

14. How far was your mother educated?
(1) No formal/school education ________
(2) First to fourth ________
(3) Fifth to seventh ________
(4) Eight to S.S.C. ________
(5) S.S.C. and more ________

15. What is your father's occupation?
(1) labourer (daily wages) ________
(2) farmer ________
(3) manual labourer (regularly employed) ________
(4) office-work (white collar) ________

16. What is your mother's occupation?
(1) labourer (daily wages) ________
(2) farmer ________
(3) manual labourer (regularly employed) ________
(4) office-work (white collar) ________

17. Who encourages you to go to school?
(1) No one ________
(2) My Parents ________
(3) My Relatives/friends ________
(4) The social-worker or teacher ________

18. If you run away from school, who sends you back to school?
(1) No one ________
(2) My Parents ________
(3) My Relative/Friends ________
(4) The social workers/Teachers ________

19. Are your parents strict about your attending school regularly?
(1) They are not strict therefore I can miss school easily ________
(2) They are strict therefore I don't miss school that easily ________
(3) They are very strict therefore I don't miss school at all ________

20. When do your parents get you your school books or school kit?
(1) At the beginning of the year ________
(2) Only late in the year ________
(3) Can't afford to buy them ________

II. *Some information about your school:*

1. Can you understand the teacher in class?
(1) No, I can't understand ________
(2) I can with some effort understand ________

(3) Yes, In can easily understand ______

2. When you find it difficult to follow the teacher in class is it:- because:

	Yes	*No*	*Don't know*
(1) The subject is too hard	____	____	____
(2) The teacher's language too difficult	____	____	____
(3) The teacher doesn't explain properly	____	____	____
(4) Inadequate facilities in the classroom	____	____	____
(5) Any other reason (Specify)			

3. How much time do you get to study on school days?
   (1) Not enough even to do my homework ______
   (2) Just enough to do my homework ______
   (3) Quite enough to do my homework ______

4. How many subjects did you fail in at your fourth std. exams?
   A. (1) None ______
   (2) One or two ______
   (3) More than two ______

   B. How many subjects did you fail in at your seventh std. exams?
   (1) None ______
   (2) One or two ______
   (3) More than two ______

5. What type of books do you read?

	Very rarely	*Sometime*	*Often*
(a) Textbooks	____	____	____
(b) Guide Books	____	____	____
(c) Story Books	____	____	____

6. What is your most favourite subject in school? ______

7. What is your most difficult subject? ______

8. What extra-curricular activities do you like?

	No	*Little*	*Very much*
(a) Games	____	____	____
(b) Music	____	____	____
(c) Drama	____	____	____
(d) Handicraft	____	____	____
(e) Dance	____	____	____
(f) Any Other (specify)	____	____	____

9. How much time do you give to them?
   (1) Hardly any ________
   (2) Not sufficient ________
   (3) Sufficient ________

10. Are you required to do farming, gardening, book-binding or any other activity for work-experience in you school?
   (1) Yes ________
   (2) No ________

11. Do you find it useful?

	Yes	*No*
(1) For you	________	________
(2) For the school	________	________

III. *Some questions on your hopes and aspirations:*

1. If you were offered a job, would you rather give up that opportunity and continue with your education? How far?
   (1) I would not continue my education ________
   (2) I would up to S.S.C. ________
   (3) I would beyond S.S.S. too.(Specify) ________

2. (For boys) Would you like to follow the same occupation as your father?
   (1) Yes ______
   (2) No ______

   (For girls) Would you like to follow the same occupation as your mother?
   (1) Yes ______
   (2) No ______

3. What occupation would you like to follow when you finish studying?

	Yes	*No*	*Don't know*
(1) Farmer	_____	_____	_____
(2) Factory-worker	_____	_____	_____
(3) Office-work	_____	_____	_____
(4) Business	_____	_____	_____
(5) Teacher	_____	_____	_____
(6) Nurse	_____	_____	_____
(7) Police	_____	_____	_____
(8) Military-serviced	_____	_____	_____
(9) Doctor	_____	_____	_____
(10) Lawyer	_____	_____	_____
(11) Other	_____	_____	_____

4. Who encourages you in your choice of future occupation?

	Yes	*No*	*Don't know*
(a) My parents	____	____	____
(b) My teacher	____	____	____
(c) My relatives or family friends	____	____	____
(d) My school friends	____	____	____
(e) Others (specify)	____	____	____

5. Name *three* persons whom you admire the most: (you ca:. name a local leader, historical person, some person from your school, a character from a story-book...)
   (1) ________
   (2) ________
   (3) ________

6. Would you like to be like them?

	Yes	*No*	*Don't know*
(1) First person	____	____	____
(2) Second person	____	____	____
(3) Third person	____	____	____

7. From amongst the following, which three groups do you think are the most advanced? -
   (1) Farmers. (2) Businessmen. (3) Regularly employed. (4) Landlords. (5) Politicians. (6) sisters-fathers-social workers.
   (1) Most advanced ________
   (2) Less advanced ________
   (3) Even less advanced ________

8. Would you like to be like them?

	Yes	*No*	*Don't know*
(1) First group	____	____	____
(2) Second group	____	____	____
(3) Third group	____	____	____

IV. *Some information about yourself*

1. Where do your best friends come from?

	Yes	*No*	*Don't know*
(a) From your class	____	____	____
(b) From your school	____	____	____
(c) From your village	____	____	____

2. Where do you meet your teacher to discuss your difficulties?

	Very rarely	*Sometimes*	*Never*
(1) In the class	____	____	____
(2) In the school	____	____	____
(3) Outside the school	____	____	____
(4) In his/her home	____	____	____

3. If you are a boarder - would you like to become a day scholar?
   Yes________ No__________ Don't know__________

4. If you are a day scholar, would like to become a boarder?
   Yes________ No__________ Don't know__________

5. Do you know of any special help for the scheduled tribes from the government?

	Yes	*No*	*Don't know*
(a) For study	_____	_____	_____
(b) For jobs	_____	_____	_____

6. While considering the other schools in your area, how satisfied are you with your school?

	No	*Yes*	*Very much satisfied*
(1) As regards the teachers	_____	_____	________
(2) " " the students	_____	_____	________
(3) " " the facilities	_____	_____	________

7. While considering the other boardings in your area, how satisfied are you with your boarding?

	No	*Yes*	*Very much satisfied*
(1) As regards the supervisors	_____	_____	________
(2) " " the boarders	_____	_____	________
(3) " " the facilities	_____	_____	________

8. Do you participate in the village - programmes/activities?
   (1) No __________
   (2) Yes; but not very actively __________
   (3) Yes; very actively __________

9. Have you anything further to add? __________

2. **Questionnaire for Parents**

Name of the village: ________ Hamlet (*Pada*):_________

Name of the household head interviewed: ______________

Name of the student interviewed: ____________

Name of the child's school: _________________

Name of the Parent's school: ________________

(1) Z.P. school or govt. school (2) Ashram school

(3) Mission school (4) Other private institution.

I. *Let us begin with some information about yourself:*

1. (a) Your age (approximately): ________ years
(b) Male or female: ________
(c) Are you: 1) Married 2) Unmarried 3) Widower/Widow..?______

2. (a) Your caste-community______________
(b) Your subcaste-community_____
(c) Your religion ________

3. How many children do you have? What are they doing?

	Boy/girl	*age*	*class* (if school going)	*Occupation* (if out of sch.)
1st child	___	___	___	___
2nd child	___	___	___	___
3rd child	___	___	___	___
4th child	___	___	___	___
5th child	___	___	___	___
6th child	___	___	___	___
7th child	___	___	___	___
8th child	___	___	___	___
9th child	___	___	___	___
10th child	___	___	___	___
11th child	___	___	___	___
12th child	___	___	___	___

4. (a) How far have you been educated? ______________
(1) No formal education at all (2) 1st to 4th (3) 5th to 7th (4) 8th to S.S.C.
(5) S.S.C and more

(b) How far was your father educated? ______________
(Clarify as above)

5. (a) What is your occupation?
(1) labourer (2) Farmer (3) Manual labourer (regularly employed/skilled unskilled (4) Office-work
(b) What was/is your father's occupation? (explain as above) _______
(c) What is your wife's occupation? (explain as above) _________

6. Do you have the following things:

	Yes	*No*
(a) Your own land	___	___
(b) your own bullocks	___	___
(c) A well	___	___
(d) A well with a pump	___	___
(e) Two crops per year	___	___
(f) Electricity in the house	___	___

7. (a) How many sets of clothes have you brought for your family last year?
____
(1) One set or less (2) 2 or 3 (3) more than 3
(b) How many times did you buy vegetable/fish/meat last month?
________ (explain as above)
(c) How often do you have toddy or liquor in a month?
________ (explain as above)

8A. How often have you been to a city or town?

	Very rarely	*Sometimes*	*Many times*
(a) Vapi or Dahanu	____	____	____
(b) Bassein or Thane	____	____	____
(c) Bombay city	____	____	____
(d) Other town or city (specify)	____	____	____

B. How long have you stayed in these cities or towns?

	less than a month	one/some months	more
(a) Vapi or Dahanu	____	____	____
(b) Bassein or Thane	____	____	____
(c) Bombay city	____	____	____
(d) Other town or city (specify)	____	____	____

II. *Now some questions on your children's education*

1. Why do you send you children to school? (1 = not beneficial 2= beneficial 3 = very beneficial)

	1	2	3
(a) Monetarily beneficial to the family	__	__	__
(b) Socially beneficial to the family	__	__	__
(c) Monetarily beneficial to the child	__	__	__
(d) Socially beneficial to the child	__	__	__

2. If you have educated one or two of your children would still want to educate all the rest?
(1) it's not necessary (2) can't afford (3) yes, if they want to (4) yes, of course. ________

3. Do you suffer any loss or hardship by sending your children to school?
(1) financial loss (2) loss of work/labour (3) no loss. ________

4. How much would you sacrifice to send your daughter to school?
(1) not willing to sacrifice (2) not as much as for my son (3) as much as for my son. ________

5. When you get an opportunity, do you read books, newspapers etc.?
(1) no don't read (2) would like to but don't get a chance (3) yes, whenever I get an opportunity. ________

6. (a) If your son is offered a job, would you rather want him to continue with his education? — upto what stage?
(1) no, would not want him to continue (2) yes, upto S.S.C. (3) Yes, even after S.S.C. ________

(b) If your daughter is offered a job or marriage proposal — would you still want her to continue with her education? — upto what stage? (Explain)
____

7. Do you know of any special help for the scheduled tribes from the government?

	Yes	*No*
(a) For education	____	____
(b) For employment	____	____

8. Would you like your son to take up the same occupation as his father (1) yes, (2) no. ________

9. What occupation would you want for your son?
(1) labourer (2) farmer (3) manual labourer (regularly employed skilled/unskilled (4) office work. ________

10. Would you want your daughter to follow the same occupation as her mother? (1) yes (2) no. ________

11. What occupation would you want for your daughter? (Explain as above)
____

12. Name *three* persons who you admire the most: (You can name any local leader, historical person, someone from the village school, a character from any book . . .)
(1) ________
(2) ________
(3) ________

13. From amongst the following, which *three groups do you think are the most advanced*?

(1) farmers (2) businessmen (3) white collared (4) landlords (5) politicians or leaders (6) sisters, fathers, social workers.
(1) ________
(2) ________
(3) ________

III. *Let us now come to your village community*

1. (a) Are the parents from your village strict about sending their children to school?

(1) they are not strict, they let their children miss school easily
(2) They are strict; they don't let their child miss school so easily
(3) they are very strict; only on important occasion, they let their children miss school.

(b) Do the villagers come to you for assistance?

	Very rarely	*Sometimes*	*Often*
(A) to write letters/forms etc.	______	______	______
(B) to seek advice on education or employment	______	______	______
(C) to go to Talathi or govt. office	______	______	______
(D) to mediate in family matters	______	______	______

2. (a) Do you attend village meetings?
(1) very rarely (2) sometimes (3) many times ________

(b) How actively do you participate in these meetings?
(1) listen but don't speak (2) give my opinion if asked (3) say no openly if I disagree. ________

3. (a) Do you attend village feast, village celebration?
(1) very rarely (2) sometimes (3) many times ________

(b) How actively do you participate in these functions?
(1) just attend (2) give my help if needed (3) take the responsibility an plan. ________

4. (a) Do you preside over any village meetings or get-together?
(1) very rarely (2) sometimes (3) many times. ________

(b) Do you hold any official post in the village (e.g. member of the panchayat or of some co-operative society, police-patil etc. state the designation)
(1) yes (2) no ________

5. (a) Do you vote in elections?
(1) very rarely (2) sometimes (3) may times ________

(b) Have you participated in any public demonstrations e.g. protest march, meetings?
(1) very rarely (2) some times (3) many times ________

(c) How actively do you participate in such demonstrations?
(1) just attend (2) attend and give my help (3) take the initiative and plan ________

6. (a) Have you worked for any social organisation? (e.g. Adivasi Seva Mandal, Gokhale Education Society, Jungle Kamgar Society etc.)

(1) very rarely (2) sometimes (3) many times ________
(b) How important has been your contribution towards these organisations?
(1) unimportant; just hold a membership (2) not very important; helped if asked (3) very important; take initiative and organise programmes.

7. How helpful are the villagers to the school?
(1) Not very helpful (2) Give help if asked for
(3) Very helpful whenever asked. ________

IV. *Some questions for Parents whose children are already in the School*

1. Why do you send your children to this particular school?

	Yes	*No*	*Can't answer*
a) Nearer to home	___	___	___
b) The cheapest education	___	___	___
c) The best school for studies	___	___	___
d) Special facilities for tribal students	___	___	___
e) Special facilities for religious instruction	___	___	___
f) Did not get admission elsewhere	___	___	___
g) Any other reason (specify)	___	___	___

2.A. What has been your contact with the school? Do you go to school to:

	Very rarely	*Sometimes*	*Seldom*
a) Attending functions for parents	___	___	___
b) Enquire after your children's academic progress?	___	___	___
c) If needed to offer some help	___	___	___
d) Any other reason (specify)	___	___	___

B. Do you feel that the school authorities need your help?
(1) Very rarely (2) Sometimes (3) Seldom ________

C. Do the school authorities visit you to enquire after your needs?
(specify as above) ________

D. Do they seek you advice on any school matter? (specify as above)

____

E. While considering the other schools in this are, are you satisfied with your child's school as regards:

	No	*Yes*	*Very much*
a) the students	___	___	___
b) the teachers	___	___	___
c) the facilities	___	___	___
d) the parents	___	___	___
(e) the help from the village community	___	___	___

On ending the interview:

1. Interviewee's response:

(1) Favourable (2) Unfavourable ________

3. Questionnaire for Teachers

Name of the School: ________________

Name of the teacher interviewed:________________

I. *Let us begin with some information about yourself:*

1. (a) Which standard are you teaching this year (1983-84)/ ________
(b) Which standard do you usually teach? 1) 1st to 4th
2) 5th to 7th 3) 8th to S.S.C. ________

2. (a) How many years have you been teaching? ________
(b) How many years have you been teaching in this school? ________
(c) How many years have you been teaching in this institution?
(institutions: (1) Z.P.School (2) Ashramshala (3) Mission School
(4) Other private institution) ________

3. Some information about your educational qualifications:

Degree	*Place*	*Class*	*Percentage*
(a) S.S.C.	______	______	______
(b) D.Ed.	______	______	______
(c) B.A./B.Sc.	______	______	______
(d) B.Ed.	______	______	______
(e) Other (specify)	______	______	______

4. How much further do you intend studying? (1) No intention of studying further (2) Do intend to study further (specify degree/ diploma) ________

II. *Now some questions on your socio-economic background:*

1. (a) Your age: ________
(b) Male/Female: ________
(c) Are you: (1) Married (2) Unmarried (3)Widower/Widow ________

2. (a) Your caste-community: ________
(b) Your subcaste-community: ________
(c) Your religion: ________

3. Number of persons dependent on you: ________

4. (a) How do you travel to your school? (1) Walking (2) By bus
   (3) By truck (4) By cycle (5) Other (specify) __________
   (b) How much time does it take to reach your school? (minutes)_____

5. (a) How far was your father educated? (1) No formal education at all
   (2) 1st to 4th (3) 5th to 7th (4) 8th to S.S.C.
   (5) S.S.C. and more _________
   (b) How far was your mother educated (classify as above) ________

6. What is your father's occupation? (1) labourer (2) farmer working on his own field and labourer (3) farmer on his own field only (4) manual labourer (regularly employed) skilled/unskilled (5) office-work __________

7. How often do you drink toddy and liquor in a month? (1) very rarely (2) twice or thrice (3) more than thrice ___________

III. Now some *questions* about *your school:*

1. (a) Are you required to have regular tests and examinations for your students? (1) No (2) yes but not regularly (3) yes, regularly __________
   (b) Do you find them beneficial to your students? (1) No (2) Somewhat beneficial (3) Very beneficial __________

2. (a) Are teaching aids made available to you? (1) Very rarely
   (2) Sometimes (3) Whenever required __________
   (b) Do you make your own teaching aids? (1) Very rarely
   (2) Sometimes (3) Whenever required __________

3. (a) Are you involved in some extra-curricular activities - at least once a year?

	Yes	No
a) Sports	______	______
b) Cultural programmes	______	______
c) Trips	______	______
d) Other (specify)	______	______

   (b) What percentage of your students are regularly involved in these?
   (1) Less than 50% approx. (2) More than 50% approx.
   (3) almost 100% __________

   (c) How actively do they participate in these? (1) Not very actively
   (2) somewhat actively (3) Very actively __________

IV. Now some *information* about *your students*

1. (a) Do your students like to study? (1) No,they don't (2) Indifferent
   (3) Yes, they do __________

(b) Are your adivasi students as capable as the non-adivasi ones?
(1) No, on their own not as capable as the non-adivasis
(2) If helped as capable (3) Yes,as capable ________

2. (a) What do you do if a student remains absent for many days - say two weeks? (1) Wait for him to come (2) Inquire after the reason and send a message (3) Visit his home ________

(b) What do you do if a student remains absent for more than two months? (1)Wait, inquire after the reason (2) Send a message the headmaster (3) Visit his family ________

3. (a) How many of your students have appeared for the Z.P. or Vidya Niketan scholarship examinations during the last three years ________

(b) Do you give any special preparation to the brighter students for the Z.P. examinations ? (1) Yes (specify) (2) No ________

(c) Do you give any special preparation to the weaker students, i.e., extra classes to help them keep up with the class.
(1) Yes (how) (2) No ________

V. *Now some information about your work*

(a) As a teacher which of the following groups make the most *demands* on you?

	Little	*Some*	*much*
(a) Students	______	______	______
(b) Parents	______	______	______
(c) Fellow teachers	______	______	______
(d) Supervisors	______	______	______
(e) Social workers	______	______	______
(f) Others (specify)	______	______	______

(b) As a teacher which of the following groups give you the most *support?*

	Little	*Some*	*much*
(a) Students	______	______	______
(b) Parents	______	______	______
(c) Fellow teachers	______	______	______
(d) Supervisors	______	______	______
(e) Social workers	______	______	______
(f) Others (specify)	______	______	______

(c) As a teacher which of the following groups have the highest *expectations* of you?

	Little	*Some*	*much*
(a) Students	______	______	______
(b) Parents	______	______	______
(c) Fellow teachers	______	______	______

(d) Supervisors ______ ______ ______
(e) Social workers ______ ______ ______
(f) Others (specify) ______ ______ ______

(d) 1. As a teacher which of the following groups is the most *appreciative* of you?

	Little	*Some*	*much*
(a) Students	______	______	______
(b) Parents	______	______	______
(c) Fellow teachers	______	______	______
(d) Supervisors	______	______	______
(e) Social workers	______	______	______
(f) Others (specify)	______	______	______

2. The next few questions are concerned with how you spend your time?
   1) What time do you set out for school in the morning? ________
   2) What time do you return from school in the evening? ________
   3) How many hours a day do you spend on school-work? ________
3. (a) In regular school-day of five and a half hours approximately how much time do you spend on the following?
   (a) in class with your students? ________%
   (b) on administration work? ________%
   (c) outside class on extra-curricular work ________%
   (d) outside class with your students ________%

   (b) In a typical term of 100 days, what percentage of the term-time do you spend on the following:
   (a) Class-work (teaching, correcting etc.) ________%
   (b) On administrative work ________%
   (c) Extra-curricular activities ________%
   (d) Outside class (with your students, making teaching aids etc.) ________%

4. Outside school hours, what percentage of your time do you spend on the following:
   (1) On family matters, with friends ________%
   (2) On students and school matters ________%
   (3) On village and community matters ________%

VI. Every institution must have someone to supervise it. Government schools have an inspector, usually the BDO/ADEI, other schools have a supervisor from the management. Please answer these *questions regarding your supervisor.*

1.(a) On an average how often does a supervisor/inspector visit your school?
(a) ________ times a month.
(b) ________ times a term.
(b) What does he usually talk about on such visits?

	Very rarely	*Sometimes*	*Often*
(a) educational matters (i.e., teaching curriculum etc.)	_____	_____	_____
(b) discipline (i.e., attendance etc.)	_____	_____	_____
(c) administrative matters (records, repairs etc.)	_____	_____	_____
(d) other facilities etc. (repairs, changes etc.)	_____	_____	_____
(e) personal matters (your difficulties problems etc.)	_____	_____	_____
(f) social matters (village difficulties problems etc.)	_____	_____	_____

2.(a) What do you think is the purpose of these visits?

	No	*Yes*	*Yes definitely*
(a) to check on your work	_____	_____	_____
(b) to evaluate your work	_____	_____	_____
(c) to assist you in your work	_____	_____	_____
(d) to encourage you in your work	_____	_____	_____

(b) How exacting/demanding have you found your supervisors/inspector?

(1) Little _______

(2) Somewhat _______

(3) Very much _______

3.(a) How useful have you found such visits?

	Little	*Somewhat*	*Very much*
(a) for your work as a teacher	_____	_____	_____
(b) for yourself personally	_____	_____	_____

(b) Would you like : the present supervisor/inspector

	Yes	*No*	*Cant' say*
(a) to stop	_____	_____	_____
(b) to continue with the same supervisor	_____	_____	_____
(c) to continue with another supervisor	_____	_____	_____

4. Do you find any difference between the supervision of government inspectors and supervisors of private institutions, as regards the following:

	No difference	*Yes (specify)*
(a) frequency of visits	_____	_____
(b) topics discussed	_____	_____
(c) purpose of visits	_____	_____
(d) how exacting they are	_____	_____
(e) how useful they are	_____	_____

VII. Now some *information* about the *organised meetings for your fellow teachers in your area:*

1. (a) How often do you have such meetings? ________
   (1) less than monthly (2) monthly (3) more than monthly

   (b) What are the topics discussed at such meetings?

	Very rarely	*Sometimes*	*Many times*
(a) educational matters (teaching curriculum etc.)	______	______	______
(b) discipline (attendance etc.)	______	______	______
(c) administrative matters (records, reports etc.)	______	______	______
(d) facilities (repairs,changes etc.)	______	______	______
(e) personal matters (your difficulties, problems etc.)	______	______	______
(f) social matters (village difficulties, problems etc.)	______	______	______

2.(a) What do you think is the purpose of these meetings?

	No	*Yes*	*Yes definitely*
(a) to check on your work	____	____	____
(b) to evaluate your work	____	____	____
(c) to assist you in your work	____	____	____
(d) to encourage you in your work	____	____	____

(b) How useful have you found these meetings? ________
   (1) Little (2) Somewhat (3) Very much

VIII. Let us now turn to the village community in which your school is:

1.(a) Are the parents of your students strict about sending their children to school? ________

   (a) They are not strict, they let their children miss the school easily. ___
   (b) They are strict; they do not let their children miss school easily. ___
   (c) They are very strict; only on important occasions do they let their children miss school ___

(b) Do the villagers come to you for assistance?

	Very rarely	*Sometimes*	*Many times*
(a) to read-write, letters/forms etc.	_____	_____	_____
(b) to ask advice on education, employment etc,	_____	_____	_____
(c) to mediate in disputes, family affairs etc.	_____	_____	_____

2. (a) Do you attend village meetings? ____________
   (1) Very rarely (2) Sometimes (3) Many times

   (b) How actively do you participate in these meetings? __________
   (1) just listen but don't speak (2) give my opinion if asked
   (3) say no openly if I disagree.

3. (a) Do you attend village-feasts, village celebrations? ________
   (1) Very rarely (2) Sometimes (3) Many times...

   (b) How actively do you participate in these functions? __________
   (1) just attend (2) give my help if needed (3) take the responsibility and plan

4. (a) Do you preside over any village-meetings or get-togethers?
   (1) Very rarely (2) Sometimes (3) Many times __________

   (b) Do you hold any official post in the village? (e.g. member of the panchayat or of some co-operative society, police-patil, etc. state the designation)
   (1) Yes (2) No. __________

5. (a) Do you vote in elections? _________
   (1) Very rarely (2) Sometimes (3) Many times

   (b) Have you participated in any public demonstrations, e.g., protest march meetings? ___________
   (1) Very rarely (2) Sometimes (3) Many times.

   (c) How actively do you participate in such demonstrations?
   (1) just attend (2) attend and give my help (3) take initiative and plan _________

6. (a) Have you worked for any social organisation? (e.g. Adivasi Seva Mandal, Gokhale Education Society, Jungle Kamgar Society, etc.)
   (1) Very rarely (2) Sometimes (3) Many times... _________

   (b) How important has been your contribution towards these organisations?
   (1) unimportant, just hold a membership (2) not very important; helped if asked
   (3) very important, taken initiative and organised various programmes... _________

7. How helpful are the people of the village to the school?
   (1) do not help... (2) give help if asked...(3) very helpful whenever asked _________

IX. Finally a *few questions to end the interview:*

1. While considering the other schools in this area, are you satisfied with your school as regards

	No	*Yes*	*Very much*
(a) students	____	____	____
(b) teachers	____	____	____
(c) facilities	____	____	____
(d) parents	____	____	____
(e) help from village community	____	____	____
(f) other (specify)	____	____	____

2. Do you feel that you can improve your prospects in your job?
i.e., by promotion, social recognition etc.
(1) little or no chance (2) depends on luck (3) good chances if I work hard.

____

3. In choosing this career, how important to you were the following reasons?

	Not impt.	*Imp.*	*Very impt.*
(a) I like teaching	____	____	____
(b) It brings a regular income	____	____	____
(c) It gives me status	____	____	____
(d) It was not my first choice	____	____	____
(e) I could not get any other job	____	____	____
(f) It is more convenient for me	____	____	____
(g) Other (specify)	____	____	____

4. If it is possible would you change this job?

	No	*Can't say*	*Yes*
(a) would you change this job	____	____	____
(b) would you do the same work in some other school?	____	____	____
(c) would you do some other work but only on a higher salary	____	____	____

5. Would you like to add any thing? ________

On ending the interview
Interviewee's response - (1) favourable (2) unfavourable ________

4. Questionnaire on the Goals of the School

One of the great concerns of education has been the goals of the school: What are we trying to accomplish through our schools. This is particularly important when we consider tribal education.

Here we have listed several goals of a school. With regard to your school could you respond to item in two ways:

(1) How important *is* each activity or goal at your school?
(2) How important *should* each activity or goal be at your school?

Estimate the "importance" in terms of the money, time etc., that *is* given or *should be* given to that particular activity or goal.

Example:

	Very impt.	Impt.	Not impt.	Don't know
to train good citizens				
(a) *is*	____	____	_x_	____
(b) *should be*	____	_x_	____	____

The answers above mean that to train good citizens for that particular school *is* not important but it *should be* important.

Please answer *all* the questions below. Indicate your answer by making a cross (_x_) in the appropriate space.

	Very impt.	Impt.	Not impt.	Don't know
1. Have a proper extra-curricular programme, i.e., games, handicraft drama, dance etc...				
(a) is	____	____	____	____
(b) should be	____	____	____	____
2. To teach students to think independently ,i.e., to enable them to criticize what they have learnt and not merely repeat it by rote.				
(a) is	____	____	____	____
(b) should be	____	____	____	____
3. To keep teachers happy and satisfied in their job, i.e., a feeling of well-being and fulfillment in their teaching.				
(a) is	____	____	____	____
(b) should	____	____	____	____
4. Have good discipline, i.e., habits or regularity, punctuality, orderliness, etc...				
(a) is	____	____	____	____
(b) should be	____	____	____	____

5. To develop sound moral values and convictions in students, i.e., to be able to make decisions on a moral basis and follow them through.

	Very impt.	Impt.	Not impt.	Don't know
(a) is	____	____	____	____
(b) should be	____	____	____	____

6 To keep teachers committed and motivated in their job.

(a) is	____	____	____	____
(b) should be	____	____	____	____

7. To train students to express and control their emotion, i.e., not to merely repress their feelings or be led by them, not to go by feeling of like/dislike, of fear/anxiety etc.

(a) is	____	____	____	____
(b) should be	____	____	____	____

8. To involve teachers in decisions of the management, i.e., not merely inform them once decisions are made but to elicit the opinion to arrive at one.

(a) is	____	____	____	____
(b) should be	____	____	____	____

9. Have efficient management, i.e., good supervision, smooth administration.

(a) is	____	____	____	____
(b) should be	____	____	____	____

10. To produce students who will be leaders for their people, i.e., play an active role in working for the good of the people.

	Very impt.	Impt.	Not impt.	Don't know
(a) is	____	____	____	____
(b) should be	____	____	____	____

11. To consult teachers regarding the running of the school, i.e., not merely expect them to carry out orders but invite suggestions, listen to problems about implementation.

	Very impt.	Impt.	Not impt.	Don't know
(a) is	____	____	____	____
(b) should be	____	____	____	____

12. Have high institutional prestige, i.e., to be among the best schools in the area.

(a) is	____	____	____	____
(b) should be	____	____	____	____

13. To teach students their own religion, i.e., Christianity to Christians, Hinduism to Hindus, etc.

(a) is	____	____	____	____
(b) should be	____	____	____	____

14. To encourage teachers to be innovative in their teaching, i.e., providing ideas and support to carry them through.

(a) is	____	____	____	____
(b) should be	____	____	____	____

15. Help students to adjust to school, i.e., helping them to fit into the school timetables and programmes.

(a) is	____	____	____	____
(b) should be	____	____	____	____

16. To persuade students to change their own religion ,i.e., from Hinduism to Christianity and vice versa.

(a) is	____	____	____	____
(b) should be	____	____	____	____

17. To reward teachers for extra work and initiative ,i.e., reward monetarily or otherwise show appreciation.

(a) is	____	____	____	____
(b) should be	____	____	____	____

18. Try to adapt teaching to the students, i.e., changing school time tables and programmes to meet students needs.

	Very impt.	Impt.	Not impt.	Don't know
(a) is	____	____	____	____
(b) should be	____	____	____	____

19. To have special facilities for backward students ,i.e., special classes or programmes for socially economically or otherwise disadvantaged students.

(a) is	____	____	____	____
(b) should be	____	____	____	____

20. To get all to work as a unified team in the school, i.e., the teacher of the school and the supervisors as well.

(a) is	____	____	____	____
(b) should be	____	____	____	____

21. Get good results in public exams, i.e., high percentage of passes and marks.

(a) is	____	____	____	____
(b) should be	____	____	____	____

22. To have special facilities for gifted students, i.e., special classes or programmes for more capable students intellectually and otherwise.

(a) is	____	____	____	____
(b) should be	____	____	____	____

23. Be a centre for community services and programmes,i.e., serving its cultural and educational needs.

(a) is ____ ____ ____ ____
(b) should be ____ ____ ____ ____

24. To give job-oriented education, i.e., bias in the school to make students more employable.

	Very impt.	Impt.	Not impt.	Don't know
(a) is	____	____	____	____
(b) should be	____	____	____	____

25. Give preference to poor students in admission.

(a) is ____ ____ ____ ____
(b) should be ____ ____ ____ ____

26. To develop self-respect in students, i.e., to appreciate their own culture and self-confidence.
(a) is ____ ____ ____ ____
(b) should be ____ ____ ____ ____

27. Give preference to students of a certain caste or community in admission, i.e., to Christians in Christian schools or Hindus in Hindu ones,etc.
(a) is ____ ____ ____ ____
(b) should be ____ ____ ____ ____

28. To have an all-round development of students, i.e., of head and heart or body and mind - intellectual, moral, emotional, social.
(a) is ____ ____ ____ ____
(b) should be ____ ____ ____ ____

5. Open-ended questionnaire for Management/Supervisors/Village Leaders/Elders

I. *The Changing Culture of the Tribal Community*

1. What are some of the *main aspects* of tribal community as you see it? Positive and negative ones? Which of these are pertinent to a relevant education.

2. How are these being affected by *changes today*?
How are these tribal coping? Where are they gaining or losing?
What is the roll and purpose for education you see?

3. What are the *future possibilities* for these tribals?
Socio-culturally, politically, educationally, economically?
What about the integration into or isolation from the national mainstream?

II. *The Historical Context of the School*

1. *Past Review.*

a. Why were these schools *originally started?*
What service were they to render? To whom?
What was the motivation behind them?

b. What *difficulties stood* in the way? From where did these arrive?

c. What role did the local village/community play?
Acceptance, support, opposition?

2. *Present Evaluation*

a What *purpose* do these schools *serve now?*
What service do they render? To whom?
How has this changed?

b. What *difficulties*/opposition do they experience?
What support? How do they cope with them?

c. How is the local/village community involved?
Is it the same? Why?
Has it changed? How?

3. *Future Plans.*

a. How do you see the further development of your schools?
What plans do you have? For expansion? For change?
For improvement?

b. What difficulties do you expect to face and how?
What resources can you get and how? Financial? Personnel?

c. What role will the local/village community play in these plans?

III. *The School.*

1. What is the *purpose of education* in general?
What is the purpose of your school in particular?
What kind of student do you want to be trained?

What kind of contribution do you want to make to the community?

2. What *means* must the school employ to secure its goal?
How far does the present system help or hinder your school?
What changes would you like to see implemented? In the syllabus?
What experiments have your tried?
How can you contribute to improve this system?

3. What *resources* are most-vital to your school?
What constraints are most crucial to your school?
How far are local resources available in terms of finance and personnel?

IV. *The Village/Community.*

1. What are the real *needs* of the village-community today?
How far are these felt needs?
Where does education stand as a real need and a felt one?

2. What *resources* can be found within and without the local community to meet its most important needs and particularly *educational* ones?
If sufficient resources aren't available, how can they be mobilised or even created?, i.e., financial, material, personnel, pedagogical resources?

3. What *means* are available to match resources to needs?
How far do government agencies, political parties, private agencies contribute?
How could these do better?

V. *School Community Links.*

1. What is the involvement/contribution of village-leaders, ex-students, educated persons, etc., to the school?
In terms of: encouraging attendance, participating/attending programmes, mobilizing-resources, etc.?

2. What is the involvement/contribution of the School teachers, and other personnel to the village-community?
In terms of:
- communicating school policy, programmes?
- organising cultural and other programmes for the village-community?
- making school facilities available to the village community when needed?

3. What is the relationship between the school and the village-community?
In terms of:
- passive acceptance by one side or both?
- active co-operation of one side or both?
- distance or non-involvement of one side or both?

BIBLIOGRAPHY

Althusser, Louis, *Lenin and Philosophy and Other Essays, New Left Books,* New York, 1971.

Ambast, N. K., *A Critical Study of Tribal Education,* S. Chand and Co., N. Delhi, 1970.

Boudon, Raymond, *Opportunity and Social Inequality: Changing Prospects in Western Society,* John Wiley and Sons, New York, 1974.

Bowles, Samual and Herbert Gintis, *Schooling in Capitalist America,* Routledge and Kegan Paul, London, 1976.

Census of India 1981: Figures of Total Population and Scheduled Tribe Population, Series 12, Maharashtra Directory of Census Operations, Maharashtra, 1982.

Citizens for Democracy, *Education for Our People,* Allied Pub., Bombay, 1978.

Comes, Henry, *A Historical Sketch of the Zaroli Mission,* Diocesan Seminary, Bombay, 1959, Unpublished Typescript.

Coombs, Philip H. and Manzoor Ahmed, *Attacking Rural Poverty: How Non-formal Education Can Help,* Johns Hopkins Univ., Baltimore, 1974.

Cosin, B. R. ed., *Education and Social Structure,* Penguin Books, England, 1972.

Desrochers, John, *The Social Teaching of the Church,* Pub. by author, Bangalore, 1982.

Dewey, John, *Education for Democracy,* Macmillan, New York, 1961.

Documents of the 32nd General Congregation of the Society of Jesus, Anand Press, Anand, 1976.

Faure, Edgar et al, *Learning to Be: The World of Education Today and Tomorrow*, Unesco, Paris, 1972, Sterling Pub. Delhi,1973.

Fuchs, Stephen, *Rebellious Prophets: A Study of Messianic Movements in Indian Religions,* Asia Pub. House, Bombay, 1945.

Gezi, Kalil I., *Education in Comparative and International Perspectives,* Holt, Rinehart and Winston, New York, 1971.

Ghosh, Ratna and Mathew Zachariah, eds. *Education and the Process of Change,* Sage Pub., N. Delhi, 1987.

Gramsei, Antonio : *The Modern Prince and Other Writings,* International Publishers, New York, 1957.

Halsey, A. H., J. Floud and C. A. Anderson, eds., *Education, Economy and Society,* Free Press, Glencoe, Ill., 1961

Handbook of Education and Allied Statistics, Government of India, Ministry of Education, Delhi,1983.

Hardiman, David, *The Coming of the Devi: Adivasi Assertion in Western India,* Oxford Univ. Press, Bombay, 1987.

Inamdar, N. R., *Education Administration in the Zilla Parishads in Maharashtra,* Popular Prakashan, Bombay, 1974.

Kanjamala, Augustine, *Religion and Modernization of India,* Ishvani, Pune, 1981.

Kumar, Krishna, "Children and the Research Mill," *Economic and Political Weekly,* Vol. XXIII, No. 41, Oct., 1988, pp. 2107- 2108.

Kumar, Krishna, "Curriculum, Psychology and Society," *Economic and Political Weekly,* Vol. XXII, No. 12., 21 Mar., 1987, pp. 507-512.

Kumar, Krishna, "Educational Experience of Scheduled Castes and Tribes," *Economic and Political Weekly,* Vol.36 and 37, 3 Sep., 1983, pp. 1566-72.

Kumar, Krishna, "Textbooks and Educational Culture, "*Economic and Political Weekly,* Vol. XXI, No. 30, 26 Jul., 1986, pp.1309-1311.

Kurien, John, *Elementary Education in India: Myth, Reality, Alternative,* Vikas Pub., N. Delhi, 1983.

Malassis, Louis, *The Rural World: Education and Development*, UNESCO, London, 1976, p. 22.

Myrdal, Gunnar, *Asian Drama An Inquiry into the Poverty of Nations,* Pantheon Book, New York, 1968.

Naik, Chitra, *Growing up at Kosbad Hill: A Study of the Vikaswadi Experiment,* Gram Bal Shikshan Kendra, Kosbad, Thane, 1978.

Naik, J. P., *The Education Commission and After,* Allied Pub., N. Delhi, 1982.

Naik, J. P., *Elementary Education in India: A Promise to Keep,* Allied Pub., Bombay, 1975.

Naik, J. P., *Some Perspectives on Non-formal Education,* Allied Pub., Bombay, 1977.

Paranis, N. R., *The History and Survey of Thana District,* University of Bombay, Bombay, 1967.

Parsons, Talcott and Gerald M. Platt, *The American University,* Harvard Univ., Press, Cambridge, 1973.

Parulekar, Godavari, *Adivasi Revolt: The Story of the Warli Peasants in Struggle,* National Book Agency, Calcutta, 1975.

Parulekar, R. V., *Literacy in India,* Macmillan, Bombay, 1939.

Parulekar, R. V., *Mass Education in India*, Local Government Institute, Bombay, 1934.

Pattanayak, D. P., *Multi-Lingualism and Mother-tongue Education,* Oxford Univ. Press., Delhi, 1981.

Rathaiah, E. V., *Structural Constraints in Tribal Education: A Regional Study,* Sterling Pub., N. Delhi, 1977.

Report of the Committee on Special Multipurpose Tribal Blocks, Government of India, N. Delhi, 1960.

Report of the Education Commission (1965-66), Ministry of Education, N. Delhi, 1966.

Report of the Scheduled Areas and Scheduled Tribes Commission, Government of India, N. Delhi, 1961.

Report on the Aboriginal Hill Tribes of the Partially Excluded Areas in the Province of Bombay, Government Central Press, Bombay, 1939.

Saldhana, Denzil, "Socialization of Critical Thought: Responses to Literacy among Adivasis in Thane District," *Economic and Political Weekly,* Vol. XXIV, No. 30, 29 Jul., 1990, pp. PE 54-61.

Sarup, Madan, *Marxism and Education,* Routledge and Kegan Paul, London, 1978.

Save, K. J., *The Warlis,* Padma Pub., Bombay, 1945.

Sinclair, M. E. and Kevin Lilis, *School and Community* in the *Third World,* Croom Helm, London, 1980.

Singh, K. S., "Transformation of Tribal Society," *Economic and Political Weekly,* Vol. XVI, No. 33, 14 Ag., 1982, pp.1376- 1384.

Upadhaya, Ashok K., "Peasantization of Adivasis in Thane District," *Economic and Political Weekly,* Vol. XV, No. 52, 27 Dec., 1980, pp. A134-146.

INDEX